c. The Arts;
i. Art History

CRAWFORD

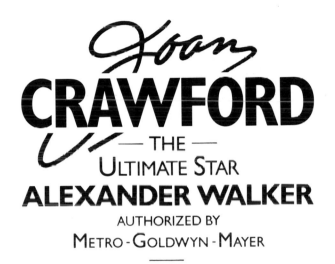

CRAWFORD

— THE —
ULTIMATE STAR
ALEXANDER WALKER

AUTHORIZED BY
METRO-GOLDWYN-MAYER

1817

HARPER & ROW, PUBLISHERS, NEW YORK

CAMBRIDGE, PHILADELPHIA, SAN FRANCISCO, LONDON

MEXICO CITY, SÃO PAULO, SYDNEY

FOR JULES DASSIN AND MELINA MERCOURI
– TO MAKE UP FOR MISSING THE PARTY

This work was first published in Great Britain.
Joan Crawford, The Ultimate Star.
Copyright © 1983 by Alexander Walker
No part of this book may be used or reproduced in
any manner whatsoever without written permission
except in the case of brief quotations embodied in
critical articles and reviews.
For information address Harper and Row, Publishers, Inc.,
10 East 53rd St. New York, N.Y. 10022
FIRST U.S. EDITION

Designed by John Gorham and Bekram Kapadia

Printed in Italy.

Library of Congress Cataloging in Publication Data

Walker, Alexander.
    Joan Crawford, the ultimate star.

    Filmography: p.
    Bibliography: p.
    Includes index.
    1. Crawford, Joan, 1908–1977. 2. Moving-picture
actors and actresses—United States—Biography
I. Title.
PN2287.C67W34 1983   791.43'028'0924 [B]   83–47546
ISBN 0–06–015123–4

ENDPAPER Crawford autographs fan photos at her Brentwood home.
FRONTISPIECE Crawford in 1933.

CONTENTS

INTRODUCTION

The temptation to write this book was formed in the very studios where most of it is set. It was while I was researching an earlier companion volume on Greta Garbo at Metro-Goldwyn-Mayer, in Hollywood, that I began sending down to the well-ordered basement vaults for the files on Joan Crawford. Curiosity, rather than necessity, was behind this. MGM nourished these two great stars; they began work there in the same year, 1925; they stayed almost exactly the same length of time; they left MGM within two years of each other; and they had almost nothing in common, except their stardom. And even in this they were opposites. In Garbo's case, it was a reluctant stardom; in Crawford's an all-consuming stardom. One woman, Crawford, could only ever think of herself as a star; she lived as a star, she insisted on being treated as a star; and she died a star. The other, Garbo, became a star virtually without trying; she used the power of stardom without caring for its attributes and when she ceased to be a star, she did not give any appearance of missing it and ever afterwards resisted the world's evaluation of her as a myth as pertinaciously as she resisted its curiosity about her as a living relic. Garbo's career, as I remarked in my earlier book, was the 'triumph of the apathetic will'. Crawford's was the victory of endless endeavour. It was impossible, I found, to be researching the one star in the very studio where both worked without yielding to the desire to discover what the great film-making machine had recorded about the other.

I was well aware that almost as many accounts have been written of Crawford as of Garbo, and I should not have added to them if the MGM archives had not contained substantial new information about the mutual relationship of star and studio. Thanks to the confidence and generosity of the MGM people named below, I believe I was the first to have access to the complete range of Crawford material, without any prior obligation laid on me except the normal courtesies of a researcher in allowing his typescript to be read for factual accuracy and, in some cases, additional valuable comments. In all cases the opinions I reached are mine.

'Joan Crawford', Richard Schickel has remarked, 'is an American phenomenon.' One could never call Garbo that. A *Hollywood* phenomenon, yes, so much is Garbo's mystery part and parcel of the movies, though even then hers is a phenomenon that overlaps with and is larger than Hollywood. In the earlier book, I tried to show Garbo plain, to suggest there was also a person who was frequently less than 'divine'. In this present book I have tried to make Crawford human, to suggest there was a raw human being inside the wrappings of stardom. It is not a full-length biography, but a portrait of a person seen from the angle of her driving will and the way it interacted with a film studio's power to create the image of a certain kind of American womanhood. No, I correct myself: certain *kinds* ... for there is not *one* Joan, but *many* Joans, each unveiled as her personal needs and career moves, her successes and set-backs dictated its necessary appearance to herself or her employers.

But I have also tried to see Crawford in a setting that is larger than her own ambitions, though, goodness knows! these were large enough. I have used letters, memoranda, contracts, cables and even pencilled marginalia to explore how a major Hollywood studio from the mid-1920s to the early 1940s conducted its relations with some of her famous contemporaries, like John Gilbert, Douglas Fairbanks Jr, Clark Gable, Franchot Tone and even that sad, self-destructive, 'instant' star James Murray. What the MGM archives reveal about the concern and care Murray enjoyed – unfortunately to no avail – should absolve the studio from the persistent charge of exploitation of his fame followed by callous disregard of him when his career foundered on his innate weaknesses.

The MGM files have been carefully preserved, in the main, by the 'civil service' of corporate officials who carry on with their own work of keeping a studio running whatever the changes in its top echelons. I hope that this book may encourage other studios to open up their company history to serious researchers. Only in this way, I am convinced, can the true corporate history of Hollywood begin to be written with an assurance and authority to match the critical history that several decades of writing have lavished on the *films*.

When Joan Crawford left MGM in 1943, the valuable framework of that great studio was lost to her, and to students of her career. She made other films, among them one of her greatest; but from this point on, the quest for

Crawford becomes a different one; and I have accordingly modulated the style and content of the book's last sections in order to follow her career more speculatively and to use hitherto unpublished material drawn from the publicly deposited papers of, among others, the columnist Hedda Hopper. But in each case, whether it is corporate history or columnist's files, my intention has been the same: to assemble in an understanding but not uncritical way the changing personality and professional aggrandizement or decline of a very American phenomenon called Joan Crawford.

A note on dates and figures: the date quoted after the first principal mention of each of Crawford's films refers to its first release in the United States or Britain, generally in New York or London. The accurate dating of some films, particularly in the silent era, is now difficult to obtain; in the main, I have followed MGM's own dating list and, for Crawford's post-MGM films, the dates referred to in the review columns. I hope this will make for an acceptable chronology. In order to avoid an unattractive text, I have left all figures in dollars; British readers may find it useful to remember that the official dollar-sterling rate of exchange for the period covered was: 1925: $4.87; 1930: $4.87; 1935: $4.93; 1940: $4.03; 1945: $4.03; 1950–66: $2.80; 1967–70: $2.40. The equivalent sterling purchasing power of $100 was 1967–70: £40; 1966: £42; 1965: £38; 1960: £45; 1955: £52; 1950: £68; 1945: £58; 1940: £75; 1935: £77; 1930: £72; 1925: £65.

Most of my research in documents and films was conducted at the MGM studios, Culver City, and my greatest debt of gratitude is to the officers and employees there: in particular, to Frank E.Rosenfelt, chairman and chief executive officer Metro-Goldwyn-Mayer Film Co., and vice-chairman and chief operating officer MGM/UA Entertainment Co; Richard Kahn, executive vice-president MGM/UA motion-picture distribution and marketing; Deanna Wilcox, director of marketing management MGM/UA motion-picture distribution and marketing; Karla Davidson, vice-president, general counsel-entertainment MGM Film Co.; Herbert S.Nusbaum, attorney MGM Film Co.; Florence E.Warner, office manager, legal department MGM Film Co.; Ben Presser, head of legal files MGM Film Co.; Dore Freeman, classic stills editor MGM/UA motion picture distribution and marketing; and those two sturdy projectionists, Mike Kaufman and Stan Wiegand, who showed me Joan Crawford movies in the basement screening rooms at MGM until the day's rushes came in.

In Los Angeles, I should also like to thank Fay Kanin, president of the Academy of Motion Picture Arts and Sciences, and the staff of the Margaret Herrick Library: in particular, Sam Gill and Tim Stansbury, who made available the remarkable collection of stills deposited by MGM in the Academy's archives. Without Carol Epstein, who aided me on the spot at the Academy, and at long distance, with my research into the Joan Crawford photo material, and who introduced me to new sources including the Hedda Hopper collection at the Academy, this book would not have the visual and human dimension that has been my aim. I am also deeply in the debt of Dorothy Barrett, administrator of the American National Academy of Performing Arts, who obtained some of the rare illustrations for me and who helps keep Joan Crawford alive in the affection of her thousands of fans; and Jane Kesner Ardmore, co-author of *A Portrait of Joan*, who encouraged me by quotation and insight to tread on ground that she broke.

In London, I was assisted by Bill Edwards, vice-president, international publicity and advertising MGM Pictures Ltd; and the staff of the British Film Institute reference library and the National Film Archive stills department, in particular Michelle Snapes and Markku Salmi.

My debt to individuals includes personal recollections given to me by Joseph L.Mankiewicz, George Sidney, Jules Dassin and Henry Rogers.

My publishers deserve my warm thanks for their encouragement and patience. For the enthusiasm they displayed throughout the project, I especially thank from Weidenfeld: John Curtis, Alex MacCormick (editor), John Gorham and Behram Kapadia (design), Sally Mapstone (copy-editor) and Tony Raven (indexer).

ALEXANDER WALKER
Davos 1981–Taormina 1982

'We can skip childhood because I didn't have any.'

'Everything I have in life, Hollywood gave me', she was fond of saying. Not quite true, but near enough. Her name, to begin with, was Hollywood's gift. The story of how Lucille Fay LeSueur, the name she had been born with on 23 March 1904, was rechristened 'Joan Crawford' by the readers of a mass-circulation movie magazine in 1925 is one that has been told often – and, like much else about this extraordinary woman, it has been told incorrectly. The truth doesn't deny Hollywood's hand in re-naming her; but it is less flattering to populist preferences. The real story lies in a flurry of coast-to-coast cables and inter-departmental memos that the harassed executives of Metro-Goldwyn-Mayer dispatched to each other in the early summer of that year. They have all been preserved in the studio's well-ordered archives. Now they make amusing reading; but, at the time, they created a minor panic in a highly cost-conscious corporation which had felt it was risking little by offering its standard 'stock company' contract, $75.00 a week with six months' option, to a twenty-year-old girl who had been 'third from the left in the back row' of the chorus-line of *The Passing Show of 1924* in New York City.

Lucille LeSueur was then earning $35.00 a week; and for that, she had to 'double up' after the show as a 'speciality dancer' in a night-club. At that time, she was abnormally self-conscious, unsure of herself, except when dancing. She weighed 145 pounds – a lot for her five feet, three inches to carry. She hated most things about her face, its plumpness and especially its freckles, which photographers later on learned to hide by considerably over-exposing their film. Paradoxically, her very insecurity made her fearless: she virtually dared people passing by *not* to notice her. On this occasion the man who did was Harry Rapf. He was a supervisor (in the coming Talkie era, he would be dignified as a 'producer') at MGM. His ranking at the film studio, number three after the studio chief Louis B. Mayer and the production chief Irving Thalberg, did not denote power so much as croney-ship. He was court jester and dining-room butt; yet he had a sharp nose for popular taste and controlled the company's output of 'B' pictures. His responsibilities were not to discover stars or monitor quality – he left these things to Mayer and Thalberg – but to provide MGM productions with attractive background 'glamour' which might be promoted to character roles in the foreground if some aspect of a girl's personality caught the camera at an attractive angle. Rapf enjoyed his job.

Where exactly he met Lucille LeSueur and asked her to do a screen test is not certain. She left it to be assumed it was back-stage. A film producer who later worked on half a dozen of the Crawford films thinks this unlikely: a crowded chorus-girls' dressing room wasn't the place for such propositions. Joseph L. Mankiewicz thinks it was made in Rapf's hotel room. Anyhow, she did a test comprising two basic positions (full-face and profile) and five rudimentary expressions (sad, mad, questioning, wistful and coy). Rapf's interest in her was fortified when, in answer to his wary query about her ambitions, she confessed that acting didn't interest her – a dancer was what she wanted to be. Rapf felt comfortable with dancers; actresses, it was left to Thalberg to groom. He ordered a second screen test, this one also viewed by J. Robert Rubin, MGM's legal counsel and Mayer's 'watch-dog' inside the studio's parent company, the theatre-owning East Coast giant, Loew's

Inc. An urbane, socially ambitious man, Rubin quite enjoyed what he saw. The result: an offer followed Lucille to her home-town, Kansas City, where she was spending Christmas 1924 with her mother and step-father. On New Year's Day, she entrained for Hollywood.

The first memo on her in the studio files shows that Rapf's own office prepared the legal contract she was to sign: they specified that she had to provide her own underwear and silk stockings for her screen roles. Rapf also had his picture taken with her. For the first, and possibly the last time in her career, she has her back to the camera: it is her protector who sits facing it patriarchally, showing if not a leg as eye-catching as hers, at least a natty length of boot. It was typical of the way that ruthless economy dictated the management of the newly-fledged MGM that within two weeks of her arrival, this girl with absolutely no acting experience was being offered on 'loan-out' terms to the neighbouring First National studio to play 'one of two parts, namely the private secretary or Ruth' in a movie to be called *The Talker*. A 25 per cent surcharge, added to her basic $75.00 weekly wage, would have gone to MGM: she would have made her bosses a profit right away. That was how things were done, though in this case, for reasons not explained, she played neither Ruth nor the secretary. Instead, she was given work on the home lot doubling for Norma Shearer – had Rapf noticed their resemblance, especially in profile? – in the latter's dual role (as judge's daughter and reform-school girl) in a melodrama entitled *Lady of the Night*. Her legs, in net stockings and patent-leather pumps, also got her into a trailer for MGM's coming attractions screened at an exhibitors' convention that April.

It is around this time that the problem of her name came up. Rapf disliked 'LeSueur'. Possibly the exhibitors did, too. It was hard to spell, difficult to pronounce and reminded Rapf of 'sewer'. He wasn't reconciled to it, either, by being told it was French for 'sweat'. It must be changed, he decreed. So Pete Smith, then studio publicity chief, arranged with the fan magazine *Movie Weekly* to sponsor a contest with prizes totalling one thousand dollars, including one of $500 for the person considered by the judges (among them Harry Rapf) to have found a new name for Lucille LeSueur which best expressed her 'energetic, ambitious and typically American personality'. The contest was to close on 2 May 1925; a week later, the re-named Lucille was due to report for her first prominent movie role in a back-stage story about three showgirls called *Sally, Irene and Mary*. This commitment dictated the choice of *Movie Weekly*, rather than a more prestigious fan magazine. As its title indicated, it went to press weekly; other periodicals usually had three-month deadlines, which would have run the contest into the movie's shooting schedule and forfeited valuable publicity for it.

'Name Her and Win $1,000', *Movie Weekly*'s readers were asked, above an article about the new player illustrated by four pictures of her by Clarence Sinclair Bull, one of MGM's leading 'gallery' portraitists. This in itself was a sign that she was basking in someone's favour, most likely Rapf's. He was quoted saying that she would soon be

PREVIOUS PAGE Imitating Clara Bow in 1925.
OPPOSITE TOP and MIDDLE In the early days of publicity Crawford's freckles were allowed to show.
OPPOSITE BELOW With protector Harry Rapf; he was the star then.

cheekbones and bold eyebrows, and hid them deep down inside me where I hoped no one would ever see them again.'[2]

But such a primal connection isn't easily severed. It was to take many years, but the world did eventually 'see' Tom LeSueur – in the features that his daughter's face gradually rendered dominant in her middle age. She even met him on the set of a movie she was making in 1934 – a fan magazine had brought them together – but it was a polite and undemonstrative encounter. By then, a new family had supplanted Tom LeSueur in her affections – the MGM studio itself.

Her childhood's restlessness continued when 'Daddy' Cassin, an amiable, feckless man glad of an industrious wife to organize his daily life, got innocently entangled in a partner's embezzlement charges and moved to Kansas City to escape the stigma. He took on a run-down hotel. Crawford helped out after classes at her elementary school, whose principal, as she recalls, praised her for trying, if not succeeding. Soon she transferred to St Agnes's Academy, a convent school. At least the nuns' discipline was a blessed

refuge from the quarrels at home, as her step-father's failure at hotel management elicited his wife's contempt and bitterness. Crawford even made work for herself, as if to shut out life's larger miseries by accepting a disproportionate amount of its minor chores. A third move, as a day pupil at a boarding-school for children from well-off families, was a step up the social scale, but a descent into slavery. She had to arrive at dawn, cook for, supervise and clean up after more than thirty children – and she was punished with a broom handle at any show of resentment. Out of the physical drudgery of these years, she acquired the broad shoulders that were to become her trademark. She also acquired something less tangible, but maybe even more character forming – an incessant, eventually manic amount of energy. She was forever on the go. Even the rare treats she allowed herself were approached with the same energy as her drudgery. 'You're burning yourself out', her dance dates would tell her as she launched herself on to the floor.

With high-school credits she had scarcely earned (the headmistress gave her them anyway, rather than risk charges of neglecting her) Crawford registered at Stephens College, Columbia, Missouri, a small girls' college whose secretary, 'Daddy' Walters, as she called him, had been her elementary school principal. This was in the Fall semester, 1922; she gave her birth date as 1906. One doubts if Mrs Cassin had been taken in by her daughter's academic 'record'. Why, then, did she allow her to go on to higher education? Why shouldn't the girl have found a job or

Top row centre is Thomas LeSueur, Joan's father. To the right of him, wearing a black bow, is Joan's aunt, Betty Johnson. In the second row (left to right) are Joan's uncle, her mother Anna Bell Johnson LeSueur holding Joan's brother Hal, Joan's maternal grandmother Mary Ellen Johnson holding Joan's sister Daisy, and far right is Joan's grandfather Sylvester Johnson. The picture was taken before Joan's birth.

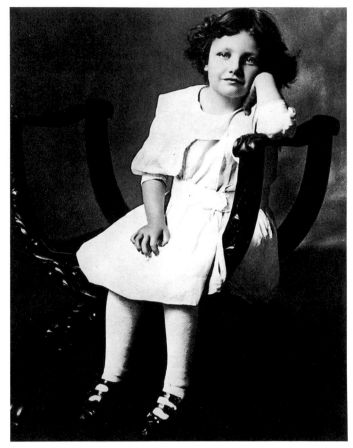

ABOVE LEFT With her brother Hal, 1908–9.
ABOVE RIGHT Billie Cassin (also known as Joan Crawford) aged about five.
BELOW Aged about nine with her mother in Lawton, Oklahoma.

helped her mother full-time in the hand laundry that Anna Cassin had started, now that she and her husband had separated? The reason may have been a desire to get her daughter away from a household which the mother now shared with one Mr Hough. This 'lodger', Crawford later hinted, was making passes at her as well as her mother.

Though she had never known her father, she was far from fatherless at this time. A constant feature of Crawford's childhood is the number of paternally disposed older men – *not* of the Mr Hough breed – who took an interest in her welfare and, to some extent, gave her a sense of security in the absence of the traditional family circle. She was luckier than she knew at the time that fate chose her for MGM. Louis B. Mayer was a stern boss, but his patriarchal relationship with his female stars insured they didn't have to submit to the *droit de seigneur* enforced by the moguls at other studios. 'At MGM we had a certain dignity,' she recalled, attaching the less ladylike rider, 'at least we didn't feel like whores.' But Mayer had his paternal predecessors. Even James Madison Wood, the long-time (1911–47) president of Stephens College, became 'Daddy' Wood to her. He was a purposeful, pragmatic, self-reliant man, a philosopher of the school of earnest endeavour popularized by Samuel Smiles and John Dewey. One day he intercepted Crawford absconding from college, rather than face academic failure. With great firmness, he commanded her never to quit: if she had to go, then she should leave in the proper manner. When her time eventually came to leave MGM, she was to remember – and act on – that advice. Another 'rule for living' which he gave her sounds presciently like the strategy for continuous renewal which she was to apply to her whole screen career: 'If you find you can do a job, let it alone, because you are bigger than the job already.' To a quite exceptional degree, Crawford's upbringing prepared her for the set-up at MGM – once she had found her way around it.

Another person with faith in her was near enough her own age to have expressed his love for her, too. Ray Sterling was only five years older: yet whenever she recalled him in later years, Crawford always singled out his sophistication rather than his sex-appeal. He seems to have been the evangelical kind of beau. He appealed to her soul, not her body. He fired her ambitions to make something of herself, but drew back from proposing any closer relationship, as if he feared to be burned by what he had ignited. If older men provided the 'rules', younger ones like Ray provided the impetus. She used to sit out the dances he took her to just to hear him talk of life and literature. He never reappears in her later years, but this first 'love' set the pattern of deference shown by her early marriages to men who were valued as much for education and *savoir faire* as for their sex-appeal, and maybe more so.

What liberated Crawford at that early age wasn't sex; it was surplus energy. It was, above all, dancing. Even doing the school chores to pay for tuition, balancing trays or juggling kitchen dishes, her body couldn't consume all her available energy. She was hyperactive from the start; not yet in the sense of being a workaholic, but dedicated to the moral ethic of physical labour. Sloth wasn't a sin in her catechism: it was something worse, it was insecurity. Dance steps were one way of siphoning off the energy without depleting the reservoir of purposeful activity. She never felt so happy and secure as when her lower limbs, in the chorus line or in speciality numbers, were giving her grace and bringing her gratification. Her arms and hands remained a problem, at least when at rest. She always had to have something to fill them: tapestry, knitting, crochetwork or, much later, a flask of 100 per cent proof vodka wrapped in a concealing napkin. The comfort this gave to an otherwise idle hand was more important – at first anyhow – than its contents. It was the sheer energy behind her desperate appeal to casting agents in downtown Chicago, to whom she had applied for work after a series of pocket-money jobs and one short-lived spell of a few weeks in a touring-company musical, that got her a re-engagement in the chorus-line. And it was her energy, spinning centrifugally from a cabaret stage in Detroit a few weeks later, that knocked over the whisky tumbler of J.J. Shubert, the New York impresario, seated at a front-line table. As in a routine Hollywood script, he offered her a place in the show he was bringing to the Winter Garden. Life, for Crawford, didn't ape art: frequently it aped bad art.

The letters that she and Ray Sterling exchanged at this time show that if her heart was still with him, his conscience was watching over her. They resonate with the warnings of the impressionable small-town boy viewing from afar the temptations of the big city. 'New York is like a melting pot of all classes, a cesspool of licentiousness ... There are

The new camera used by studio publicity caught her at her most athletic.

bound to be flies gathering around a sugar bowl like show business, but there must be many good people in the city too. May God keep you and give you the aid I cannot.' It is this tone that echoes through the thousands of letters that Crawford herself wrote in future years. Licentiousness, it is true, was seldom part or parcel of her correspondence, but she rarely failed to end the humblest note without a prayerful invocation or blessing.

Even after the most gruelling evening at the Winter Garden, Crawford had enough energy left to move over to the West Side and do a speciality dance at a speakeasy run by the singer Harry Richman. She had got an audition there through yet another 'Daddy' figure – though this one was actually called 'Granny' Granlund – and he was stage manager at the Winter Garden. And 'Granny' it was, too, who drew Harry Rapf's attention to her when the MGM executive came East on one of his talent-scouting jaunts.

Timing can be as valuable as talent in launching a screen career. Crawford could not have arrived at MGM at a better time. The studio production machine in 1925 had to feed new films into the 110 cinemas in the East owned by Loew's Inc., and it was rapidly shifting into top gear. Mayer aimed to turn out a movie a week. And he nearly succeeded in the first full year since Marcus Loew, already in control of the Metro studio, had combined it with Mayer's own under-employed company and the foundering Goldwyn one to form MGM. Working a six-day week, MGM made forty-six features in 1925 and a net profit of $4,700,000 at the end of its first fiscal year in August 1925.

Mayer's reconnaissance trip to Italy at the end of 1924 to salvage the *Ben-Hur* epic by moving it out of Italy and back home to Hollywood, where costs could be controlled, showed the managerial instinct that characterized his control of MGM and made it the most efficiently run Hollywood studio of its time. *Ben-Hur* began reshooting on the back lot at Culver City, then a suburb of Los Angeles, the very month Crawford reported for work. She also saw the tail end of the temperamental tempest precipitated by Thalberg's *démarche* against the extravagance of Erich von Stroheim, then finishing *The Merry Widow*, another troublesome 'special' inherited by MGM from Goldwyn. In 1925, no fewer than three Lon Chaney films were released; Crawford would shortly be co-starring with Chaney, who ranked with Chaplin, Fairbanks and Pickford as one of the silent cinema's biggest draws. She would also be cast with John Gilbert, whose phenomenal career as the Great Lover of the silent screen was about to be recast even more popularly in the shell-holes of the First World War epic *The Big Parade* released in 1925. Buster Keaton created one of his funniest, most continuously inventive comedies, *Seven Chances*, in that year. Other established stars at MGM included Jackie Coogan, Norma Shearer, Ramon Novarro, Mae Murray, Conrad Nagel, William Haines, Lionel Barrymore and Marion Davies. Lillian Gish arrived in 1926 to join the 'family' and add to its prestige and (for a time, anyhow) its profit; and before *that* year was out, the greatest female star ever created, Greta Garbo, outshone everyone in the MGM heavens.

Affluence was in the air – and the pocket. Mayer's salary was $1,500 a week in mid-1925; Thalberg's, $680; and both were entitled (along with J. Robert Rubin) to a share in 20 per cent of the net profits. Well inside the year, Mayer and Thalberg were rewarded for their success with even-handed generosity: each was put on $2,000 a week (Rubin took $1,500) and given a guarantee that the 'net' to be shared by the triumvirate would not be less than $500,000, plus hefty dividends and stock options.

Names and figures like these are essential to show how low a risk was involved in engaging speculative talent like Crawford – and also how swift an ascent she made in the star roster and the studio pay-roll once she got her 'break'. But it came as a sobering surprise at first to learn that her 'five-year contract' had an option clause allowing the studio to drop her after six months. Her congenital refusal to face inactivity of any kind now had the imperative of a deadline to galvanize her. Each morning at the church opposite the studio's colonnaded entrance on West Washington Boulevard, she got down on her knees and prayed for strength – and picture roles. Having nowhere specific to go in the studio, she went everywhere. In those silent-era days, each set was an 'open' one, with a teeming social life. Stars 'visited with' each other between shots: a newcomer was unremarked or welcomed. Crawford took the chance to observe everything. She showed a desire to please everyone, from the highest to the lowliest, who might have anything to do with *her* part, *her* career. It is not simplistic, or sentimental, to observe how desperate a need to be loved this suggests. For this is the very definition of stardom. A star, at that era anyhow, was someone who was *loved* by all the millions of film-goers out there. Then, too, being still very insecure, she intuitively made her earliest friends from among the studio's 'little people', as they were patroniz-

ingly called, whose technical crafts sustained the artistic illusion. The cameraman Johnny Arnold and his electrician Tommy Shagrue, who together did routine tests of all contract players within a few days of their arrival to alert the higher-up supervisors to the available new talent, sensed a quick and willing learner in her initially uncertain responses. Arnold, later head of the camera department, became the man who assigned photographers to directors – and photographers could take care of stars they liked, even when directors were uninspired. It was the same with make-up. 'Background talent' like Crawford was not made up individually. She was simply handed cosmetics and told to get on with the job herself. But she watched, asked for advice, experimented back in her drab little hotel room.

Her need to make friends, to be loved, has an almost holy zeal to it: for time was flying. Her urgency, her insistence on standing corrected at any professional slip-up, was so different from the hard-boiled superciliousness affected by others who were beginning their careers, that studio personnel spotted a 'difference' in her even before her screen image began to define it. 'You weren't like the others,' Carey Wilson, then a writer, later a director, assured her, 'you were just plain scared to death.' It quickened her own perception of herself. 'I was beginning to realize that I wanted to become an actress,' she recalled, though she was not yet quite ready to forswear the thing she knew she *could* do, for she added, '. . . maybe a dancing actress.'

Pete Smith found Crawford's highly visible vitality was just the thing that publicity needed at that time. Smith had been a newspaperman. The Speed Graflex camera, which had recently come into use, was the favourite of sports editors, for its swiftness in freezing athletic action could dramatize the static. Smith adapted it to studio publicity and employed a *Los Angeles Times* lensman, Don Gillum, to take action shots of the MGM talent. Not the *star* talents: they needed the protection of the exquisitely lit gallery portrait to project their unique looks and already proven appeal. But the stock-company talent, whose female members especially were put into swim-suits, athletic vests and track shorts and endlessly snapped 'in action' at the University of Southern California sports stadium or on the beaches of the Costa Del Mar at Santa Monica. Virtually every MGM acquisition, if she had the right physical form, was exposed as an 'outdoor girl' on these locations, even Garbo, who predictably detested the 'humiliation' she felt standing next to beefy athletes or feeling their coach's biceps. But Crawford, just as predictably, found these photo-calls a channel to release pent-up energies with a profitable pay-off across the pages of the nation's newspapers. She and another *débutante*, Dorothy Sebastian, played beach ball, wrestled, lifted (fake) dumb-bells, punched a sparring dummy, even danced to something called a 'portable radio', which was really an empty box with a horn on top devised by the props department to cash in on the mid-1920s radio craze which hadn't then invented a portable set. Back at the studio, Crawford was asked to leap in the air – which her impatient dancing legs did gratefully – and the 'frozen' image made the front pages: it

OPPOSITE On a Santa Monica beach with Dorothy Sebastian.

Energy demonstrated to order at the studio.

A girl for all seasons: a 1925 calendar.

20 had the 'modern' and 'peppy' look demanded by the pacy decade. Even in repose, Crawford's own looks were striking. 'Your face is *built*,' Johnny Arnold told her.

The calendar itself co-operated in displaying her. Every significant annual festival featured a seasonally dressed (or undressed) Crawford or an appropriately posed saint's day girl. She was ejected from an enormous Independence Day cracker, face smudged by the 'explosion', shorts titillatingly tattered; she hoisted a long limb over a studio chimney as one of Santa's delivery girls in a fur-fringed one-piece; she commemorated Hallowe'en as a peek-a-boo witch riding a broomstick; and another view of her at her dressing-table torn between competitive millinery was sent out to the nation's Press by the M G M caption writers with the somewhat wishful statement: 'Joan Crawford, M G M player, shows how a million girls will spend their Easter morning.' The fashion angle that was to play such a vital part in her stardom – eventually an overwhelming one – was set in these early days. No chance was lost to reflect (or create) a dressy trend or a cajoling, flirtatious, attention-getting bit of fashion business. The gilded beauty-mark shaped like a cupid's bow as if some lover had branded her on the shoulder; the man's black bow-tie worn below her knee like a trophy of the chase which required her to raise her already short skirt in coy display; the ready-rolled stockings ('saves having to roll your own') favoured by the era's flapper girls; or the new-fangled hip-length stockings ('a necessity with shorter-than-ever dresses'): from the very first, Crawford was identified with novelty, novelty, novelty. Sometimes even Pete Smith's inventiveness was strained. A story he put out to accompany one photo illustrates the way that the studio publicity machine linked players, public and commercial tie-ins so that each sold the other: 'Asking the time is going to be one of the most popular pastimes if the new garter watch, the latest whisper in timepieces from Paris, catches on in Los Angeles. The watch is of platinum and has a clasp on the back and the garter is of flexible metallic material. It is worn half-way between ankle and knee so as to be readily visible with the new short skirts decreed by fashion. Miss Lucille LeSueur, M G M featured player, was the first to introduce the new fad to Hollywood.' A pencilled note on the memo usefully (and ironically) 'dates' the fashion as well as its wearer: 'Name changed to Joan Arden', it says.

Crawford's co-operativeness in the fashion-publicity game became legendary: 'I probably had more pictures taken than any girl who'd ever been signed at the studio.' The still camera did something even more valuable for her at this time: it enabled her to experiment with her looks from photo to photo – perhaps even to glimpse the latent stardom beneath the fleeting fashion item she was wearing. 'Lots of newcomers to films undoubtedly think that posing for [calendar, art and fashion] photos is a waste of time. It doesn't need to be. I have made a careful study of every single still picture that was ever shot of me. I wanted these stills to teach me what not to do on the screen. I scrutinized the grin on my face, my hair-do, my posture, my make-up, the size of my feet.'[3]

What did she do after work at the studio? The answer is, she worked – her playtime was simply an extension of her personality display. She had not been many weeks in Hollywood before she started dating men – but only the boys who could dance. Romance was defined by her as the

One of the most revealing of the early publicity shots; later on, they kept adding the clothes.

supply of dance-floor partners, not sexual ones. She could convert romance into money, too. She and her current escort would enter competitions for the Charleston or Black Bottom at such supper clubs as the Montmartre or the Coconut Grove, or even the *thés dansants* held by the big hotels on Saturdays. Studio contract talents were always welcomed (and rarely charged) if they gave the tourists a taste of Hollywood glamour. Her winning trophies – 'soon I had more cups than the Brown Derby' – were negotiable for cash if returned the next morning; and $15 to $20 in return fees meant a lot to a $75-a-week player. Soon the publicists found she was manufacturing stories for *them*. Adela Rogers St Johns, the journalist and screenwriter, saw her at the Montmartre and noted her feverish vitality. 'From her too high heels to her too frizzy hair, she was all wrong; yet she stood out as though the light was too bright for anyone but her.' Such a comment may have had a slightly self-serving edge: for it was one of the St Johns stories, adapted for the screen as *Pretty Ladies* (6 September 1925), in which Crawford received her first credit (still as Lucille LeSueur). She had advanced a little bit farther than providing background glamour for its Ziegfeld Follies story, but not so much farther that any reviewer noticed her. 'Living chandeliers and undressed ladies usual revue adjuncts', *Variety*'s critic tersely commented.

Until very recently, film historians accepted that the rechristened Crawford was then put into a costume romance, *The Only Thing*, concocted and 'supervised' by Elinor Glyn and starring Eleanor Boardman. It took Stephen Harvey, an acute author and researcher for the Museum of Modern Art, to notice that some MGM employee, in 1925, had confused this film with another costume picture, *The Circle* (22 September 1925), also starring Eleanor Boardman, to the extent of transferring some of the latter's credits to the former's cast list! *The Circle*, adapted from Somerset Maugham's play, was directed by Frank Borzage. Harry Rapf had alluded to Crawford's being cast in it and, in fact, she appears in the prologue, set in England in 1895, playing Young Lady Catherine, who abandons her husband for her lover and lives outside society. In the main story, Lady Catherine, now an older woman whose daughter-in-law is about to repeat family history, was played by Eugenie Besserer. The confusion is understandable, but until the error was spotted every filmography has listed *The Only Thing*, instead of *The Circle*, as Crawford's second film. Crawford's comment on *The Only Thing* in her autobiography was, 'I remember nothing about it,' which is very reasonable in the circumstances, although she then allows herself – how persuasive scholarship is! – to acknowledge that she may indeed have been in it. And perhaps she was, as well as being in a third Eleanor Boardman vehicle, *Proud Flesh*, also released in 1925. However 'positive identification' has only been made in the case of *The Circle*, where the captions on the stills in the MGM Collection at the Academy library refer to 'Lucille LeSueur', notwithstanding the change of name, which had become official by the time of its release.

Old Clothes (9 November 1925), her next film, released six weeks later, co-starred her with Jackie Coogan, which at least got her picture in the papers along with Chaplin's child discovery. Louella Parsons even wrote: 'The girl,

ABOVE Dancing lady; with more cups than the Brown Derby.
BELOW Her first film, *Pretty Ladies*, with Paul Ellis and Tom Moore.

Joan Crawford, is a discovery of Jack Coogan Sr. She is very attractive and shows promise.' One suspects another 'Daddy' relationship here; perhaps so, though she later recalled she literally danced into the part. For Jackie Jr, then 'on the sunny side of eleven', as critic Mordaunt Hall put it in *The New York Times*, was to be presented in the movie as a precocious brat, doing things that adults did, like golfing . . . and Charlestoning. Crawford was hired to tutor him in the dance steps and stayed on to co-star with him.

By now she was getting noticed by MGM executives. It is not uncommon for impressionable film people to start to believe the publicity they themselves put out. Pete Smith's planted stories of Crawford's date-and-dance night-life seemed like the life-style then being 'sold' by films in every studio's production roster as the Jazz Age roared to its climax. Edmund Goulding was an MGM contract director. An Englishman with a taste for fast living and faster women, he had a good instinct for working with female players whom he would try to involve romantically off screen. Witnessing Crawford perform on the Montmartre's dance floor, he cast her in *Sally, Irene and Mary* (13 December 1925). A back-stage story of three chorus-girls each matched by a suitor (a sugar daddy, a ladykiller and an honest Joe), it was, as Crawford said, 'my own life . . . the characters were true and well observed'.

LEFT and BELOW In the Prologue to *The Circle* and with Frank Braidwood.
OPPOSITE ABOVE Crawford played young Lady Catherine.
OPPOSITE BELOW Frank Borzage (seated centre) directs Crawford on location.

Jackie Coogan was the star in *Old Clothes*, but at least he got her picture in the newspapers.

Goulding had taste in decor as well as women: he suggested the artist Erté to design the film and advised Crawford to tone down her unrestrained vitality. It was the first time anyone had instructed her in acting. Perhaps, she felt, dancing wasn't all that life was about. Her good friend Johnny Arnold was cameraman on the film: she felt in safe hands. Her co-stars, Constance Bennett and Sally O'Neil, were more self-assured than she; but by exposing Crawford for the first time to someone she could admire, a strong emulative drive was released, and it is from this moment on that conscious efforts are apparent in the steps she is taking to establish her screen image. This involved her in physical changes. She had her teeth fixed. The film's new hair-style with its centre-parting had emphasized her face's plumpness so she began dieting in order to force the iron of her jaw-line into the camera's view. Self-control was starting to shape her. Goulding taught her a basic training exercise she never forgot – to slip her shoes off and, standing in stockinged feet, suck up into herself the power she felt from her own gestureless immobility.

Crawford's role, as Irene, was not the showiest in the film, though, like the haughty Bennett and the cheeky O'Neil, her sentimental 'in love with love' character benefits from the realism with which a chorus-girl's life is depicted – the sweat, powder and propinquity of the overcrowded dressing-room and the razor-edged calculation needed to extract the maximum of pleasure from one's man and still elude the risks of being used by him. The world of the gold-digger and womanizer requires Crawford, cast as a 'good girl' rather than a good-time one and still tucked up in bed at night by her police-cop father, to adopt a fairly passive attitude. Refusing to be seduced by a cad in a brocaded smoking jacket, she is cynically bundled into her coat and hat with the advice, 'Promise me you'll always stay as you are now.' Instead of sexiness, fatalism is what singles her out of the trio. On the rebound, she runs off with a playboy to get married. Both are killed at the railroad crossing, and Crawford comes back to the footlights as a spectre, Charlestoning as furiously as she did in the flesh and causing the rest of the chorus to fall into the orchestra pit!

Though wildly out of key with the rest of the film, hers is the sort of Fate (intense and capitalized) that causes filmgoers to remember a role – as very soon they would the player. F. Scott Fitzgerald certainly remembered the Crawford he saw, at the end of the 1920s: 'The best example of the flapper ... dancing deliciously, laughing a great deal, with wide, hurt eyes. Young things with talent for living.' Later on, when he was, in a sense, her employee at MGM, writing scripts for her, Fitzgerald's focus was understandably harder. The very vitality which transfused the character she was playing imposed limits on her acting talents – and on her writers. 'She can't change her emotions in the middle of a scene without going through a sort of Jekyll and Hyde contortion of the face, so that when one wants to indicate she is going from joy to sorrow, one must cut away and then back,' Fitzgerald told his friends the Gerald Murphys. This is a sizeable over-statement, but it does contain a modicum of truth. Crawford's acting was instinctual; she never received training, but the discipline which Goulding advised her to acquire was as good as training. Reconciling instinct and discipline remained difficult for several years and accounts for the dislocation that Fitzgerald detected. Yet his complaint is essentially irrelevant. Crawford had always to be taken at face value, and her face learned to acquire total conviction in what she was playing. Another instinctual actress like Garbo was suited, by role and temperament, to withhold a part of herself from an audience, which then had to penetrate the collusive mystery that was created. Crawford left nothing to be guessed at, but projected herself, as if on a saluting stand, towards her loyal fans as they trooped by: 'Eyes right!' and there she is, God bless her, *acting*!

When MGM picked up her first contract option and raised her pay to $100 a week, she celebrated a securer future with a move to a more independent life-style – from hotel room to a rented bungalow on Genessee Street. A sure sign that she was prospering was the unexpected arrival of her brother Hal, who hoped to take a share of her good luck and higher earnings. To look after him, she had then to invite her mother to join them. Hal proved reckless in borrowing and crashing her second-hand car and her mother proved spendthrift with her daughter's weekly pay-check. Such people could have come out of a movie: the fact that a similar family situation did come to figure in a number of her later movies suggests that Crawford, never behindhand at indicating scenes to her writers, knew exactly how impatience at being exploited could propel a working girl on and upwards into the story's more glamorous reaches. Why, then, didn't she make a quick, profitable marriage to one of the wealthy playboys she dated, like nineteen-year-old Mike Cudahy, heir to a meat-packing fortune, with $1,500 in allowance a month? The reasons she later gave indicate how her priorities were forming. In romance, she said, she sought one thing – perfection. She compared it to a new dress, treasurable at the start of its life, but soon patched beyond wearing. No wonder that a cheap wire coat-hanger out of place in the closet among all the expensive dresses would rouse her to such a pitch of intemperate, yet not irrational fury. The compulsion to make everything over anew and throw away what no longer served inflicts its own damage sooner or later; but at that time, it only seemed to serve her ambitions.

ABOVE With Henry Kolker as a stage-door Johnnie in *Sally, Irene and Mary* and (right) a publicity still for the film: 'Hearts or icicles – either sign can be displayed at will', says the caption.

BELOW Crawford (centre, as Irene) with her co-stars Constance Bennett (Sally, left) and Sally O'Neil (Mary, right) in the well-furnished dressing-room.

PREVIOUS PAGES Crawford, circa 1926, in Clara Bow attitude.
ABOVE Urban sophistication, 1926: pearls are for simplicity.

BELOW LEFT Fashion plate: pockets are for pets.
BELOW RIGHT Pirate Joan: any costume goes.

To Louis B. Mayer, informed by the studio's intelligence services, these characteristics appeared highly laudable. The work ethic that drove her touched his sentimental nerve. To him, she quickly became Joan the breadwinner, keeping her family together, supporting her mother, bailing her big brother out of messes, being careful with the dimes and wary about her playboy dates. However, his paternalism did not yet get her the roles she craved. These were largely in the gift of Irving Thalberg, who had scarcely deigned to notice Crawford when she arrived at MGM. It was a definite handicap, she discovered, to resemble Norma Shearer, for Shearer, whom Thalberg married two-and-a-half years later, was his favourite MGM actress. Her rise was so swift as to be privileged. By mid-1924, Shearer was on $450 a week, and MGM had an oral agreement with her mother always to send her on location with her daughter, all expenses paid. Shearer's salary was raised to $1,000 a week in 1926, the year Thalberg wrote personally to the Los Angeles Tax Inspectors appealing against their decision to disallow the use of a Buick for Shearer, 'who is one of our stars'. After March 1926, Shearer's salary was $2,000 a week, a suitable consort fee for marriage to Mayer's second-in-command. Crawford felt keenly the advantage Shearer had derived from arriving just before her at MGM and engaging Thalberg's affections and sponsorship. Until Thalberg's death in 1936, Crawford's appeals for the best roles that were going inevitably conflicted with the prior claims of 'the boss's wife'. The fact that Crawford had stood in for Shearer in her first appearance on screen was an omen neither lady would forget.

But Crawford soon had her own affectionate sponsor at MGM. In retrospect that studio seems to have been especially rich in men, immigrants themselves or the sons of immigrants, who used their studio rank and salary to enjoy a life that would have been outside their class back in Middle or Eastern Europe, particularly where the company and entertainment of women were concerned. It was not quite akin to keeping a mistress – Mayer's rectitude would never have permitted that. But directors and producers at MGM did gravitate towards female contract artists who were especially susceptible to being, for want of a better word, groomed. The German-born Paul Bern was one of these men with a Pygmalion-like temperament. He had the innate good taste that shaped movies he produced. Outside the studio, he chaperoned the patently glamorous women who appeared in those MGM movies, giving them social confidence, creating a more sophisticated image of them and, of course, enhancing his own masculine authority. A writer for Lubitsch and Von Sternberg, he became story consultant to Thalberg at MGM and soon supervised Garbo's silent films; and he succeeded Ray Sterling as Crawford's platonic confidant. She was flattered to have him as arbiter of taste and chaperon around town; and to him, this ill-educated but vitality-packed girl was pliable material for improvement. It is an echo of Bern, surely, that one detects in the confession she was soon making to a press interviewer: 'I want the Joan Crawford of this year to be only a building block for the Joan Crawford of next year.' It is unlikely that the attraction between Bern and Crawford was basically sexual. Bern later married Jean Harlow, and one can detect the appeal that women like Harlow and Crawford had for him. He committed suicide while

Joan as Hamlet, more sultry than gloomy.

married to Harlow, but as Samuel Marx (then an MGM writer) made clear in his 1975 book *Mayer and Thalberg*, Bern was not a victim of his own sexual impotence, whatever subsequent innuendo made out. His method of wooing women was to flatter them into a better appreciation of parts of themselves other than their sex-appeal. It was a narcissistic pleasure: the man who took pains to explain the provenance of a fine wine to his dinner companion showed not only his high regard for her (and the wine), but his own *savoir vivre*. When he took Crawford along one night after a theatre show to the dressing-room occupied by Pauline Frederick, it was most likely done with the aim of presenting her to an actress who, like her, had started in the chorus-line, and had now become one of the finest stage and silent-screen players. Frederick's advice may have been less practical than Bern thought his *protégée* needed ('Dream your dreams, little one,' she reportedly said), but his instinct in exposing Crawford to this role-model was a correct one. Observers noted that for a time after the encounter, Crawford took to emphasizing her resemblance to the established actress who, four years later, was to play her mother in *This Modern Age*.

But even Bern's social tutoring did not bring her an early stardom and may even have exacerbated her discontent as she was dropped into one kind of film, one kind of role, after another, generally supported by a far better-known male star, in the restless experimentation with public taste which was the hit-and-miss technique used to 'make' a star in the studio system of that era.

The Western Association of Motion Picture Advertisers named her a WAMPAS Baby Star of 1926: other players of promise so nominated included Mary Astor, Dolores Del Rio, Janet Gaynor, Fay Wray and Dolores Costello. Pete Smith celebrated with a fresh batch of Crawford photos, including one of her as Hamlet. Her films did not match this ambitious pose.

She was cast with George K. Arthur as a Prohibition agent in a hick comedy called *The Boob* (17 June 1926); loaned out to First National to be a bill-board 'Dream Girl' and peripatetic inspiration to Harry Langdon, the baby-faced clown undertaking a transcontinental hike in *Tramp, Tramp, Tramp* (13 June 1926); and then, with relief, passed back to Edmund Goulding again to play an *apache* dancer in *Paris* (13 June 1926) torn between her brutal partner and the kind of silly-ass American millionaire who makes no distinction between night and day, but wears his dinner jacket continuously. The picture was built around Charles Ray, whose heavy clowning knocked it down again in every scene. A pity, for Goulding's unconventional taste in eroticism scarcely gets the chance it hankers after to develop Crawford's perverseness as the girl who prefers pain and low life with her raffish dance partner to conventional happiness with the jejeune playboy. It may

ABOVE WAMPAS Baby Stars of 1926: (from left to right) Joan Crawford, Marcelline Day, Mary Brian, Dolores Costello, Mary Astor, Edna Marion, Vera Reynolds, Janet Gaynor, Sally O'Neil, Dolores del Rio, Fay Wray, Sally Long and Joyce Compton.
BELOW LEFT A morning walk with her Belgian police dog for protection.
BELOW RIGHT In her film *The Boob*. The caption says: 'Knee-length stockings, which solve the problem of rolling your own.' Worn with a dress of brown satin trimmed with orange ostrich feathers described as 'practical as well as beautiful'.

ABOVE With baby-face clown Harry Langdon in *Tramp, Tramp, Tramp*.

BELOW With a group of real, but unidentified, Parisian *grisettes* assembled for the film *Paris*, but eventually excluded from it for reasons of prudence.

Crawford as the 'Virginia belle' in a dime-a-dance emporium in *Taxi Driver* with Douglas Gilmore as the 'Bowery sheik', and (right) taking the title literally for a publicity shot.

have personally amused Goulding to reverse audience expectations, but it did not amuse the audiences of that time; and in her next film, *Taxi Dancer* (5 February 1927), again with Douglas Gilmore as her erstwhile *apache* lover now turned West Side ballroom dancer, conventional morality was slavishly served. Crawford, feeling more at home than the director Harry Millarde in what, after all, had been 'home' to her , did some of the dance-hall scenes in the film *her* way and the reviewers spotted it. 'Here is a girl of singular beauty and promise,' wrote Lawrence R. Quirk in *Photoplay*, 'and she certainly has IT. Just now she is very much in need of good direction.' *Variety* didn't go as far as to identify an 'IT' factor in her, but allowed that 'every so often comes a flash of power that may indicate this girl has something'.

'IT' or simply 'something' did not emerge any more definitively in the two unlikely movies that followed. Raven-haired or wearing a platinum wig, she played an eighteenth-century general's daughter, René (*sic*) Contrecoeur, beloved by Tim McCoy, a gallant Army officer caught in the wars between French settlers and the Indians in *Winners of the Wilderness* (15 January 1927), one of a series on Frontier history for which MGM had signed Col McCoy, a stickler for authenticity who insisted on having genuine Cherokees: he was not at all pleased when Pete Smith put out some publicity stills showing Crawford teaching Chief Big Tree to Charleston. In *The Understand-*

ing Heart (19 July 1926), the *raison d'être* for the production was MGM's bargain purchase of some reels of forest fire-fighters at work. Crawford played a look-out girl in the Rangers. The fact that some reviewers found her 'attractive, but at the same time clever enough to impress us with the idea that she is not quite aware of it', shows she was developing a sense for playing a character, though in highly unpropitious circumstances.

For her next 'acting lesson', she found a bizarre tutor in the 'rather frightening' Lon Chaney playing the supposedly armless knife-thrower in *The Unknown* (26 June 1927). Chaney knew the value of keeping his myriad make-up secrets to himself, leaving the public to guess which face was really his. He had already advised Greta Garbo to make herself that little bit mysterious; not that *she* needed any encouragement. For Crawford, who sought exposure rather than concealment, he had different advice. 'Concentrate,' he commanded. 'When he worked,' she recalled, 'it was as if God were working, he had such profound concentration. It was then that I became aware for the first time of the difference between standing in front of a camera, and acting.'[4] To play the role, he kept his arms (needlessly) strapped to his sides for hours at a time until they were quite numb. She was appalled, overawed by his masochistic dedication. Her own coming stardom was going to be sanctified by this kind of self-sought Calvary. Working on a Crawford film set was seldom without its

ABOVE Surrounded by authentic period colour in *Winners of the Wilderness*.

BELOW With Lon Chaney (left) in *The Unknown*, and John Gilbert in *Twelve Miles Out*.

pains. Even her insistence on keeping the temperature down to a frigid 58° Fahrenheit was a way of 'concentrating' people's minds on the work. '*Ardua Gratia Artis*' (Pain for Art's Sake) would have been a better motto at MGM for Crawford than the company slogan of '*Ars Gratia Artis*'. As others shivered in the cold climate she created, her own concentration burned up her energy.

That quality was useful to cope with the undiluted ardour of John Gilbert in *Twelve Miles Out* (9 July 1927) as the bootlegger who highjacks her. It was Gilbert's totally uncritical ability to surrender to his feelings as he panted them out (silently but potently) on screen which gave him his self-charging energy. He was a romantic by conviction who was keyed to the highest pitch of excitement during the first few takes of a scene and was never as good thereafter. By now, Crawford had discovered this was her nature, too: 'Rehearsals rob me of spontaneity,' she said. A romantic liaison might have developed off screen as a result of this compatibility except that Gilbert was already in thrall to Greta Garbo and infatuated or infuriated at their on-again, off-again affair. It was Crawford's first experience of acting with an MGM superstar and the lesson of how he had turned acting power into real studio power was not lost on her. His sheer 'worth' impressed her: he was then on $3,000 a week, it would rise to $5,000 a week by the end of the decade and he insisted on all the appurtenances to which he considered himself entitled. He had had his own bungalow dressing-room at the old Metro studios; he demanded the same facilities at MGM. Records disclose that the studio met the $15,000 bill for this structure, but prudently kept the indulgence a secret from other top stars. Yet it refused to pay an additional $7,000 for furnishings and kept passing the bill back to Gilbert or around the departments accompanied by memos sprinkled with cautionary 'You know John ...' marginalia on them. This was the first contest of strength between MGM and the star, whose shockingly sudden drop from popularity and box-office power after his early Talkie débâcle in 1929 opened the breach into an embittered gulf. Not enough study has been made of the effects on fellow contract artists of such tragedies as Gilbert's – and others that will be mentioned shortly. But the dethronement that was possible to the most apparently secure screen idol was a fate that weakened the resolve of some and stiffened that of others: it certainly played its part when Crawford's hour for bargaining with MGM came.

Meantime, she had made another important friend. Frank Orsatti is hardly mentioned in official MGM records, yet every studio employee knew this gregarious Italian-American as one of Mayer's most companionable cronies. He dealt in real estate, he dealt in illicit liquor, he dealt in speakeasies – Frank Orsatti dealt – period,' says someone still at MGM today who recalls this powerful 'fixer'. He was an Italianate *padre-padrone*, who moved into Mayer's business circle and eventually into his family circle. Orsatti and Mayer shared an attitude to their wives and children which was much the same mixture of sentiment and authority. Orsatti was Mayer's gin-rummy partner and travelling companion and even accompanied him to the White House when the MGM chief (who was also Republican Party treasurer in California) met the newly elected Herbert Hoover. According to Samuel Marx, Orsatti used to throw beach parties at which he offered to 'fix the boss up' with some of the girls passing through his talent agency. It is doubtful if Mayer's powerful inhibitions about mixing business and pleasure let him take advantage of this. Orsatti is unmentioned in Crawford's memoirs, so their relationship must remain speculative. But his name crops up in a memo dated 1 July 1927, couched in one of those asides which, in the studio's intramural semaphoring, mean so much more than the actual words. By then, Crawford's patience at putting up with her family was exhausted: she wanted a place of her own. M.E.Greenwood, an MGM executive who appears to have handled the internal memos he wrote to *himself*, communicated with Charles A.Greene, head of contracts: 'According to Miss Crawford's explanation, the price [of the house she wanted to buy] is $28,000, completely furnished. I arranged with the Culver City Bank to lend her $6,000. We guarantee it. She says this $6,000 is for the first payment ... Since she is rather hazy about the details [she] is bringing Frank Orsatti to explain.' Orsatti presumably 'explained' to everyone's satisfaction. Crawford got a studio-negotiated mortgage of $10,000; MGM also backed a trust deed for $12,500. In addition to the $6,000 loan against salary, this put her monthly obligation at nearly $500. She was then on $500 a week for the first half-year, $400 a week for the rest of the year 'payable on Saturday'. Her commitments were not excessive; but for the studio to guarantee a substantial capital sum indicates how satisfactorily her career was running, or how persuasive Frank Orsatti was. In those early years, Joan Crawford certainly knew who her friends were at MGM.

The house at 513 Roxbury Drive, Beverly Hills, was dark inside with poky rooms in the way that such a surprising number of film-star homes seem to have been in the 1920s. Its shaded interior was made even more sombre by black-wood furnishings in the Spanish style, ornately carved and polished. But a short staircase lent it a certain dignity and a tapestry she had bought from the studio props department hung in stiff folds. Not quite Old Castile, but certainly Beverly Hills – and her own.

Another event that happened at this time is small in itself, but shows the anxiety that MGM manifested when a promising property ran into trouble. Literally, in this case, as Crawford in her second-hand coupé – 'white, of course' – had almost collided with an employee of the nearby DeMille studio. The woman fell in avoiding the car. Early in the New Year, 1928, a flustered and worried Crawford appealed for help to Charles A.Greene. 'The girl is suing her for damages as a "hit and run" driver,' he noted, 'and for bribing the Culver City police. According to Joan, the girl was not even knocked down and is suffering from asthma, making this an excuse for confinement from her injuries. Do we do anything about stopping publicity or about helping her in any other way?' The MGM hierarchy decided it did, very much, want to do both. MGM foresaw the unpleasant consequences if not of a near-collision, then of the conjunction between a rising star of theirs and a major studio brought into the public arena by a certain

ABOVE The house that Metro bought: Joan's first Hollywood home.
BELOW The dining-room of a star-to-be.

'young lawyer, attorney for [the plaintiff], very anxious to make a reputation and without any scruples about bringing the matter to a court hearing if he can get a big indemnity for his client. On account of the several undesirable angles, that is [the plaintiff's] statement that she was run into while crossing the street in a safety zone, that Miss Crawford did not stop her car, and that the money paid to a police officer constitutes a bribe, all gives this case a very bad complexion.' The insurance company's attorney 'pledges his word to get the company to pay at least double [the sum thought reasonable compensation, i.e. $500] to settle the case'. But MGM took no chances: some sympathetic pressure brought by a DeMille studio executive on its employee won an out-of-court settlement. Thus the young attorney had his starring role snatched from him; Crawford's image remained unblemished – that was the important thing. And MGM tightened its links with the Culver City police, whose chief, 'Whitey' Hendry, later headed the studio security staff.

The local police were a Distant Early Warning system for the studio's publicity department. MGM was tolerant towards its contract artists' private misdemeanours, though ever since the Fatty Arbuckle scandal of 1921, which had painted Hollywood as a modern Sodom, and made the film companies fearful of Federal censorship, contracts had contained a 'morality clause'. Crawford's required her to conduct herself 'with due regard to public convention and morals and commit no act prejudicial to the motion picture industry in general'. This covered a multitude of sins; but the most grievous one an artist could commit was unprofessional conduct that cost the studio time and therefore money. This was not only unforgivable, but uncancellable, since the time lost while the player was incapacitated or suspended was added on to the term of their contract – a form of peonage that, in theory, could be indefinite. (It was not declared legally invalid until the early 1940s and then only after the high-priced stars who fought it had compared themselves to the similarly indentured but far less generously treated labourers in the Californian vinefields.) Sexual misbehaviour, cocaine addiction or just plain liquor were the temptations of the 1920s which claimed stars who were unused to high living or high pressures. The disgrace or downfall of any personality sent a shiver through those remaining on the favoured roster.

Crawford co-starred with an actor who exemplified just such a personal tragedy. It always stayed in her memory as a warning to her. The year after she joined MGM, in 1926, the director King Vidor had picked an unknown extra named James Murray as leading man in a film then entitled *The Mob* (later *The Crowd*). Murray brilliantly personified the Little Man overcoming all the vicissitudes of daily life in the big city with such homely truth and understated sentiment that he looked, in retrospect, to be the Spencer Tracy of the silent era. He was placed on $60 a week, a five-year contract, with six-month options rising to $500 a week, and the studio advanced him $1,500 for a Buick and cast him with Crawford in a silent version of the operetta *Rose Marie* (19 February 1928), which was shown publicly, of course, with a theatre orchestra playing the score. Crawford made the best of an unpromising adaptation which turned the Rocky Mountain melody into a murder melodrama. At least it turned out a better picture than two

ABOVE With William Haines (and a useful make-up mirror) in *West Point*.
OPPOSITE Crawford's hair goes frizzy for *Rose Marie*.
OVERLEAF Melodrama played a bigger part than melodies in the silent version of *Rose Marie* – with the doomed star James Murray.

previous pot-boilers she had made, a golfing comedy called *Spring Fever* (9 July 1927) and a sports comedy called *West Point* (8 January 1928), both of them with the light comedian William Haines well to the fore and Crawford collecting such throwaway notices as 'Joan Crawford is charming as Allie' (in the first film) and 'Joan Crawford is quite charming as Betty' (in the second). For the first time she got star billing in *Rose Marie*, and the physical passion she put into portraying the French-Canadian outdoor girl was complemented by James Murray's manly naturalism. But within months of the picture, and when plans were advanced to team them again, she saw Murray's career and personality fall utterly to pieces.

The MGM files contain a minutely detailed, even moving account of the studio's endless efforts to redeem Murray from the consequences of becoming an alcoholic. Contrary to the allegations usually made against the heartless 'studio system', they show how a highly promising talent was worth the trouble and expense of salvaging.

On 9 April 1928, M.E.Greenwood informed other MGM heads: 'We were advised that James Murray was at 1216 Highland Avenue in a much intoxicated condition ... His right eye was extremely cut and swollen. He was taken to the Porter Sanitarium that afternoon. He remained there until Saturday 7 April, until about three o'clock in the afternoon, when he called me and asked permission to go to the Catholic Church in Hollywood. He wanted to stay in

Hollywood overnight, so that he could go to the early Sunday Mass and to the sunrise service at the Bowl, and he promised to return afterwards to the sanitarium. Dr Zin reported that he was in very good condition and recommended that we give our permission, the idea being that if he failed us this time, it would be the end of him. He did not report to the sanitarium and at eight o'clock, Sunday night, 8 April, I was informed that he had gone to 2322 Highland Avenue, the residence of Mr Lubin, and broken in to get some whisky and was terribly intoxicated. [We] had the Culver City police go over and bring back our Buick, which is now in the lot. Other than that, we have paid no more attention to Mr Murray.' But this was *not* the end. The studio paid constant attention to Mr Murray; again and again, it accepted his sincere repentance, concealed his weakness, even managed to loan him out to other film companies, where he acquitted himself so well that Mayer and Thalberg wiped the slate clean of the money which his 'incapacities' had cost MGM and which had been charged against his salary. This evidence of a charitable side to corporative management – seldom recognized as even existing in most accounts of the studio – is punctuated by fastidiously kept records of the moneys paid by the studio to police officers for 'taking care' of Murray during his spells of intoxication (officer L.O.Lindsay, 72 hours: $72.00; officer G.C.Truschal, 43 hours: $43.00, and so on).

Marriage sobered Murray, but only for a time. All too soon, he was authorizing MGM to 'appoint such person or persons as you may designate to act as bodyguard for me'. Even with this 'attendant', Murray gave the film unit the slip, vanished off the location of *Thunder* and had to be pursued into the Mojave Desert, where he was recaptured and 'worked on' for two or three days before he could complete his role. He was found to have been taking 'some kind of harmful drug, as he was nervous and all shot to pieces'. Only then did MGM give up. Mayer terminated his contract – serving no fewer than three notices on him to ensure that one at least reached him – and he quit the studio in mid-1929. He worked his way through other film companies and a number of undistinguished films until he fell, or jumped, into the Hudson River in 1936. Some film historians have made him out to be a Hollywood martyr; the MGM evidence does not support this.

His self-willed fate constantly reminded Crawford and her peers that however slow their advancement and insecure their status, they were part of a system that could sustain them as well as extinguish them.

One evening in October 1927, Paul Bern escorted Crawford to the Los Angeles opening of *Young Woodley*. It starred Douglas Fairbanks Jr as the schoolboy who falls in love with his housemaster's wife. 'Very tall, very thin and boyish', was how she recalled him. He looked even younger than his nineteen years and – like Crawford – had deducted a couple of years from his official age. He was to become Crawford's first husband.

It was said later (but not too much later) that Doug's social standing, the son and step-son respectively of Hollywood's demi-Royals, Douglas Fairbanks Sr and Mary Pickford, was the attraction he held for the ambitious girl with no background and a still insecure status in the studio. But this misses the point completely. Crawford had not much use in those days for social standing; she defined her goals in terms of constant work and hard-won success. Though her career had not yet taken off, it was in a more active and promising state than the younger Fairbanks's. A liaison with his family wouldn't necessarily have assisted her. At that time, Doug Jr and his father were estranged by the older man's resentment of another 'Fairbanks' in the movies as well as the reminder that Doug Jr's mere presence held for his father, then in his mid-forties, of how the years were flying. Crawford had already met the son in the MGM dining-room and thought him uppish and clannish. So what made her take to him now, so spontaneously that she could hardly wait to get back home from the theatre to write and tell him of her feelings? Well, the theatre where she observed him this time was a place that always threw a spell over Crawford: appearing in front of all those people was a fearful experience she never felt herself up to. And the play, as well as its *jeune premier*, made a great impression on her. No wonder: for the sentiments uttered by Laura Simmons, the housemaster's wife who avoids taking advantage of Young Woodley's puppy love and surrenders her own happiness to spare him disillusionment, were exactly like the kind of thing that Crawford was wont to express to the rich but callow young escorts with whom she went on the town but took care to quit. One can see her lips forming lines by playwright John Van Druten ('Don't let me be a bitterness and a reproach to you always ... Don't let me spoil love for you'), as she heard them repeated night after night on her subsequent visits to the play. One knows the attraction she felt assimilating sentiments like 'building blocks' to give her life a new dimension. If Doug Jr's performance determined her to believe that the moment was now ripe for love (and she felt secure enough), then what subsequently occurred between her own tougher, maturer nature and the younger man's impetuous romanticism resembles a *Young Woodley* being played out to a happier conclusion in real life.

Crawford, as critic Richard Schickel reminds us, enjoyed demonstrating mastery over her career. She was unlikely to have felt that Doug Jr had made as much of his at that date as she had of hers. Despite good looks and an agreeable personality, his heart didn't seem to be in acting. Where he did score over her was in education, taste and discrimination. He moved easily among life's better things, which Paul Bern was still helping her sense and acquire. 'We seemed to be each other's good-luck charm,' she wrote of the constant dating that now ensued between them. He was certainly her cultural talisman. Whatever Doug approved, she attempted to absorb: the romance was an extension course in aesthetic appreciation long before it became a proof of social acceptability. Doug had his father's instinct for self-improvement, though he didn't have to sweat over it. When he told Crawford, 'Nothing is important from yesterday save what we learn for tomorrow,' he sounded as if he was mouthing one of those moralistic aphorisms which his father liked to emblazon on the end-titles of his silent film-epics to raise the audience's aspirations as they left the cinema. A whirlwind romance became for Crawford a crash course in literature. 'He mentioned books he'd read and I tried to devour Shaw, Ibsen, Proust and Nietzsche all at once. I read my way to mental indigestion.'[5] More than ever, as a result of such courses at the 'University of One', she craved 'valid' parts, yet continued to draw 'programme' pictures like *Rose*

ABOVE Sailing by with Ramon Novarro in *Across to Singapore* and (right) stealing scenes from a moustacheless John Gilbert in *Four Walls*.

BELOW Crawford shows off her slave anklet. 'Does this mean anything?' asked the caption. Yes, marriage was pending.

Marie, or *Across to Singapore* (6 June 1928), a square-rigger melodrama co-starring her with Ramon Novarro. But at least Doug accompanied her on location to Yosemite national park and listened to her singing the 'Indian Love Call', or waved at her sailing ship as it passed Long Beach. On the last day of December 1927, he proposed marriage. He bought their wedding ring before the engagement one; and except that a film editor devoid of romance would have re-edited this out-of-sequence event, it was a love affair that might have been made in the movies. They kept their romance secret while waiting to fix a date for marriage.

Courtship made another Tim McCoy Western endurable. Propinquity helped while they waited. Doug's studio was First National, but he was on 'loan-out' to MGM as Garbo's dissolute brother in *A Woman of Affairs*, which was being shot on the set next door to the gangster melodrama *Four Walls* (26 August 1928) which Crawford was shooting with John Gilbert. The time they might otherwise have had to spend commuting between studios was now consumed in frolicsome flirtation between shots. By now, Gilbert's infatuation with Garbo had cooled and the distance between them showed in the scenes they shared in *A Woman of Affairs*; paradoxically, Crawford's romantic arousal by Fairbanks enabled her role as Gilbert's moll in the *Four Walls* film to distract the fans' eyes from the male star. MGM executives sensed this as they viewed the daily rushes: for the first time, the script department was ordered to construct additional scenes for Crawford.

About the same time as she met Fairbanks, Crawford read a serial story in one of the Hearst newspapers. It was called *The Dancing Girl*, and was intended to be turned into a film for William Randolph Hearst's movie company, Cosmopolitan, which released its productions through MGM. Testing stories for their public appeal in this way, before spending money in turning them into a scenario, was one of the few bonuses which MGM derived from its links with Hearst, whose film company was simply one way of promoting the career of his mistress Marion Davies, vainly as it usually turned out. Emboldened by having a film role tailored for her in *Four Walls*, Crawford purloined the new script. Immediately she read it, she begged producer Hunt Stromberg for a part in it. MGM had sensed something different about the story, but was not quite sure what. It was a studio which put more reliance than most on the title given a film. The technique was to poll several executives until a consensus was reached. Several dozen titles might be run through and discarded. Sometimes the indecisiveness revealed doubts about where audience tastes might lie in times when trends were changing, sometimes it suggested corporate uncertainty about casting, content or style. 'Personally like title *These Modern Girls* for *Dancing Girl*,' cabled one MGM executive. 'Also have suggestion *Dancing Daughters*. We like either of these much better than *Dancing Girl*.' On 7 March 1928, when shooting had got underway, another title was registered: *These Naughty Times*. This, too, fell by the wayside, until, on 16 April 1928, Howard Strickling cabled J. Robert Rubin in New York: 'Final title of *The Dancing Girl* is – *Our Dancing Daughters*.' This time, there was no further change; and by then, the girl who herself had undergone some fateful name-changes was well into playing the role that made Joan Crawford a star.

44 The same vitality that shaped Joan Crawford's physical restlessness and fuelled her career transfuses itself into 'Dangerous' Diana Merick, the flapper girl of *Our Dancing Daughters* (1 September 1928). Rhythm and role are now one. The opening shot, an emblematic figurine celebrating the madcap spirit of the Jazz Age, dissolves into Crawford's lower limbs, so impatient to take their owner to an all-night party at the yacht club that they are already doing a tap-dance as she steps into her undies. 'Mother, how vicious!' she cries spotting the orchid on her parent's gown – for flappers like Diana have modern parents, too. Then roguishly advising her father not to stay out late, she rushes off on her own wild fling, first making provision for the distance she means to travel with a sip out of a succession of champagne glasses offered by her dancing partners and a toast 'to myself. I have to live with myself until I die. So may I always like myself!'

The impression is of spoilt exuberance, youthful audaciousness, heedless abandon. Finding herself improbably encumbered by a party gown that can scarcely have weighed an ounce in the first place, she whips it off and finishes Charlestoning in her slip. 'You want to take all of life, don't you?' asks the wealthy playboy she is dating and confidently expects to marry. Comes the pat reply (in silent-era titles): 'Yes – all! I want to hold out my hands and catch at it.'

Our Dancing Daughters was a declaration, a manifesto. It didn't just speak to the younger generation of film-goers: it spoke for them. If they couldn't aspire to Diana's wild life-style, they could live the vicarious thrills of it through the film's promotion of youth, pace and modernity. The fans who disregarded fire regulations and stood five deep behind the last row of seats at the film's first performance after the shops had closed that opening Monday night at the Capitol theatre, New York, were Joan's generation. They were ready and able in all except what their purses held to go along with her lack of inhibitions about all the really important things life held – boy-friends, party-going, having a good time generally and waking up not to a hangover but a happy ending.

Yet the appeal is not quite so simplistic as this suggests: nor is Crawford's conquest simply a matter of story-rigging. The film divides the interest, if not film-goers' sympathy, between three well-balanced characters. Crawford herself is the good-bad girl, whose snappy, syncopated movements are perfect for the short cuts she takes to the pleasures of the time, but whose wildness is ultimately defined as simply being a good sport. Headstrong she may be, but she is true to herself and incapable of being false to any other. Then there is Anita Page, another 'daughter' of the times, only devious rather than dance-mad. Her baby face is the badge of the flapper-age vamp. Acting innocent and virginal, egged on by her mother out of a need to replenish the family purse, she entices Joan's millionaire beau into her own arms. ('Does this signify marriage?' Her mother slips the question in like a knife-thrower after the pair return from an innocent moonlight walk.) It forces Joan into a redemptive bit of moral stock-taking – and gives disadvantaged film-goers the pleasure of enjoying wealth in the short term while immediately approving of virtue as a long-term investment. The lesson is rubbed in – *scrubbed* in, rather – when Anita, who has gone to the bad, falls fatally down the stairs at the private club after standing at

PREVIOUS PAGE Very nearly an Art Deco object. Cedric Gibbons's Art Deco sets for *Our Dancing Daughters* (above and opposite) influenced the fashion of the times and enhanced the style of flappers like Crawford's 'dangerous Diana'.

the top sneering drunkenly at the charwomen washing them. The story's third 'daughter', Dorothy Sebastian, is a victim, too, but of male chauvinism: her husband cannot cope with the revelation that she has played around before marriage. The moral: never tell all.

'None of us was starred in the picture,' Crawford recalled, 'but theatre owners, sensing the audience response, "starred" me. My name went up on their marquees.'[6] Crawford's is indeed the name – and *Our Dancing Daughters* the movie – most often cited by impressionable teenage children surveyed in the years 1919–33 by the Payne Fund established to find out the effect that movies had on adolescents. One girl, a delinquent, admitted that when she went to parties after seeing the film, 'of course I mingled the drinks as [Diana] had done. I also sang the theme song of *Our Dancing Daughters*.' But wanton hedonism was not the lesson that most children absorbed. Far from it. 'No matter what happened,' said one girl in her teens, '[Diana Merick] played fair, even when she lost her man ... The older generation [think] that when a modern young miss wants her man back, she'd even be a cut-throat; but Joan Crawford showed that even in a crisis like this she was sport enough to play fair. And "play fair" is really the motto of the better class of young Americans.'[7]

Fifty years later, the grand-children of 'our dancing daughters' showed the same sort of generational response to John Travolta, thrusting him into what the inflation of later times called 'superstardom'. In a simpler age, when movie-going and not discoing was the mass stimulus, teenagers' identification with a star who appeared to *be* the character she played was not confined to Saturday night fever.

Crawford's stock soared in ways that MGM couldn't ignore, even if it had wanted to: in the box-office grosses of all the Loew's theatres, and in the suddenly increased volume of fan mail arriving at the studio. Some of it came addressed to 'Diana', but the mail room needed no other clue to its destination. People wrote to Crawford as if they knew her. At a stroke, she had found 'that incredible thing, a public ... From this moment on, I had a sense of audience, warm living people who would care for me in direct proportion to the energy and talent I could give, a public to whom I owed a loyalty and from whom I've always received loyalty.'[8] She answered every letter personally, or so she claimed. Perhaps this was true of the first couple of

tons of mail-bags, until she saw the rising cost of loyalty in time and postage. An MGM internal memo suggests that the machine had soon to take over. 'This is your authority', M.E.Greenwood wrote to a Miss Farrell, re. 'Joan Crawford Fan Mail', to 'take charge of [this] mail until further notice. I would suggest we reply to all the intelligent letters and keep a record of the cost.' On 18 February 1929, Crawford's stardom, already accorded her by her fans like a commission on the field of battle, received its official confirmation at HQ. 'Is Joan Crawford to be considered a star?' W.K.Craig, head of accounts, asked Floyd Hendrickson, studio attorney, and added with a bluntness indicating how such intangibles as 'stardom' had a practical application to studio management: 'And is all her accumulated salary to be charged to the pictures in which she works?' Back came an unwavering 'Yes.' Crawford's new sense of identity was also formally registered. 'Joan Crawford', wrote Craig, 'is asking that we issue salary checks from now on to "Joan Crawford", instead of Lucille LeSueur. Will you find out from the attorneys if this is okay.' Unsurprisingly, it was – though, strangely enough, some memos, even those from Mayer himself, continue to be addressed to 'Miss LeSueur' until well into 1931.

Her contract option had been picked up at $1,000 a week on 28 November 1928. Following *Our Dancing Daughters*, it was raised by a further $500 and there was to be no 'lay-off' period – the stretch of time that an artist was officially on holiday without pay. In other words, she was now considered so valuable a property that she was to be given a paid vacation.

Crawford now entered a phase in her professional life that was familiar to front-office executives, but not always welcomed by them. In taking stock of what had happened to her and evaluating her capacity for even greater success, she began defining that success not, alas, in terms of

With John Mack Brown and other admirers in *Our Dancing Daughters*: party girl, but at heart a good sport.

corporate profits accruing to the generous employers who had given her that chance, but in terms of 'valid pictures, significant parts' for herself. She was asking what the part might do for her, not what her presence in it might do for the part (and the picture). In such contradictory views of stardom lies much of the strain and stress and occasional total and acrimonious breakdown of the relationship between stars and their studios which has, frequently unfairly, made the term 'studio system' a pejorative one. As yet, though, Crawford's champagne glass was so overflowing that she was not ready to dash it ungratefully in the face of her employers. The fact that she was put into two pot-boilers straight after *Our Dancing Daughters* signifies nothing except that public reaction to her Jazz Age incarnation had taken MGM by surprise, with no vehicle of similar horse-power ready for her. Hence *Dream of Love* (30 December 1928), another doomed Ruritanian romance in which her guitar-strumming gypsy child opens the eyes of Nils Asther's playboy Crown Prince to the joys of true love and, one hopes, constitutional monarchy, and *The Duke Steps Out* (16 March 1929), 'in which I was again background' for William Haines as a wised-up preppy at West Point. But by the time these were out and already forgotten, MGM had *Our Modern Maidens* ready to go into production.

The trio of 'daughters': Crawford (in front) with Dorothy Sebastian and Anita Page.
BELOW Stopping the party.

As this is being written, Hollywood is locked into what could be called 'filming by numbers', or the 'sequels syndrome', placing hope and huge budgets on the proposition that not only do people know what they like, but, even more, they like what they know and will continue to like it if given it often enough. This nowadays seems a product of terminal desperation; five decades ago, it was a confident and buoyant trend. What this new movie proved, along with its predecessor *Our Dancing Daughters* and its own follow-up film *Our Blushing Brides*, was the bank-ability of fans 'loyalty – not only to pictures with 'Our' in the title, but with the name 'Joan Crawford' above the title.

Much more than the first film in the series, *Our Modern Maidens* places the accent of interest squarely on Crawford. It opens on the same high note of speed, youth and pleasurable promiscuity. After dancing the night away at some country club, the girls and their beaux, jam-packed into open roadsters, race each other back to the school gates where an impromptu fling – 'What are our thoughts on leaving school? All together, girls – MEN, MEN, MEN!' – is staged under the art deco hoarding advertising the products of Joan's motor-magnate father, J. Bickering Brown. There's the customary Crawford dance, peppy, preppy and provocative, and then she is seen off to the dorm by the young man she has secretly promised to marry. He is played by Douglas Fairbanks Jr.

Six weeks before shooting started, after a courtship lasting a year and a half, Crawford and Fairbanks had publicly announced their own engagement. Louis B. Mayer opposed the match the minute he got wind of it. Romance between a movie company's contract artists was one thing. It was good publicity, for a start. Life seemed to be an extension of art and the fans could imagine themselves privy to the real romance while paying to see the scripted one. But marriage was another matter. An alliance of talents consecrated by marriage, a knot much trickier to untie than an option-loaded film contract, could work against a studio's plans for the independent careers of husband and wife, especially if one of the partners was more popular at the box-office than the other. Fairbanks was under contract to First National studios: employing him on loan could be expensive if his wife-to-be, under contract to MGM, wanted him as her co-star. Anyhow, Mayer's instinct, which at this period was seldom wrong, told him that Crawford's box-office appeal rested on her image of zestful independence, not settled matrimony. On the other hand, Crawford assured him that she and Fair-banks had no intention of making more than one picture together – they didn't want to commercialize their love, she explained. Mayer made the best of the situation, yet managed to have his own way, too. For although Fairbanks was cast as Crawford's fiancé, he was never, as it was worked out, destined to remain her celluloid husband.

Our Modern Maidens is a less well-known film than *Our Dancing Daughters* and it is often assumed that if its

TOP TO BOTTOM Between location shots Anita, Dorothy and Joan take in some plain old food.
With Nils Asther and Dorothy Sebastian.
Girl friends comfort each other: Crawford and Dorothy Sebastian.

ABOVE Ruritanian interlude: with Nils Asther and her gipsy guitar in *Dream of Love*

BELOW With Douglas Fairbanks Jnr in *Our Modern Maidens*: they were secretly engaged off screen too.

ABOVE The Roaring Twenties: Douglas and Joan (left) drive on to the next party.

BELOW Making her own music in *Our Modern Maidens*.

Clowning on the set of *Our Modern Maidens*: director Jack Conway watches Rod LaRocque put his leading lady in jeopardy.

romance doesn't run smoothly, at least it ends happily. The reverse is true. Half-way through the story, Fairbanks slips off from his fiancée's houseparty with her best friend, played again by Anita Page. They cross the ornamental lake in a gondola, and before the fade-out in the shrubbery on the island, the champagne has gone to Doug's head and Anita is in his arms. The girl's consequent pregnancy, conveyed by Anita Page in protracted gasps and shakes as if she had just escaped a hurricane, is revealed just too late to stop the engaged couple's wedding, but it throws their honeymoon plans into instant disarray. 'What do you think of a groom-less honeymoon? "Modern", isn't it? I'm just setting the fashion.' And with that, Crawford deserts her new husband, swaggers off alone through the aghast and gossiping guests, gets shunned by Society and picks up an annulment in Paris. She later turns up in South America to wed Rod LaRocque, who has been the film's jilted lover – while Fairbanks, presumably, does right by Anita Page.

The film was another huge success, largely because of what *Variety* called Crawford's 'far-fetched but vivid' performance as the girl who has everything, including a private railroad car in which she shoots craps, an inexhaustible penchant for dancing in her underwear and generally living it up every hour of the night (the day was for sleeping) in a Cedric Gibbons set of millionaire's art deco which runs to a living-room apparently three storeys high and a staircase that incorporates what looks like a high-diver's spring-board at its apex. Yet some critics and public felt Crawford had married the wrong man: they

preferred Fairbanks to LaRocque. The earlier film had provided a handy staircase to do away with inconvenient Anita Page: it shouldn't have been beyond the wits of the eight writers who worked on the screenplay to convey the accident-proneness of someone who lives in precarious art deco decor as well as by promiscuous sex. In one version of the script, Crawford and Fairbanks were re-united. But Louis B. Mayer had the final say. Crawford was to marry inside the MGM ranks, which meant her fellow contract artist Rod La Rocque.

However, real-life compensation was quick in coming. Immediately the film finished shooting, at the end of May 1929, Joan and Doug set their footprints side by side in wet cement outside Grauman's Chinese Theatre, a ritual that admitted them to the status of fully-fledged (or fully-shod) stars – then they slipped away to New York to be married. The reason they had waited so long was nothing to do with rumours of opposition by Doug's father and stepmother. The marriage of Douglas Fairbanks Sr and Mary Pickford was breaking down at this very period: he had begun to snap at her; he made the filming of their first talkie together, *The Taming of the Shrew*, into a trial of temperaments between as well as during takes. These two were much more worried at the likely effect of divorce (which was to follow their 1933 separation) on their own images and careers than at the consequences of marriage between Doug Jr and a fast-rising MGM star. The person who did oppose the match was Doug Jr's own mother. Beth Sully's bitterness towards her ex-husband had caused her to try and run the acting career of her son, then aged fifteen, in competition with his father's. Now she saw another woman with the power to plan her son's future for him. However, Doug Jr had become twenty-one in December

ABOVE The heiress who has everything including her own private railroad car for craps shooting and (below) the film star who has just acquired her own smart town car.

ABOVE Undergoing one of the rites of stardom: 'signing in' outside Grauman's Chinese Theatre.
RIGHT The new Mr and Mrs Douglas Fairbanks Jnr.

1928, and the mother who had had custody of him could no longer withhold her consent to marriage. So Beth and *her* husband-to-be, Broadway song-and-dance star Jack Whiting, were witnesses at the wedding on 3 June 1929. Significantly, the way the newly-weds relayed the news back to their respective studios showed how confidently they believed it would affect their earning power as well as their happiness. Crawford wired MGM: 'If I have worked hard in the past, just watch me now.' Fairbanks, in his cable to First National, got to the point more bluntly: 'Joan and I were married yesterday. Now that I have a wife to support need raise in salary.'

But as her husband was nearly $15,000 in debt, it was Joan who provided the roof over their heads – at 426 North Bristol Avenue, Brentwood, midway between Beverly Hills and the Pacific Coast.

The house cost $57,000 and, to a visitor three months after the married couple had moved in, it looked 'furnished for a perpetual honeymoon'. Rustic stepping-stones across the front lawn led up to the hall door with its knocker sculpted in the shape of two heads, male and female, their lips pressed together in a kiss. Its ten rooms were done in green and gold, silks and brocades, with Spanish wrought-iron gates separating the dining and living areas. The taste displayed was meant to be cosmopolitan, but it looked, as a more sophisticated Crawford later admitted, 'a hodgepodge' of French brocaded settees, Early American chairs, Italian occasional tables, and Joan's cherished Burmese drape, now

deployed not as a wall covering but as a grand-piano spread to enhance a large portrait of herself and Doug which stood next to a vase of constantly renewed cut flowers. Smaller-than-life statues of the newly-weds defended each side of the fireplace like household gods and right in the middle of the mantlepiece was a bust of Doug. Crawford allowed another rare shot of her with her back turned to the camera to be taken by *Photoplay* magazine, which was making an inventory of the house for its readers – she was pictured reverentially embracing Doug's bronze head. (Her adoration, however, ended when she saw the print: 'Do Not Use' is scrawled on the back in her imperious handwriting, thrice underlined. It was not used in the article.) The fans may have wondered at husband and wife maintaining separate bedrooms: Doug's was furnished in a masculine style with some of his own pen-and-ink drawings 'in the manner of Gustave Doré' adorning the walls, Joan's was 'thoroughly feminine', and *Photoplay*'s reporter, Alma Whitaker, was particularly struck by the numbers and orderliness of Crawford's clothes closets: 'forty dresses, thirty street hats, five dinner hats ... sixteen pairs of sports shoes, nineteen pairs of street shoes, eighteen pairs of evening shoes ...' (At this point, the article gives out: no wonder.) But the most extraordinary room was the sun-porch. Its shelves were stacked with dozens, and eventually hundreds, of dolls, as well as mechanical baby pigs, clucking hens, and Doug's electric railway, which was his wife's Christmas present to him. There were three live-in servants, cook, maid and chauffeur (for the Cadillac), as well as the master's bulldog, the mistress's chow, a Persian cat, a marmoset monkey and two love-birds twittering away in a cage in the breakfast room. Miss Whitaker's sharp eyes noted Wells's *Outline of History* and Ludwig's *Life of Napoleon* beside the gold-upholstered settees in the living-room. '"Yes, I am really reading them", says Joan smilingly. "Doug is crazy about Napoleon just now ..."'[9] The house was called 'El Jodo', a playful amalgam of Joan's own name and her nickname for Doug – 'Dodo'. One wonders if the gracious couple up the hill, in the mansion called 'Pickfair,' took this as a compliment or as a slightly disrespectful joke that people of Doug and Joan's generation would play on the honoured alliance of talents also enshrined in the name of *their* house.

In fact, relations with Mary Pickford and Douglas Fairbanks Sr were not nearly so chilly as has been often reported. And it is not at all true to assert that Hollywood's 'First Family' disdained the newly-weds or suspected Joan of social climbing and Doug Jr of wanting to usurp his father's throne. The older couple, as has been noted, had their own marital problems. But Mary's niece Gwynne (later the wife of George 'Bud' Ornstein, head of United Artists production in Europe in the 1960s and the man who, more than anyone else, fostered the 'New Wave' of British films in that decade) reported to this writer that her aunt admired Crawford's determination and followed her film fortunes as avidly as any fan-club member. Mary Pickford had made a vain attempt in 1929, when she was thirty-six, to break away from her imprisoning 'Sweetheart' image by playing a modern swinger in her first talkie, *Coquette*. She won an Oscar for her efforts, but not the new audience she desired – the very audience of sixteen-to

ABOVE The master bedroom, complete with the master on the side table.   BELOW The dolls' room for a dolls' house marriage.

twenty-five-year-olds whom Joan's flapper-girl performances had won over so completely in the same year. It is true that Mary waited for months before extending a white-gloved hand to her stepson and his wife at a 'Pickfair' dinner party in honour of Lord and Lady Mountbatten – who, ironically, were crazy to meet the star of *Our Dancing Daughters* – and saying graciously, 'Welcome to "Pickfair", Joan dear.' But the two women already had a lot in common. Despite her eminence, Mary possessed, and used in private, a vocabulary every bit as salty as Joan's. Mary sensed the same sexuality in Joan which she had had as a girl when she eloped to Cuba in 1911, at the age of eighteen, with her first husband Owen Moore. She sensed that Joan also comprehended the power-play of studio politics at which Mary herself was such a skilful and ruthless manipulator – she was, after all, part-owner of United Artists. According to Gwynne Ornstein, Mary Pickford would have bet on her step-daughter-in-law to make rings around Doug Jr in the ceaseless quest for ways and means of getting to 'the top of the heap' in Hollywood.

Gwynne helped ease Joan's *entrée* into Aunt Mary's world of 'Pickfair' society. It was like attending a finishing school. If the place's stately pretensions gave her an inferiority complex, it was soon overcome by the way she was now getting used to meeting any challenge which presented an opportunity for personal advancement. She absorbed it, as if it were a part in a film, making herself over into the new look or the new experience until she had become so much a part of it that further concealment was unnecessary. She used her Sunday visits to Pickfair throughout the autumn and winter to polish her deportment, gain social poise, pick up practical hints for entertaining guests, laying a table, dressing for company and making conversation with a wider range of more significant – she might have added '... and valid' – acquaintances than the residents of Hollywood, where people who did not talk of movies usually did not talk at all. Mary did not have any gift for entertaining folk informally: her social occasions, like her pictures, were 'produced'. Joan was often glad she had brought her tapestry needle with her to 'Pickfair'. It kept those hyperactive hands of hers busy during the afternoons when Mary retired to rest, for Joan did not dare depart for an hour or two to freshen up before dinner, lest Mary should find her gone if she unexpectedly broke her siesta and came downstairs. Fairbanks father and son usually went off to disport themselves at some mutually admiring male activity, like muscle-toning in the private gym which Fairbanks kept on the United Artists lot. Doug called his father 'Pete', his father called him 'Jayar' – it got them over the self-consciousness of calling each other 'father' and 'Junior'. Being 'big brothers', so to speak, maintained the older man's illusion that there was less than twenty-five years between him and his son. He was grateful to Joan for bringing them together.

Doug Jr and Joan renamed their own home 'Cielito Lindo' (Little Heaven) as their own absorption of gracious living gained ascendancy over their flirtatious sense of fun. Towards each other they now behaved with that high-pressure attentiveness which people who are worked hard by their jobs or their own inclinations display as proof that although their time is rationed, their love is still limitless. Both were worked hard, *very* hard by their respective

A star without losing the homely touch . . . but famous enough to be caricatured.

studios – they left their home at 8.00 a.m. and were not back much before 7.00 p.m. To Joan, that did not matter so much. Life to her was work. But for Doug Jr, life was play. The strain was bound to tell; but for the time being, 'El Jodo'/'Cielito Lindo' might have been mistaken for the 'Doll's House' of the Ibsen play, before anyone started slamming doors, that is.

Doug and Joan entertained in the style to which 'Pickfair' had accustomed them. At other people's dinner parties, they exchanged jokes or badinage in the secret 'lovers' language' they had invented, which put an additional syllable like 'op' or 'po' before vowels or consonants in order to baffle outsiders who were not 'in' on their connubial bliss. His pet name for her was 'Billie'. She had been called that, too, when Harry Cassin was her step-father; but Doug's 'Billie' referred to the character she had played in *Our Modern Maidens*. She kept adding rolling-stock to his electric train set. He set a new doll for her on the sun-porch shelf almost every week. And her hands knitted sweater after sweater for him and his father, the way an expectant mother would busy herself with providing a layette for the baby on the way. One of her own hand-knit sweaters was covered in Pop Art-type graffiti expressing her love for Doug. It wasn't worn much, though: Mary thought it vulgar. A heart on the sleeve, maybe, but Doug's profile on the bosom . . . Joan dear, please!

Doug's screen career received a much-needed boost when a reluctant Hollywood accepted that the Talkies were here to stay. Stage experience like his was in demand for the short-lived but agonizing period when it was believed that only trained professionals could utter screen dialogue satisfactorily. Crawford never doubted *her* ability to talk; but she bought a Dictaphone in 1929 and Doug supervised her reading verse into it – the English love-poets, of course. When she took her place on the sound stage at MGM, however, it was the verse of the American song-writer Nacio Herb Brown that provided her graduation exercise. The man who had 'discovered' her, Harry Rapf, was again by her side. He had been assigned the crucial task of producing *Hollywood Revue of 1929* (7 December 1929) in order to prove that the film company which boasted of 'more stars than there are in Heaven' could also muster enough voices to get into the Talkies.

Virtually every MGM star was in it, except Garbo. Her contract frustrated MGM's wish to have her in the film because it stipulated that although she could be starred alone in a film, or co-starred (with another player), she could only be co-starred with a male player. Everyone in *Hollywood Revue* was, more or less, a co-star on this occasion; but some of them were female. Crawford took only three days to film her segments. She sang and tap-danced with the Biltmore Trio's backing; and she appeared in the 'Singin' in the Rain' finale with Buster Keaton, Marion Davies, George K. Arthur and others, all of them very wet despite their waterproof slickers, and trying to hold their own vocally against the torrents of studio-made rain which in those primitive days had to be recorded at the

LEFT and OPPOSITE PAGE Marriage to Doug adds to her social poise . . . but it is still such a fresh experience that they are more like lovers than newly-weds . . . and Joan's own design for a sweater even includes Doug on the bosom.

same time as the songs. In her first real talkie, *Untamed* (23 November 1929: a film made after *Hollywood Revue* but screened slightly before the latter's general release), she played Bingo, child of the jungle ('Hear its chant Lang-uid and plain-tive', she crooned in the opening reel) and made the transition from jungle rhythms of South America to the snappy ones of the Jazz Age as she moved into well-heeled New York society life and back again. She was another spoiled brat, tamed this time by the Wild West rather than the East Side, in *Montana Moon* (28 March 1930). She had lowered the timbre of her voice, it recorded well – and some people at MGM spoke of a new singing star.

Meantime, Depression Era realities were beginning to enter even into Hollywood's calculations of what film-goers expected to see on the screen. The third and last of the 'Our' series of movies, *Our Blushing Brides* (19 July 1930), unexpectedly belies its frolicsome title. It has the usual trio of girls: Crawford, Anita Page, Dorothy Sebastian, but this time they are working girls holding down a job in the Big City rather than fun-loving society flirts out of the *Social Register*. All of them work in a department store, as good a place for being picked up by a man as the old stage door of *Sally, Irene and Mary*. Crawford is the girl with her head screwed on the right way, playing den mother to the other girls between modelling dresses in a sort of permanent fashion display which suggested that the ten screenwriters used on the film were still somewhat uncertain where shop-girls' values might be at in 1930 and decided to put some of them on her back. But not all of them. Though the boss's son, played by

PREVIOUS PAGES A face that reminded people of other stars like Garbo (left) or Jean Harlow (right).
ABOVE Her first talkie, *Hollywood Review of 1929* with (centre front) Buster Keaton, Marion Davies, George K. Arthur and everyone 'singin' in the rain' and trying to make themselves heard above it.
LEFT Peace and quiet again in the great outdoors of *Montana Moon*.

Robert Montgomery, proposes marriage, she rejects his millions. Quick wealth that's unearned by love is therefore unvalued by the working-class heroine of the new decade whose outline, whenever it can be seen under the outrageous fashions, Crawford is starting to sketch in this film. Her acting now is far less nervy: it shows a great gain in self-possession. It is as if she has been physically slowed down by the mannequin show. Instead of life being a permanent St Vitus dance she now takes her time in registering her effect. Her make-up is more modern, too. It is a movie that sounds the death knell of the flapper era. Even Cedric Gibbons's plutocratic sets have totally parted company with reality, as if the rich have no place in real life. The ultra-modern love-nest where Montgomery takes Crawford is literally off the ground, situated in a tree and reached by a staircase that lets down and can be drawn up again. The film's downbeat mood is clinched by the cautionary tale of Miss Sebastian, who falls for a crook, and of Miss Page, who kills herself after the store-owner's other son has jilted her. Shopgirls of the Thirties, beware – a girl's best friend is . . . another girl.

In spite of its following a sternly moral line, some individual scenes got the film into trouble with State censorship boards. The studio appealed against the cuts; and Louis B. Mayer's own memos to his executives show how shrewdly such incidents were anticipated and discounted in advance. 'Massachusetts censor board who have jurisdiction only on Sunday exhibition ordered dressing-

Our Blushing Brides: Crawford, Page and Sebastian have now to earn their living as department store girls.

Work comes before play in the big store even when it's the boss's son, Robert Montgomery.

Director Harry Beaumont instructs Crawford in the 'working girl's friend', the time clock.

Dorothy Sebastian finds a girl's best friend is . . . another girl.

Joan, the den mother, prepares breakfast.

Art Deco into fantasy land: Crawford (in a blond wig) receives Robert Montgomery's proposal in the tree house conversation pit.

gown scene eliminated in *Our Blushing Brides*,' Mayer noted on 29 July 1930. 'We immediately appealed and are asking permission to use a different dressing-room scene which I have had in Boston for censor board from last week ... You must bear in mind that no elimination was ever made weekdays in state of Massachusetts, but that for Sunday exhibition it is almost traditional and almost impossible to get by anything in nature of drinking, semi-nudity close-ups, chorus dancing, pistol shots, kept-woman incidents, etc.' The studio won its appeal – 'permitting us to put back entire drunk scene and to use substitute Crawford-Montgomery kimono scene'. Mayer continued: 'Always bear in mind that censor reports that go out from these boards to Hays Office [the industry's own self-regulatory board] are always appealed and that we always reduce them by at least 75 percent and many times 100 percent ... But the boards hardly ever issue statements showing that they withdrew eliminations, as they like to keep records that suggest they made extensive eliminations.'

Lucius Beebe, the gay *Social Register*-ite who also wrote a gossip column, declared that 'Joan Crawford in *Our Blushing Brides* ... plays the part of a mannequin with enough assurance for a *marchesa* and enough virtue for a regiment.' But the lady herself was less merciful: 'Personally, I had wearied of the part – to me it was totally *passé*. If I'd proved I could play the dancing girl I'd once been, fine. Now let's have a new objective.'[10] But when that came, it turned out an unwelcome prospect.

Unfortunately the production file on the film entitled *Great Day* has not survived in the MGM archives; but then the film does not exist, either. It was begun in or around September 1930; and after no fewer than eight weeks' shooting, or twice the time it took to film the usual Crawford picture, it was abandoned on the personal orders of Louis B. Mayer. The cost of aborting the production was $280,000 – 'a tremendous amount of money', Crawford rightly said. The reason for the débâcle can't be precisely established, but certain clues suggest it was a decisive moment in Joan Crawford's career. *Great Day* was based on Vincent Youmans's Broadway musical, which the Talkies had now rendered a most attractive vehicle for a star who could sing as well as act. Thalberg seems to have had no doubt about Crawford's ability to do both. He personally requested her services, even though she had previously had little direct contact with the studio production chief: she invariably pursued parts she fancied through Hunt Stromberg or, in the last resort, Mayer himself. The explanation she gave for the film's being abandoned was that she could not play the *ingénue* role in it – a 'baby vamp' from the Deep South. 'I just can't talk baby talk,' she told Mayer after she had viewed the daily rushes 'with mounting concern – they were God-awful'. Mayer viewed them, agreed with her, and scrapped the film: as Crawford never tired of saying, he knew how to build *and protect* his properties. But the Culver City archives contain not one note on a decision that must have singed the cable wires between the Coast and New York. Instead, they indicate MGM's tenacious retention of the film rights to *Great Day* and a long and sometimes contentious series of dealings with Youmans (and, later, his estate) over the company's plans to re-mount the production for Jeanette MacDonald, the singing star who had joined the studio in 1933. Therein, perhaps, lies the clue to Crawford's panicky dissatisfaction with *Great Day* which led her to appeal to Mayer over Thalberg's head. She said later that Thalberg hadn't seen the rushes, a statement flatly contradicted by Thalberg's practice of seeing the rushes of every MGM film in production at 2.30 p.m. sharp, the day after they had been shot. Why, in short, was she so desperate to be out of the picture?

It can only be an informed guess: but suppose Crawford had made a *success* of a role that was essentially a singing one? This was a crucial moment in her career. She was determined to go into 'straight' dramas; but she had already been employed in musicals, or films with song-and-dance numbers. With the coming of sound, virtually every major Hollywood studio had bought into the music-publishing industry. Sheet music made the sort of huge profits that disc recordings were soon to notch up: between 100,000 and 150,000 sheets of a song could be sold, and almost as many discs, within a month of a successful musical film's release. Every studio sought a musical star, or wanted to use the singing and dancing talents of what stars it already had. If *Great Day* had repeated its Broadway success for Crawford, she would have found it increasingly difficult to continue her career as a dramatic actress. She would have been typecast as a musical star. We have no way of verifying if her baby-vamp talk was inadequate because she couldn't play it. But everything about her, every move she had made in the past, every challenge she accepted indicates a will to succeed at any cost. It is highly unlikely that she couldn't have given *some* acceptable interpretation with all the dialogue coaching and other resources available at MGM. But she did not. Instead, she willed the contrary – and now she was powerful enough to cause a whole production to be folded around her.

It is leaping ahead in her story, but there exists a memo dated 9 November 1938 that may have some relevance to this incident. Signed by Floyd Hendrickson, the studio attorney, it reads: 'Joan Crawford's singing in *Ice Follies* [the skating spectacular] ... Our contract with Miss Crawford provides that we will not require her to appear in a musical in which she is required to sing several numbers prior to 28 February 1939. We should therefore get a letter from her waiving this restriction.' The letter was duly given: Crawford, by 1938, was in a weaker bargaining position. But this restriction on doing musicals had been inserted in her contract, at one of its periodic revisions, exactly seven years earlier: she was taking no chances of being deflected from the direction she meant to travel.

No wonder she referred to her next film as 'a moment that was crucial career-wise'. One thing about the script for *Paid* (20 December 1930) was comfortingly certain: this story of a department-store girl jailed for a theft she did not commit and revenging herself on her boss by marrying his son had no singing numbers, no dancing sequences. It was drama, all drama. Mayer and Stromberg initially hesitated over assigning her the role. The switch of personality it demanded from the girl who had been the symbol of flaming youth undercut the very basis of stardom, which is constant rotation of what is familiar and well-loved. *Paid* was a clean break. What if it cost MGM's valuable new star

OPPOSITE How she looked in the role she never completed in the picture that was never finished: *Great Day*.

Two more scenes from *Great Day*: (above) with John Miljan and (below) with John Mack Brown.

ABOVE Stripped of glamour and ready for gaol in *Paid*.
RIGHT Social realism in *Paid* brings Crawford closer to her fans – with Marie Prévost.

one well-established fan following without gaining her the loyalty of another? They yielded, though, and one reason was the indisposition of the other MGM star originally intended for the role – Norma Shearer was pregnant. Bearing Thalberg's only child, a son, made a present of the role to her rising rival.

It is indeed a 'new' Crawford who stands up in court for sentencing in the first scene of *Paid*. She is all in shop-girl black, a tone to match the severity of her make-up – her face looks set in emotional plaster. Harsher lighting brings out unsuspected hollows in her cheeks; her eyes glow almost phosphorescently inside their worried mascara; the prison pallor is enhanced by the unexpected size and vividness of her tight-pressed lips. Crawford had had her teeth capped for the second time and this painful operation, which compelled her to go on a liquid diet for several days, naturally stretched her mouth. From now on in her films, one can see her use of lip make-up to emphasize a character's emotional intensity by exaggerating still further the apparent size of her mouth. The first words she speaks after the court has shown her no mercy presage the way that Crawford was going to redefine her screen image almost entirely in terms of feminine will-power – 'You're going to pay for everything I'm losing in life.' Behind the revenge story, in which she exchanges her prison number for the family name of her oppressor, Crawford is forming the image that a legion of admirers came to accept as archetypal. She is the working girl, initially at an economic

ABOVE Fans who demand glamour are still served when the ex-gaolbird marries Robert Armstrong as the boss's son.

LEFT MGM portrait photographer Hurrell prepared the way for Crawford the glamour symbol even in a piece of social realism like *Paid*. OPPOSITE What Hurrell did for Garbo he could also do for Crawford. OVERLEAF Two more Garboesque studies by Hurrell.

disadvantage, who uses her sex appeal as a climbing rung on society's ladder to status and success. It is, of course, a metaphor for film stardom itself, but it is unnecessary to interpret it in this way to understand why it appealed to Crawford over and above the demands of a role which allowed for emphatic confrontation, but little shading. Her prison scenes are brief. Yet they allow her to empty trash cans, battle for a place in the communal showers and outface a segment of tough female society that was much more commonplace in the 'Big House' melodramas of a male-oriented studio like Warners. It was a thrill for her fans to see her literally stripped of her finery, though she gets it back swiftly enough on release from prison when her successful management of a 'heart-balm' racket, prising money from rich old men in return for silence, brings her the Adrian wardrobe that is the wages of extortion. It includes a huge black fur-collared coat which gained instant fashion status in Fifth Avenue stores when she wore it: her head, in a black skullcap, rises from it like a cobra about to strike. A vivid image. But she also seems at this stage to be emulating another image – Greta Garbo's. The fly-away eyebrows are Garbo's. So, too, are her bleak, all-passion-drained intonations when she confronts the father of the callow young man she has seduced by her very show of reluctance to be seduced by him: 'Don't you understand, I married your son, Mr Gilder.'

But the impact Crawford made in her own right (and image) was indisputable. 'Just wait till you see [her] in this powerful dramatic role!' cried *Photoplay*. The film made MGM a profit of $700,000. For many years, *Paid* was a title that made Mayer weep with gratitude. Even before such grosses were in, he knew what he had got. Almost every MGM film in those days was tested at previews, in theatres equipped with double-headed projectors (for separate sound and image) which made re-editing or re-shooting feasible before the laboratories produced a married print. But there was no need to alter a frame of *Paid*. Mayer demonstrated his gratitude in a way that was equally unmistakable. 'In appreciation of the co-operation and excellent services rendered by you, we take great pleasure in handing you your check made payable to your order in the amount of $10,000,' he wrote to his star, though corporate prudence compelled him to temper his gratitude with the reminder that 'this does not affect the terms of the contract dated 2 November 1928.' This was then worth $1,500 a week to her; and Mayer knew he was soon going to have to revise it. One reason: he had just seen the final cut of the next Crawford film, which MGM rushed on to screens throughout the land less than three months after *Paid*.

Its title was *Dance, Fools, Dance* (14 February 1931) and her co-star was a youthful 'heavy' who was hoping for a film career following the hit he had made on stage in a gangster play. It was only his second film at MGM, though he had been freelancing around the studios, and in that first year was to appear in no fewer than fourteen pictures, sometimes shuttling from set to set to play the different roles. Clark Gable was being given screen exposure in exactly the same way as Crawford had. His role in *Dance, Fools, Dance* was simply a chance to see what he could do – and whether *anything* he could do would make people want to come back and see him do it again and again. He played a Chicago gangster, speakeasy king and ruthless bootlegger. He had not yet grown his lip-line moustache that later put a smudge of highly visible masculinity on a cheeky face; his ears (contrary to myth) were no larger than average, but, being placed somewhat higher on his head than most people's, appeared more protuberant and added to his alley-cat allure. He already has 'presence'. It does not require the deferential attitude of his henchmen, who have recruited Joan's brother, a society ne'er-do-well from a family ruined in the Wall Street Crash, to tell us this man is dangerous. Gable has perfected gangland's authoritative gestures – the trick of helping weaklings to their feet by pulling on their lapels, the habit of having his cigarettes lit by an ever-attentive moll whose thanks is to have the smoke blown back into her face. But when he meets a woman who is unlike the others she blows the smoke back first. The woman is Crawford. And from then on, the pleasure is watching two consummate performers sparring for dominance, the sexuality they each possess sparking like crossed wires when they lay hands on each other. It is unlikely that the word 'chemistry' was then in use to express this potent reaction, much less the word 'synergism' that a later Hollywood with more pretensions than Mayer's used to connote the additional thrust imparted to a film's box-office performance by such a union of forces. But whatever it was, Mayer knew it when he saw it; and Crawford soon enjoyed the spectacle of Norma Shearer

standing in line to get the rough treatment from Gable in a movie entitled *A Free Soul*. 'You make no more bargains with anyone but me,' he cries, slamming the gracious Norma into a chair, 'You're mine and I want you.' 'A new kind of man . . . a new kind of world,' she murmurs. It was indeed: one where women receiving manhandling are not cheap molls, worth at most a breakfast grapefruit in the kisser, but highly desirable, well-groomed ladies, like Crawford's society girl in *Dance, Fools, Dance*, before Daddy's fortunes are dissipated and she goes to work as a cub reporter, covering poultry shows at first, but soon promoted to 'human interest' beats like the city morgue, where feuding gangland's wives and sweethearts are always dropping in to view the bits of their beloveds. The movie is an opportunistic amalgam of *Our Dancing Daughters* and *Scarface* and was based on the St Valentine's Day massacre and the Chicago underworld's slaying of a newsman, both offences which are laid at Gable's door. To get the goods on him, Crawford enrolls in the cabaret at his speakeasy – she dances vigorously in a silver mini-skirt, but becomes a 'lady' once again by clipping an ankle-length one over it.

The movie achieved a reputation for daring in its own day – one which it has kept – because of its opening sequence, a midnight party aboard a yacht where the Bright Young Things go for an impromptu dip, without swim-suits, in their underwear. ('Lights out and off with your clothes!') Nowadays, the same scenes would be done entirely nude; but it was bold in 1931 for a mixed company to frolic in slips, vests and underpants which clung more tightly and transparently to their forms when soaking wet. MGM again successfully fought off the local censorship prudes – except, curiously enough, in Germany, where the film entirely failed to inflame movie-goers just prior to Hitler's coming to power. In Munich, where the box-office averaged only 600 Marks, against the customary 2,500 Marks, MGM's representative reported, 'Critics very bad and public protesting bathing scene. My personal opinion: no business expectations because [film] does not suit German mentality at all.' It was whistled at at all performances at the Kurfurstendamm cinema in Berlin. But the rest of the world was more appreciative. A film that cost $289,000 returned more than $900,000 profit. Mayer's understanding of the reason for such success transcended the fascination with midnight dips in transparent underwear. It was the teaming of Crawford and Gable that made the difference. The partnership, he ordered, must be repeated at once, even if this meant re-shooting the scenes in her new film *Laughing Sinners* (30 May 1931) where John Mack Brown played a Salvation Army officer – or did until Mayer put the uniform on Gable and had their scenes filmed again. Their sexuality played off even more forcefully against each other when restrained by Salvation Army dress that was as good for warding off local moralists as the Production Code seal which was originally refused the film on account of its earlier title *Complete Surrender*.

The period between the release of *Paid* and *Dance, Fools, Dance*, roughly the turn of the year 1930–31, can be said to

OPPOSITE ABOVE *Dance, Fools, Dance* and strip off too for yet another party aboard millionaire Lester Vail's yacht.
BELOW 'Ready, steady, go.' Today the scene of midnight frolics would be played nude, but it was still shocking in 1931.

be the time when Crawford consolidated her stardom for the rest of the decade, and Hollywood, in turn, confirmed it in the most realistic way that the film industry knew – in money terms. In addition to a $10,000 bonus, her old contract was torn up and she was awarded a new one. Behind this contract, dated 7 April 1931, lay the whole power-play of stardom – the star and her studio each trying to secure their self-interest, each implicitly recognizing their reciprocal indebtedness, each holding out for the least and the most that could be yielded or taken. A letter from Crawford's agent attests to the edgy way these things were managed in the studio-system era. She had written to Phil Berg on 31 January 1931, requesting him to be her personal manager. And on 21 March 1931, Berg sent Mayer a letter (it is doubtful if Crawford ever saw it) which shows the delicate footwork required of agents in those days, who had not only to advance their clients' claims but also keep themselves safe from the growling lions of the studios.

'Dear Mr Mayer,' Berg wrote, 'I keenly regret your attitude regarding the Joan Crawford matters and I am hereunder taking the liberty of reviewing them for you. Joan approached me to handle her business. I was very careful not to intrude upon the situation without permission. However, when it was tactfully granted, and we entered in[to] our discussion, you asked what her ideas of money were. I told you that she had been led to believe that she was worth an exorbitant salary of $6,500–$7,500 per week, but in the same sentence I stated that I considered

any such demand preposterous, in as much as you had developed her, and asked what your idea of salary was. You told me that, with her viewpoint, it was impossible to discuss her salary, but, when we continued to talk, you offered to start a new five-year contract for Joan at $2,500 per week and later raised this starting point to $3,000 per week. I told you that I would discuss the matter with Joan, but that I did not think I could make a good deal starting under $4,000 per week. I further informed you that Joan was ill and in a highly nervous state. That evening I visited with her and discussed the matter. We reached no conclusion and the following Thursday I again saw her. I purposely refrained from seeing her on the set [of *Laughing Sinners*] as I did not want to upset her when she was working. Please believe me that I am cognisant of the fact of how marvellous your studio has been to me and accordingly I have always felt it part of my job to speak to my clients not only as their representative, but very strongly from your angle. It is my aim to serve you, as well as my clients, with the minimum of friction. Friday morning, I informed you that with Joan's reduced idea of $4,000 per week and you adamant at $3,000 per week, I was doing everything in my power to consummate a mutually equitable agreement. My point is that I am very anxious in the interest of my client and yourself to come to an agreement.'

Eventually, one was consummated. Crawford did not insist on her own stiff terms. Probably the example of John Gilbert counselled prudence. By this time, the erstwhile Great Lover, though protected by a golden contract which brought him $250,000 a picture, signed before his Talkie débâcle, had been reduced by the sudden drop in his popularity rating to doing pot-boilers and was locked into a self-destructive relationship with MGM. Crawford also

OPPOSITE Crawford by Hurrell.
BELOW The Salvation Army girl stayed the same in *Laughing Sinners*, but John Mack Brown (left) was replaced by Clark Gable (right) with a gain in glamour.

listened to Mayer's advice; he used to invite the stars he loved to come and tell him what they wanted, and then let him talk them out of it. Anyhow, she settled for a new contract, signed on 7 April 1931 but back-dated to 30 March 1931, at $3,000 a week, with four options of one year each rising in steps of $500 a week until she would reach $5,000 a week in 1936. Only two other MGM actresses had better deals: Garbo, whose compensation was $250,000 a picture, and Shearer at $110,000 a picture. If Crawford's career hadn't yet taken her up to these figures, it had well out-distanced her husband's screen worth. In 1931, when MGM paid Crawford $146,000, First National paid Douglas Fairbanks Jr $73,000.

To Crawford, this was not just a disparity between their box-office worth; it was a reflection of the different amounts of effort that each of them put into work. She was coming to realize that Doug was more attracted by the social pleasures of life than by devoting himself to the long and lonely climb to stardom. Once the closeness of their honeymoon was over, they began to see each other in terms of their separate ambitions. Doug, she felt, didn't want a wife so much as a hostess to entertain their growing guest-lists of people who represented positions in society more frequently than credits on the screen. She began reproaching him for not trying hard enough, for not going after better pictures, bigger roles: he hadn't the inclination or the muscle for fighting, she told herself.

Among Doug's alleged shortcomings, as she itemized them years later, can be read the values that she herself set great store by: ambition (he hadn't got it), perseverance (he tired quickly), determination (he was happy just coasting along, not summoning up that extra burst of speed to put himself out in front). It seemed to her sometimes that his studied indolence was a way of saying 'I'm not really an *actor*, I'm not one of *them*: I have my own crowd.' Crawford saw her husband's after-hours life turning into an imitation of his father's energetic socializing and she realized she was being asked to divert the energies she stored up for work into the hours he kept for play. Celebrity of two different kinds had made them strangers to each other. The heady tempo of the *Dancing Daughters* series had coincided with the enraptured pleasures of assimilating the privileged world of 'Pickfair'. But now her hit films portrayed her as the working girl who has either never known high society or has abandoned it by necessity of earning a living. The work ethic had replaced the pleasure principle; and Crawford, who tended more and more to see life in terms of pictures, did not feel that Doug was much touched by this new motivation.

Her co-star Clark Gable, on the other hand, seemed much more 'her' sort of man. Like her, Gable had come to movies 'hungry'. Like her, he was the child of a broken family. Like her, he had been a neglected kid subjected to the uncertainties and often genuine fears of a precarious working-class existence. Like her, he had used elbow grease in a variety of manual jobs from telegraph linesman to oil-field rigger. Lastly, he had fallen under the spell of an older woman with ambitions for him in the same way Crawford had always been susceptible to the advice of 'Daddy' figures kindly disposed to her even if, in some cases, the kindness was also self-serving. His first wife, Josephine Dillon, his senior by fourteen years, had groomed him socially and taught him the dramatic techniques of personality projection with the stern affection that some mothers reserve for sons whom they wish to see do well, yet fear to spoil. Gable had inherited his father's acute restlessness: he hated 'doing nothing' between takes – a phobia of Crawford's too. His impatience, and, really, his inability to amuse himself on the set except in work, made him highly professional. Like her, he began a scene with his engine already running; and she found it familiar and reassuring to note his dislike of personal disarray, his fetish for the spick-and-span appearance which he generally liked his screen roles to reflect and which, fortuitously, was ingrained in the MGM way of presenting stars to the public. Gable might have been Joan Crawford's big brother; instead, he became her lover. In the more permissive era ahead of her, she expressed it to the interviewer David Frost by saying, 'He had balls' – something that big brothers were not supposed to have, for kid sisters anyhow. His preference was for the woman 'who has seen more, heard more, knows more', in short, a woman much like Crawford. Of his five wives, three were down-to-earth, companionable types and two were socialites. His marriage to one of the latter, Rhea Langham, had a lot of similarities, in the sense of acquiring social status, with Crawford's union with Fairbanks.

The sexual reaction that worked so potently on screen was now repeated before the cameras started turning. Each had to be discreet; but both had cast-iron reasons for being together at their employers' studio, and their early arrival before the day's shooting started let them make love without the risks that might have attended covert meetings after hours in the Hollywood social community. It was easy for two impressionable people like they were to persuade themselves that life as well as the screenwriter had shaped them for each other; and this in turn affected the spontaneity of their roles together. Crawford was never as good with any other actor as she was with Gable.

CAREER GIRL

'If you want to see the girl next door, go next
door.'

Joan Crawford and Clark Gable were teamed together for the third time in *Possessed* (21 November 1931), the last of four Crawford films to be released in 1931. It had been rushed into production after the disappointment of *This Modern Age* (29 July 1931) which, despite its title, was as *passé* as its characters, drunken playboys, worldly Frenchmen and reckless rakes. The only satisfaction for Crawford was playing opposite Pauline Frederick (cast as her mother *and* her lover's mistress). The cultured speech of the older actress influenced Joan's own tones in the lady-like roles ahead of her.

Possessed is arguably the best film she made in the 1930s. Without a doubt, it is the one that presented her definitive portrait of a working-class girl's morality in Depression era America: her upward mobility, her gift of assimilating herself into the new class, her near-neurotic need to succeed and her interpretation of success as marriage, wealth and status. Its director, Clarence Brown, could reveal the grain of MGM's star actresses, show what they were made of inside, better than anyone else; George Cukor sometimes gave them more 'edge', but seldom that straight through view to the heart of the material. And so confidently, too, so immediately!

The opening scenes of *Possessed* can hold their own with the neo-realist movement in Italian cinema twenty years later. A paper-box factory in some worn-down little town empties at the end of a long, hot day and Crawford exits with the throng. In a few seconds, Brown sketches the authentic background of working folk, their frame houses by the railroad, the housewife drawing water from a stand-pipe by her front gate, a husband tipsily arguing to be let in with another wife resolute on keeping him out. Brown shot on location; a newly acquired 360° camera platform puts the depth into this vivid glimpse of proletarian life. And Crawford and her factory-gate beau, played by Wallace Ford, prove how well they can hold a scene in the long unbroken tracking shot accompanying their homeward amble beside the railroad lines. 'Tired?' he asks. 'Not just tired... dead.' 'What do you want anyhow?' 'I don't know. I only know I won't find it here.' Lines like these with their familiar echo of desperation substantiated the existence of millions of working-girl film-goers who heard them, engaged their understanding, enlisted their sympathies. Brown timed the shooting perfectly: it is the 'magic hour' at the end of the day, when the sun has set, but its borrowed light from over the horizon gives a feverish glow to Crawford's declaration, 'I can't wait.'

And then as she halts alone beside the tracks to let a train haul slowly by, a vision of the Other America passes with miraculous smoothness in tantalizing review in front of her. Behind the loco is a private railroad car; the lights are already a-glow inside; and as Crawford watches it, her back to the camera, images of affluence go by as though across a cinema screen, each compartment dangling the luxury of those who 'have' before the eyes of one of those who 'have not'. Oysters are being fastidiously shelled in the kitchen, next door a pre-dinner cocktail is being shaken, a maid is caressing a silk slip with an iron, a manservant shines his master's shoes ... and so on, along the length of the carriage, past a couple in evening gown and tuxedo dancing

PREVIOUS PAGE Crawford in *Grand Hotel*.
BELOW *Possessed*: Working girl finds temptation and champagne when she meets Skeets Gallagher's Manhattan millionaire in his private railroad car.
OPPOSITE Gable and Crawford share a reflective moment between takes on *Possessed*.

ABOVE Director Clarence Brown insisted on a neo-realist approach to the working-class *milieu* shot on location in *Possessed* . . .

BELOW . . . but Brown (left) also knew when the studio glamour was needed for Crawford and Gable living in affluent sin.

to a portable phonograph, the man bending seductively over the woman, all wordless, wistful and Gatsby-like, until the locomotive grinds to a halt and on the observation platform exactly opposite her, a middle-aged Manhattanite pouring himself champagne impishly offers a glass to the mesmerized Crawford. Is there any other scene of social seduction which hits its mark so impeccably in every sense? Skeets Gallagher's affluent stranger pouring out the wine starts Crawford pouring her heart out; and the dialect of her dream versus his experience is a brilliant bit of shorthand for the way that America interpreted the class struggle in terms of social opportunity. 'I mean to get away.' 'Off to the big city to be done wrong?' 'To be done right ... my clothes, my shoes, my hands, the way I talk, everything's wrong with me.' He gives her his card with a Park Avenue address; a little tipsy now, too, she accepts it the way she might take an unexpected bonus from the boss, not quite believing it is meant for her. The wine is what emboldens her to leave home a few dramatic minutes later: the address on the card is where the American Dream begins. Not only is the economy of this sequence masterly, the acting, too, is perfectly on pitch, catching undertones of longing on Crawford's part, modulating Gallagher's lurking cruelty into perceptible pathos.

P. G. Wodehouse might have had a hand (at least a line) in the following sequence when Crawford, her ambitions clutched as tightly as her slim purse, appears at Gallagher's apartment just as the man who dangled opportunity in front of her is pulling out of a hangover. Politely, sheepishly, he bows at her, and water jets out of the icebag on his sore head. 'The damn thing isn't house-broken,' he snorts at his manservant. 'Ambrose, take it out for walk.' He quizzes her: 'What are you here for?' She is just as direct: 'For me.' He counsels her: 'There's only one way for a girl to get along in this town – find a rich man ... Never look [men] in the eyes, take a peek at their pocket-book ... Don't tell them too much about yourself – men are like Christopher Columbus, let them discover America.' The lesson over, she is about to leave. 'Down?' asks the elevator man. A split-second hesitation, then: 'No, not *down*.' And back into the apartment she goes, to try out the lesson on the two men who have just entered it. 'Are you rich?' she asks the older one. 'Awful.' 'That's nice. I couldn't waste my time with you, if it were otherwise.' But it is on the other man that she scores. 'Careful, she's after your money,' Gallagher warns him. 'Are you?' he asks. 'Yes.' His moustache expands along a lip that curls with disinterested amusement; his eyes twinkle with flattered curiosity; his whole presence doesn't just betray his interest in her, but registers it frankly. Thus is the Clark Gable image fully rounded at last.

One doesn't need to believe in the story of *Possessed*. All that's needed is for one to believe in Crawford and Gable. They make it easy. It is not just a case of good casting: it is an *attachment* to each other that has the tangible completeness which only players who are at ease or involved with each other manage to register so satisfyingly on the screen. But the story matters, too. For its time *Possessed* was a bold film. It recognized that love without marriage was sometimes desirable. It is the truth of the relationship that preserves its boldness despite the way that time has turned its singularity into commonplaceness. Gable's rich attorney will not marry Crawford even though divorce has left

Possessed was one of the greatest hits that Crawford and Gable made in the early 1930s; each brought out the star in the other.

him free to do so. His last wife left him for their chauffeur. 'Losing a sweetheart is a private misfortune,' he says in a Wilde-like quip, like an olive in the dry Martini, 'but losing a wife is a public scandal.' To avoid a second 'scandal', he grooms Crawford as his mistress, turning her into a working-girl's fantasy of *soignée* assurance and gaining her love so completely that she is willing to live in the luxury apartment he rents under her name ('Mrs Moreland'), which suggests her support comes from some other man's alimony and not from his account. Again thanks to its stars, the movie makes a strong case for being a kept woman without regrets. 'I left school when I was twelve,' Crawford says, 'I've never known how to spell "regrets".' Marriage is weighed, and found wanting. 'I wonder how many wives would be so understanding,' Gable muses, and receives the full withering force of his mistress's realism: 'These things don't happen to wives.' Even when Crawford later offers to withdraw from the situation, fearing she'll hurt Gable's political ambitions, and incites a row to make the parting easier, one does not feel the audaciousness has been neutered; for she still gives the go-by to the narrow, conventional nature of her *petit bourgeois* beau from long ago who shows up in New York, prospering and courting Gable's influence, but lacking all his generosity and boldness. Her old lover simply wants what she has already acquired: money and power. But she is a woman and has risked all to get them. It is one case of the 'double standard' working out to the woman's advantage.

It is a truism of star acting that players don't take off their make-up at the end of the day. If so, then there are plenty of good reasons in the script of *Possessed* why Gable and Crawford should have fallen in love during the shooting. Lines like 'The surest way to lose a woman is to marry her', or 'Even if married, I couldn't respect you more than I do', might have been calculated to keep an illicit relationship going after work, too. It did, if Crawford is to be believed. But it never came to more than a 'relationship'. The reason throws light on the awesome responsibilities that stardom carried for two people who were, as she put it, 'peasants'. Both were bemused by the suddenness of their celebrity, and not a little fearful that they might lose it as fatefully as they had gained it. Ultimately, this is what deterred them from provoking the sort of scandal which in the film comes near to wrecking the political ambitions of the Gable character. In *Possessed*, scandal has its origins in their not being married to each other; in real life, it would have originated in their being married to others. Neither star dared risk a double divorce at that point in their careers. Indeed, there was a fifth party whose interests had to be considered – namely MGM. The penalties were already spelled out in the contracts' morality clauses. But there is other, inferential evidence of Mayer's watchfulness over Gable and, obliquely, over Crawford. It is spelled out in his response to an attempt at this time by Gable's first wife, Josephine Dillon, to profit from her old relationship with him. Not two months after Gable had married Rhea Langham – *remarried* her, to be precise, since an MGM lawyer had discovered that their first marriage was not legal under Californian law – Mrs Dillon wrote a shrewdly calculating letter to Mayer. She had, she pointed out, 'received a number of offers for the story of my experiences as the wife and coach of Clark Gable. I have prepared such a story and have it ready for mailing to a publication.' The letter, dated 2 August 1931, continued: 'Mr Gable has given me no cause to be concerned for his welfare, but your company has never done me any harm and this story will probably damage one of your properties. If you would rather buy this story from me . . .'

The point was easy to get. Lyn Tornabene has published the letter in full in her biography of Gable, but unaccountably omitted the studio's reaction to it. It would seem that Mayer himself was out of town at the time, since his unwaveringly loyal secretary, Ida Koverman, sent a memo about it to Thalberg on 18 August 1931. 'Mrs Gable called yesterday to know how much longer she should wait for Mr Mayer. Said that she had received another wire from New York asking her to send on her manuscript and she didn't know what to do until she heard from Mr Mayer relative to this matter. Mr Loeb [of Loeb, Walker and Loeb, outside attorneys retained by MGM] today advised through his secretary that if possible you might get in touch with Mr Clark Gable and find out what he is going to do. Mr Loeb recommends that you use no pressure on Mr Gable and if Mr Gable doesn't want to come through, Mr Loeb advises we can then tell Mrs Gable that we are not interested in buying the manuscript. He [Mr Loeb] cannot take very seriously the consequences that might result from the publication of any article . . .' Perhaps Mr Loeb couldn't. But Mr Mayer could – and *did* – when he was acquainted with the matter. Mayer immediately wrote a letter to Mrs Gable. Unfortunately, it has not survived; but its contents may be readily guessed from her reply of 31 August 1931, addressed to Mayer personally. 'This is an acknowledgement of my debt to you for your great kindness. The world looks much brighter than it did . . .' It was, in fact, $200-a-month brighter, for this was the sum Gable had agreed, at Mayer's stern urging, to pay for his first wife's silence.

How much greater, then, would Mayer's fury and retribution have been had he been confronted with the damage which double divorce suits might have inflicted on two of his top contract artists, Gable and Crawford, one of whom was gaining in popularity with every picture he made while the other was now a hugely lucrative part of MGM's corporate profit? Fortunately, he never needed to face it. He may have warned them: we do not know, for no record has survived which suggests a rebuke of this nature. But both stars backed off for the moment; and later, when one of them was matrimonially free, MGM, as will be recounted, had ensured the continuing good conduct of the other by links that were stronger than marriage.

But if the appearance of rectitude was preserved by such manoeuvres, morality elsewhere was distinctly disturbed by the relationship of Crawford and Gable in *Possessed*. Film censorship in England was much stricter than in America at the beginning of the Talkie era. Though then (as now) a tiny self-perpetuating private body, answerable to no one for the way it conducted its affairs, the decisions of the English censors were backed by the laws of cinema licensing: if the censors withheld approval from a film, it was denied public exhibition. And early in 1932, MGM was informed that *Possessed* would be banned in England in its entirety due to its pair of lovers living in sin *and enjoying it*, as if a man-mistress relationship were more natural than

OPPOSITE Hurrell's Crawford in a more relaxed mood.

the mixed blessings of wedlock or even the miseries of adultery. (At this time, three other MGM films, *Freaks*, *Night Court* and Crawford's *Letty Lynton*, the film following *Possessed*, were also banned in England for various reasons.) Getting round the ban was Thalberg's responsibility. It involved re-shooting parts of the film, so as to give a different interpretation to the story. This was quite practicable (for a price) at a studio where the artists were always contractually available. But as may be imagined, it would cause quite a bit of re-jigging in this case. How MGM went about it sheds rare and hence valuable light on Hollywood morality, on the lengths that the studio was prepared to go for two 'money' stars like Crawford and Gable and, finally, on Thalberg's frequently praised but seldom illustrated talent for remaking movies after they had been shot so as to make them more popular or, in this case, more acceptable.

On 26 February 1932, Thalberg cabled MGM's New York office asking, 'Will British censors pass *Possessed* if story is reconstructed as follows? Gable is scion of the important family. [In the film as shown in America, he was simply a rich lawyer.] Prior to opening of picture he has made one unfortunate marriage and been threatened with disinheritance. [In the original, his marriage had failed because, as stated, his wife had eloped with their chauffeur.] When Gable realizes he cannot have Crawford without marriage, he agrees to keep it a secret to the world – therefore to the world she appears his mistress ... Meanwhile, political enemies, counting on mistress angle, discover marriage and destroy record of it. Gable, outraged, wants to admit marriage and fight enemies. [In the original, he had defended his right to a private life.] Crawford realizes he loses his inheritance if he proves marriage, or career if he does not. [Originally, he had just risked losing a gubernatorial election.] She steps out, leaving balance of story as is.' Thalberg added, in something of an understatement, 'Naturally dialogue will be changed in many scenes.' But on 9 May 1932, he was advised by cable from London that even this ingenuity did not soften the English censors. 'Suggest you send another detailed synopsis,' he was told. So Thalberg and his writers tried again.

On 4 October 1932, he cabled MGM's London office: 'Would censors accept the following reconstruction of *Possessed*? Gable married to hopeless invalid and spends time in European spas. Has great regard and affection for her and believes loyalty lies with her despite everything. His relations with Crawford based on this and they enter into their equivocal position rather than disrupt his marriage and hurt helpless woman. Emphasizing Gable's respect for marriage relationship. Later, when both hopelessly in love and have suffered together because of sacrifice, wife dies. They grateful at prospect of sanctifying union when his proposed running for office comes up. He is asked to give up mistress and, when approaching marriage is announced, is told it will ruin his career to marry mistress on eve of election. Now plays as before, with Crawford sacrificing her happiness for Gable's career ... Please advise immediately, Thalberg.' Eventually this was substantially the form in which Britain saw the picture. It did good business. But its business generally was record-breaking and it is easy to see what MGM considered was a primary cause of this in the memo sent on 31 October 1931,

from Howard Strickling, at the studio, to Howard Dietz, the New York-based head of publicity and advertising: 'In future advertising *Possessed*, we will play up Gable larger and if okay with you will read as follows Joan Crawford (100 per cent-size type) with Clark Gable (60 per cent) in Clarence Brown's Production (50 per cent) *Possessed* (100 per cent).' Crawford's name was still above the title, as big as it, and in front of Gable's; but the day would come when she would be locked in combat over which of their names, by then equally aggrandized, should come first. In Hollywood, it is easier to surrender a lover than surrender a credit.

It is said that Crawford begged Mayer to cast Gable opposite her in *Letty Lynton* (7 May 1932), in which she played a woman who kills for love, but that Mayer turned her down because he wanted to keep the distance between the stars wider than a camera two-shot. *Letty Lynton* was based on one true-to-life scandal (the Madeleine Smith poisoning case) and Mayer didn't wish to provoke another less lethal but possibly more expensive one. Unfortunately, like so many good Hollywood myths, this is untrue. Gable was simply not available at the time, since William Randolph Hearst, anxious to put some pep into the amiable but anaemic screen reputation of his mistress Marion Davies, had successfully requested Gable's stud-like presence in *her* next film. *Sally of the Circus*, however, did nothing for either of them.

Robert Montgomery took the role of the man who falls in love with Crawford aboard ship from Buenos Aires to New York, only to have her jealous, brutal lover (a badly miscast Nils Asther) turn up at the pierside and later blackmail Crawford into coming to his bedside. In desperation, she poisons him – or, at least, doesn't hold back his hand when he gloatingly drains the champagne she has heartbrokenly doctored for herself in a mood of suicide before dishonour. It is an astonishing narrative twist for its time. It comes as near to condoning homicide as any Hollywood film possibly could before the Production Code was stringently revised to ensure that girls like Crawford paid the penalty. She gets off, much as Madeleine Smith did. The film was based on Mrs Belloc Lowndes's novel, inspired in turn by the Edinburgh poisoning case, though MGM had wished to buy a play entitled *Dishonored Lady*, which told the same story. But as the Hays Office banned the use of such an 'inflammatory' title, the studio settled for the novel – and later on had to settle a plagiarism suit that made legal history (see Filmography).

The suit may have had more suspense than the film. The trouble is, Crawford in this kind of role has no aura of mystery, only a past; and Robert Montgomery has no sex-appeal, only a personable charm. Gable was obviously much missed. Only Garbo could have made Letty a compelling character – and Garbo by this time was heartily sick ('Always the vamp, I am always the woman of no heart') of *femmes fatales* like Letty, a woman with a secret past, a moral though far from insolvent outcast, a traveller through the impermanent world of hotels *de luxe*, ships' state-rooms and *boîtes de nuit* where Society and the Underworld thrilled each other. She avoids all commitments except the one forced on her by destiny. One can hear Garbo sepulchrally keening a line like, '"Home" and "mother" ... who ever put those two words together?' One imagines at times that one sees Garbo, too, in Adrian's cartwheel-collared fur wraps, skullcap hats and even in Crawford's gaze (usually so candid and direct) now focused on the place where Garbo usually melted into myth, namely 'infinity'. She even changed her hair-style to Garbo's page-boy cut – though in fact Crawford's was created by Sydney Guilaroff. She had found him working in a New York salon, got him to style her hair for *Letty Lynton*, then carefully preserved it on the 3,000-mile train ride back to Hollywood, where it was so successfully copied that she persuaded MGM to engage the man who became their outstanding stylist for over three decades. To those who thus 'protected' her, Crawford gave life-long loyalty.

The English censors rejected the film on the understandable grounds that it 'justified homicide without penalty'. After their experience in Germany with *Dance, Fools, Dance*, MGM took no chances there, but asked Arthur Loew, then at the company's Broadway office, to sound out opinion in Berlin. 'Staff [in Hollywood] doubtful of German public reaction,' he was told. 'They feel German public will not consider girl has sufficient motive for attempted suicide because of previous love affairs.' Loew wired back laconically: 'Personally believe girl has sufficient motive attempt at suicide in any language.' The fears were groundless. The film made a world wide profit of over $600,000 for an investment of half that figure. It also demonstrated the immense influence of Crawford when it came to 'selling' fashion through her screen wardrobe.

One of Adrian's creations for the film became the most copied film-gown in the world. This was a sensationally

ABOVE The dress worn in *Letty Lynton* that sold a million replicas.

BELOW Rehearsing *Grand Hotel* with (left to right) Purnell Pratt, Murray Kinnell, Edwin Maxwell, Tully Marshall and a rather unimpressed Wallace Beery.

Grand Hotel's director Edmund Goulding, himself an artist, used a story-board technique to sketch out the seduction scene between Crawford and Beery in order to anticipate any objections from the censor.

ABOVE Crawford and Beery in a dramatic moment in *Grand Hotel*; the drama is provided by the (unseen) body of John Barrymore.

ruffled dress in layers of white organdy. Macy's stores claimed to have sold 50,000 inexpensive copies of it; and the impact it made on Seventh Avenue's garment district confirmed Hollywood as a source of high fashion scaled down to purchasers of modest means and exploited so successfully that it outsold Paris. How much this fashion 'connection' was worth to MGM is impossible to determine, but right up to the end of her stay at the studio, what Crawford had on her back was of major concern in building a film around her. In a few years' time, Adrian would switch styles and establish the severely tailored outline with the wide, wide shoulders that became her sartorial and assertive trademark. But what is not well known is that this, in turn, was a reaction to Crawford's very practical desire simply to be comfortable inside her glamorous clothes. To facilitate her unusually wide collarbones, Adrian had to cut the gowns full across the shoulders, which required him to pad her shoulders even more generously so as to support the fabric. What started off as a structural necessity was absorbed into her dramatic persona: it even seems to grow with the melodrama. Don't worry about the plausibility, one thinks, admire the width!

Crawford apparently *did* worry over the comparison which the film prompted between Garbo and herself. She never made a secret of Garbo's influence on her: in later, more relaxed times she jokingly remarked that Garbo was the only star who made her sorry not to have been attracted to her own sex. But it was not in Crawford's nature to define her own appeal by reference to another female star.

'I admire Garbo,' she said at this time, 'I think she's a great talent, and because I said so they started whispering, "She's imitating Garbo – ah, ah!" That's so unfair, so untrue. I don't have to imitate anybody. I don't – I'm my own personality.' Years later she was to boast that nobody could imitate *her*: this went unchallenged.

Yet comparison between the two stars was inevitable when both appeared in *Grand Hotel* (12 April 1932). Sadly for those who believe goddesses should bump into each other occasionally, they did not share a scene, not even a room in the Berlin hotel where Garbo played the ageing Russian *prima ballerina* in mid-life crisis and Crawford the bold stenographer on the make. Her working-girl's frocks are starkly plain, but she compensates for this with startling *décolletage* – and when this is coupled with her bare yoke of creamy collarbone, even John Barrymore's attempts to steal their scenes by deployment of his left profile is nugatory.

Crawford was again working with Edmund Goulding, and there is some evidence of the especial attention he gave her in the seduction sequence with the brutal business tycoon played by Wallace Beery. These scenes pack more sensual power than even the bedroom ones between Garbo and Barrymore and lend support to the story that Crawford feared they would suffer much more from the censor than Garbo's and thus diminish her impact in the film. They did not, perhaps because Goulding very carefully 'story-boarded' the camera angles for the *décolletée* Crawford, seated beneath the imperiously lecherous gaze of Beery, and thus indicated precisely how they were to be manoeuvred into a sensual but acceptable physical relationship.

Crawford's stock now stood so high at MGM (the box-office of *Possessed* was defying the accountants' speed in counting grosses and *Letty Lynton*'s rushes were causing excitement) that one has to take seriously the story that MGM were prepared to shift the story interest in *Grand Hotel* from Garbo to Crawford. It was later believed that this threat was used to pressure Garbo into renewing her contract, which had just expired. In fact, neither tale is true. Garbo had already agreed to the most generous – and secret – deal ever made between MGM and one of its stars, one which rewarded her with her own production company inside MGM. The contributions of the two stars are complementary, not competitive. Crawford provides *Grand Hotel* with its melodrama and drive; Garbo, with its magic and sense of autobiography, since for the first time on screen she is heard speaking the celebrated catch-phrase, 'I want to be alone.'

Crawford, anyhow, had no need to share a scene with Garbo to catch the infection of being a Great Actress. But the experience of actually being in a film with Garbo did seem to give her resolve to become that kind of sacred animal an appropriately holy zeal. To an anonymous *Variety* reporter, with shorthand fortunately fast enough to pursue her confessional outpouring, she said on the eve of *Grand Hotel*'s première:

> I want to do some really fine things to be remembered by, and then I shall say goodbye, thanks a lot, it was lovely. But how to know it when the time comes? That's why I'm always groping, seeking to learn, trying to improve myself. I want so much to fight off conceit. I must never allow myself to become self-satisfied. But I don't think I ever will. My ambition is too driving – too relentless to permit me to grow complacent. I would never, for instance, talk over the radio, 'When I did this, when I did that' – those silly, stupid interviews all about oneself. Who cares? If you're important enough, people will talk about you. You don't have to do it yourself.

It was on this note of aspiration, matched by the peak of her power at MGM, that she attempted to climb even higher in her endeavours – and suffered a humiliating and frightening fall from grace and favour which she was never to forget or forgive herself for inviting.

'A proven play ... a great play', was how Crawford had described *Grand Hotel*. She seldom got such tried and tested vehicles: her scripts were mostly cobbled together by studio writers from unpublished stories or unperformed plays that MGM had frugally acquired and stockpiled while waiting for the right stars to give them box-office lustre. How much more proven, then, how much greater than even *Grand Hotel* was the play entitled *Rain*. It had been adapted from Somerset Maugham's short story of 1917 originally called *Miss Thompson*, about the flashy, blonde prostitute in Pago-Pago whose generosity in enhancing the lives of others locks her in fatal conflict with the repressed sexuality of an evangelical missionary. It had already helped confirm the star aura of Jeanne Eagles (on stage) and Gloria Swanson (in the 1928 silent film).

Nicholas Schenck, president of Loew's Inc., was asked for Crawford on a 'loan-out' basis by his brother Joseph, president of United Artists, which had produced the Swanson film of *Rain*. It was a very attractive deal for both companies. The files disclose that United Artists paid MGM $12,500 on signature, then $3,500 a week for a minimum ten-week period. (This was Crawford's weekly salary at the time). MGM also participated in the profits after United Artists' distribution surcharge had been met – this was usually thirty per cent of the gross, but ran as high as fifty per cent in continental Europe. Crawford recalled

PREVIOUS PAGE Crawford as Sadie Thompson before redemption.
ABOVE For *Rain* Crawford deliberately cheapened herself.
BELOW Walter Huston as the repressed evangelist prays for the soul of Sadie Thompson while lusting after her body.
OPPOSITE A bad girl reformed: Crawford's prostitute in *Rain* gets religion and kinder lighting.

that Joseph Schenck had been very persuasive; at these rates, one can see why. Crawford hesitated. Playing the role would give her prestigious parity with Eagles and Swanson, but these predecessors gave her an inferiority complex too. This was the first time she would have to withstand direct comparison with a celebrated forerunner. Schenck told her not to worry: he would assign Lewis Milestone to the film. Milestone would 'protect' her, he was 'good' with actors and fresh from directing *All Quiet on the Western Front* and *The Front Page*.

It was a fateful decision – and it almost ruined Crawford's confidence from the start. For it turned out that Milestone had no faith in *Rain* (19 October 1932): he thought it badly dated and, anyhow, nobody could touch Jeanne Eagles's performance. 'Also,' he added ominously, 'after [Eagles] had played it on Broadway for about three years, you couldn't enter a vaudeville house that didn't feature an act sending up Sadie Thompson.'[11]

To ease the tedium, and protect himself against 'the big star and very sultry dame' foisted on him by the front office, he 'blueprinted' scene after scene before shooting them. Crawford's spontaneity was undercut from the start by this insistence on rehearsal. She made much of the film away from the friendly family of MGM. Location shooting often brings out the worst in actors cooped up together, far from the amenities of home and the attributes of stardom; Crawford's position was the more vulnerable since the minor players were bonded together by their stage background and disparaged this contender for Eagles's allure who had only her movie pedigree to plead for her. In short, she was thoroughly rattled – and the notices she received completed her disintegration. The critics' comments on her performance were bad enough. What must have distressed her more was the violent antipathy of her fans: her performance didn't just disappoint them, the letters she now received contained a vehemence she had never experienced. They thought Sadie Thompson 'vulgar' and 'cheap' – words repeated again and again; and in Crawford's lexicon, that meant only one thing – they thought she was no longer (for the moment, anyhow) a star. It was a fearful lesson in rejection, so severe it was to cause a temporary but penitent physical withdrawal from the company of her friends, colleagues and even husband.

Yet, in retrospect, how unfair and unfortunate this revulsion was, for a viewing of *Rain* reveals how severely under-rated the film was in its time and how unperceptively Crawford's critics rated a performance whose dramatic gain in horsepower is amazing, quite apart from the nerve it required in the circumstances to take such risks with herself. Next to *Possessed*, of the year before, and *Mildred Pierce*, which was still eleven years ahead, *Rain* contains one of the best and certainly the least characteristic of all the performances Crawford was to give. From start to finish, she is unsparing of herself, unpredictable in her playing and almost unrecognizable in her looks. The physical change she has worked in herself is the first surprise. She has developed the high, protruding bosom, tight waist, accentuated hips and ramrod straightness more commonly associated with her later career. She gives a superbly controlled impression of a woman battered by life to the point where she cannot be hurt by any more knocks. Her entrance is done in graphic, staccato close-ups of her gaudy appurtenances – a bangled arm, a be-ringed hand,

white high-heeled shoes almost stamping defiance at convention, and, suddenly, *there she is*, giving a rakish salute to the marines, lolling against the doorway with the casual, negligently provocative posture of a woman thoroughly sure of what men want from her. She is as direct in her dealings with life and her voice sounds made for transacting business on her terms. Technically, Crawford proves herself ready for the most exacting roles. She can handle the long monologue almost as skilfully as Walter Huston, playing the evangelist, orchestrates his self-inflammatory sermons against the flesh. As he prays *at* her, assaulting her, as it were, with the words of the Lord's Prayer, and Milestone's camera, too, looks down on her from an altitude of holier-than-thou aloofness, Crawford latches her tongue on to his fervid pitch and, like someone at a revivalist meeting, begins to follow his hysteria up the scale, while the camera duplicates the effect in a crane shot that carries it up to roof-top level and leaves the two small figures locked in embattled prayer far below.

Sadie's 'conversion' is less satisfactorily managed. But Crawford to her credit refuses to rely wholly on the face tissues and cleansing cream to remove the visible 'taints' of her profession. By substituting a still, *very still* composure for her former restless and jerky metabolism, she shows how carefully she has thought through the character, despite her later *mea culpa* protestation that 'I hadn't the vaguest idea what [Sadie] was like inside. I didn't even know then that you could work from the interior to the exterior.'[12] Maybe, but instinct gets the better of her ignorance; boldness masks her uncertainty. What *does* show is the probably unanticipated contribution made to her performance by an 'actors' director' like Lewis Milestone and the way he reveals the male will that inhabits Sadie's assertively female body. This is precisely the conjunction that fascinates many of Crawford's admirers today, even those who do not find her sexually attractive. She is a woman with power over men – and part of that power is the disconcerting discovery a male makes that the power is of the same gender as himself. It proved too unexpected a change, too raw a demonstration, for Crawford's fans to accept in 1932. It was to be many a long year before she attempted another 'bitch' role like Sadie's – and then she took care to play it with a hyper-feminine style.

Horribly rebuffed by her experience, the first thing she did was quit her Brentwood home and make a temporary retreat to a rented cottage at Malibu, where she spent hours alone, cooking her own meals, brooding on the fans who had disowned her and the husband whose life-style distanced him from her more and more. On long walks by the Pacific, she would stop and plant her bare feet solidly on the sand, sucking up fortitude from the basic element the way she had been taught to brace herself before a film take. She also committed herself to Christian Science. This is a faith well tuned to offering consolation to stars in her despondent mood. It recommends positive thinking on the lines of 'I wish' – FADE OUT – FADE IN – 'I got'. It concentrates one's mind on one's career, as well as counselling resilience on the occasions when the disciple has to recognize that 'I wish' is not going to be followed by 'I got'. But then why should one be surprised that at this of all times she embraced the absolutism of Mary Baker Eddy? After all, Sadie Thompson had 'got' religion in much the same mood of penitence for her hubris. The feeling of a just God again in control, sending the moral courage coursing through her to overcome critical rebuffs and win back disaffected fans, precisely fitted Crawford's needs at the time. These hardships were sent to anneal her: all she had to do was endure them, and she would emerge toughened. Of course this same tenacious belief that mind overcomes matter and wishfulness changes everything can obscure the fact that nothing has really changed; and a certain exaggeration develops in order to deal with inconvenient normality that refuses to adjust itself. It is probably at this time, in some spasm of withdrawal, that Crawford started to overcompensate in advance for what insecurities her life, character and career held for her; so that what she strove to excel in, she came to dominate. When she offered support to friends, she demanded total loyalty in return; when she braced herself against disappointment, she repressed all her vulnerable feelings; when she sought to protect those nearest her, she caused more actual hurt than the harm she feared.

She broke her Malibu seclusion for a 'second honeymoon' with Fairbanks taken in England at the suggestion of Mayer, who hoped it would bring them together again. MGM and Warners paid for it, and got useful publicity for the couple's respective new releases. Noël Coward, the Duke and Duchess of Kent, Ivor

The 'late' Crawford face appearing before its time: two portraits taken in the early 1930s (above) by Hurrell and (below) by Clarence Sinclair Bull.

ABOVE Gable and Crawford on the steps of the portable dressing-room which was a wedding present from her husband, Douglas Fairbanks Jnr.

Novello, Laurence Olivier and his then wife Jill Esmond were nightly escorts to plays, clubs, restaurants and movie premières; and Crawford had it brought home to her, better than a ton of studio mail, that she was a world-wide star, fêted everywhere she went and carried by policemen over the heads of the crowds to get her into Coward's *Cavalcade* unscathed and exhilarated.

Returning to California was a predictable let-down, and worse. Like spent momentum, what was left of their once affectionate union had been reduced to a state of played-out exhaustion. Crawford filed for divorce and sent a new agent she had acquired, Mike Levee, to break the news of it to Fairbanks (whom he also represented), while his chauffeur was simultaneously collecting her husband's clothes and effects from her home – by such proxy methods were the gentler kind of Hollywood separations arranged. Even the subsequent charge of 'mental cruelty' was merely formal: 'He would sulk for days at a time and refuse to speak to me,' Crawford testified. 'He began to make uncomplimentary remarks about my friends.' Fairbanks behaved like the gentleman he was and his own social circle closed protectively around him. After their divorce, on 13 May 1933, Crawford soon found herself dropped by Doug's friends; it may by then have been a relief to her. Many years later, when she was living in New York, her first husband perceptively observed of her: 'It was only in the theatrical world [of New York] that she lived, and, even then, only the film part of that theatrical world. Everything else was strange and undesirable and unattractive to her.'[13]

Crawford's divorce left her free and she profited for a time from the avid speculation attaching to an 'available' star: who would be her 'next'? Clark Gable, said many. But if one obstacle to that union had been removed, another was

being employed to block it. At the start of 1932, MGM had established a trust fund for Gable, undertaking to pay into it $500 a week for the next six years. Gable was then earning an additional $2,000 a week; and this was satisfyingly topped up in mid-1932 when he felt his stardom was secure enough to stop paying Josephine Dillon her $200 a month 'hush' money. The trust fund swelled with Gable's salary and 'loan-out' bonuses: the year 1933 brought MGM receipts of $50,416 for lending Gable out to other studios, and nearly $20,000 of this was clear profit. The studio could afford to be generous to him – and it was. The phrase 'you are a pretty nice guy' keeps cropping up in letters from studio executives; and he was granted a favour akin to Papal dispensation by being sometimes exempted from having the time not spent in work (perhaps when he was ill) added on to the term of his contract. But the trust fund could be broken if Gable's conduct terminated his employment – i.e., if the 'moral turpitude' clause were invoked, or if his wife Rhea initiated a divorce action which would compel a division of community property – and even then, the studio had a preferential claim on his estate. This indeed is what was to happen some years later, when Gable wished to marry Carole Lombard. The trust fund then amounted to nearly $40,000, and Gable's additional assets to over $175,000. Mrs Rhea Gable took exactly half of all this for agreeing to relinquish her matrimonial rights to Lombard. Gable was crippled financially, and a curious feature of the settlement was an agreement by MGM to pay Mrs Gable's income tax. The attempt to reclaim this from Gable caused endless, intricate, increasingly acrimonious exchanges between MGM and Gable. When he enlisted in the US Army Air Force – against the desire of Nicholas Schenck of Loew's Inc. – it was not just to ease the pain of Lombard's death in an air crash, but to seek sanctuary for himself from the unforgiving argument of the lawyers over his debt to the studio. Even when peace was declared and he returned to MGM, there was no peace from such harassment; it only ended when an MGM lawyer discovered that a statute of limitations made the debt's recovery beyond any power except that of persuasion.

Gable was always pursued by memories of his own needy childhood and avoided unnecessary expense at all times. To have divorced his wife in 1933 and married Crawford would have been inviting financial woes much earlier in his career than he was prepared to bear. Crawford, for her part, understood such anxieties well enough not to goad Gable into matrimony. And thus, except for the fade-out clinch on the screen, he remained beyond her possession – or, as a few of the studio wits put it as they contemplated a sequel to the couple's biggest screen hit, her *Repossession*.

Had they married, it is more than probable that they would have run through each other's attractions even more quickly than Crawford and Fairbanks had done, for they were too alike ever to 'extend' each other into regions where Crawford's first marriage had taken her. But very soon, she found a new man who offered her that sense of uncharted experience, like a new film role, which she could explore and make her own.

OPPOSITE Crawford as a fresh-air girl; portraitist Clarence Sinclair Bull usually saw Crawford in a softer light.

Crawford met Franchot Tone when she learned that MGM was assigning her to an Air Force melodrama provisionally entitled *Turnabout*, for direction by Howard Hawks from a William Faulkner script. The idea was highly unwelcome to her: what part was there for her in this all-male milieu? Came the answer: none. But as she was on a 'play or pay' basis, work had to be found for her, and Faulkner was instructed to write in a feminine-interest role. She became Diana Royce-Smith, English débutante in love with Claude, a British Naval officer (played by Robert Young), but seduced by Gary Cooper's American pilot who was known, promisingly, as Bogard. Women's interest was also imparted by a change of title: *Turnabout* became *Today We Live* (21 April 1933). It is easy to imagine what cynical quips this produced on location at March Field, a Californian air base which none other than General Douglas MacArthur had freed from red tape so that MGM could film the First World War flying scenes. Crawford's sole consolation was her screen brother, played by Franchot Tone. She asked to see his screen test and what impressed her at once was his voice, the tones of a self-confident Easterner, the reason he had been picked to embody an 'English type' (called Ronnie, oh dear!) in his second film for MGM.

Tone was then twenty-eight. He had family wealth in his background – his father was president of the Carborundum Company – and something that often went with such unearned wealth, namely moral discomfort. Tone was a forerunner of those romantic radicals who were soon to settle in Hollywood and try to purge themselves of the extravagant fees some of them earned, and of the comfortable material circumstances of life in the sun, by subverting what they interpreted as the privileges around them and contributing money or sympathy to the causes they left behind them. Tone had been baptized Stanilas Pascal Franchot and his political ideals were even enshrined in the names he gave one of his own sons by a later marriage to the actress Jean Wallace: the boy was called Thomas Jefferson Tone. Franchot's upbringing in prep school, Cornell and the University of Rennes not only matured his outlook and veneered his worldliness, but fed his capacity for creating disorder. He defined himself by opposition to 'the system', whether it was private schooling, Broadway establishment or Hollywood front office. He helped found the left-wing Group Theater (Harold Clurman, Stella Adler, Lee Strasberg, Clifford Odets were other members). He had made one film, *The Wiser Sex*, in 1931, co-starring with Claudette Colbert by day at Paramount's Long Island studio while acting on Broadway at night. When he accepted an MGM contract a few months later, a New York columnist wrote: 'Mr Tone is one of the best of the young actors in the New York theatre and the most promising in his chances of development. He does not have to go to Hollywood to get a good role: many roles in the theatre are open to him. And for the same reason, he doesn't have to stay in Hollywood when he gets there.' No doubt this was Tone's view, too – then. He calculated cynically that within a year or two, on Hollywood's scale of inflated rewards for strolling through a few movies, he could use the money to subsidize the social conscience of the Group Theater.

Though he had approved MGM's signing him, Louis B. Mayer never took to Tone from the start. One reason may have been Tone's role in his first Hollywood movie, *Gabriel Over the White House*, produced by a fellow left-winger, Walter Wanger, and shot so secretly (for Hearst's Cosmopolitan Pictures) on MGM stages that not until its final cut reached Mayer in his private screening room did the studio boss discover its pro-Roosevelt sympathies. Mayer was a staunch Hoover supporter (Hoover's ex-secretary Florence Browning was taken on the MGM payroll and sent to be Mayer's eyes and ears in the Broadway office) and he ordered extensive re-takes so as to keep the film off the screen until 1 April, 1933, by which time Hoover would have just vacated the White House. Tone's part as the secretary of a fictitious US President of energetically liberal principles was not large, but Mayer associated him with it and mistrusted the actor's pursuit of 'socially valid' roles during his MGM days. The politically committed (or even motivated) movie wasn't a type that flourished on Mayer's acres; and Tone was thus being constantly 'loaned-out' (at a profit, of course) to other studios where the soil was more politically fruitful. The occasional gratification this gave him was continuously defeated when he returned to MGM to be cast as a white-tie-and-tails socialite in pictures that endorsed the very society values he made a show of rejecting in his off-screen hours. This was indeed an unlikely man to become enamoured of Joan Crawford.

What did fascinate Tone was 'Hollywood politics', the power-play of the studios. He had come to the first meeting prepared to dislike Crawford as the prime type of consumer-object created by a capitalist movie industry to distract and corrupt the disadvantaged masses. She nearly confirmed his prejudices by misinterpreting his privileged East Coast background and serving him tea on a silver tray in the most gracious 'Pickfair' style. Each speedily disabused, then attracted the other. He provoked Crawford's interest by his earthy use of a word like 'dames' (later, it would be free use of words with one letter less) with which he gave warning that he wanted no truck with Hollywood gentility, and she stopped being the lady and started being her forceful self. He expected vanity and found a hard worker; she expected disdain and found idealistic commitment. Two unlikely people quickly discovered they were meant for each other: which explains, much more than the money, why Tone's intended trip West to pick up a fat pay-cheque lengthened into weeks and months and an increasingly intimate liaison with Joan Crawford.

He helped Crawford recharge herself at a low time in her life, just as he would later try to redirect her career so that it led away from the film studios and back to his own home ground of off-Broadway theatre-land. For the moment, though, Crawford needed no one's help in constructing a new mythology for herself. This was her 'gardenia period', for example, when she adopted the somewhat overpoweringly fragrant flower as her personal emblem, perfumed her home with bowls of them, interlaced them with the presents she handed out to the 'little people' on the film set, and liked to be presented with a fresh one daily when she appeared on the set. A 'fee', so to speak, for her personal appearance. Most people humoured her; some, like the

OPPOSITE Fred Astaire took his first dance steps on screen with Crawford.

ABOVE LEFT Saturation publicity for *Dancing Lady*.
ABOVE RIGHT Clark Gable was the rough-neck Broadway producer.
BELOW and OPPOSITE One of the numbers in *Dancing Lady* supposedly set in a Broadway theatre but obviously geared and decorated to the demands of Hollywood fantasy.

future director George Sidney, then a sound technician at MGM, rather sceptically suspected that her reading had acquainted her with 'the other lady' in Paris who had been known around town by her posies of camelias, amongst other charms, 'and as camelias aren't as easy to come by in California, she went for gardenia'.

She also took to manic spring-cleaning sessions at her home, whether it was spring or not, personally scrubbing it from top to bottom as if to obliterate an imperfect past. But contrary to later legend, she did not at first insist on guests removing their shoes before they walked on the all-white carpets that were part of her friend Billy Haines's refurbishment scheme. This was a fan-magazine writer's invention: but the papers picked up the story and guests acted as they had been 'cued' by the fiction, until the lady of the house was soon insisting on it from every caller, as a sort of hygienic obeisance.

Some eccentricities seem related to her insecurities; and at that time, following the flop of *Today We Live*, she was declared to be 'on the verge of ruin' by no less a prophet than David O. Selznick, who had become an MGM vice-president in 1933 and had his own production unit on the lot. One guesses this phrase to be the exaggeration of Selznick the compulsive cable-sender; for MGM soon showed its faith in her credit-worthiness by re-teaming her with Gable in *Dancing Lady* (24 November 1933). Another good reason for putting the studio's resources behind Crawford was its temporary loss of Norma Shearer. Irving Thalberg had suffered a heart attack on 26 December 1932, and his recuperation in Europe kept him away from MGM until August, 1933. Shearer was constantly at his side; so Garbo, Crawford and Jean

Publicity for *Sadie McKee* tells the story . . . and Crawford, as a working girl, ensnares a millionaire played by Edward Arnold, who shows another night-club customer where to get off.

Harlow had to be worked hard and successfully at a time when costs were rising and the box-office was showing the first faltering signs of being affected by the Depression. (The business outlook in 1932 was so uncertain that even Shearer, who then got $110,000 a picture, agreed to let Nicholas Schenck decide when, 'and if', she could get a rise if 'conditions materially improved in the United States'.) Fortunately for all, *Dancing Lady* was one of those films that showed the market was still there. Selznick wrote that 'for years [it] was rated by MGM as the 100 per cent commercial picture by which all other pictures were measured'. It certainly set Crawford on top again. Throughout the production, she was highly strung. George Sidney recalls her demanding (and later retracting) his dismissal after his alleged clumsiness with the playback music, which was then recorded on 35mm sound-track stock, had broken her shooting by keeping her waiting. It was an accident-prone production. Nelson Eddy got his role in it only because the original male vocalist slipped a disc as he leaped on to the podium for the 'Rhythm of the Day' number; fortunately, the camera was shooting a rear-view angle, and as Eddy had the same physique, he stepped into the role when the shot cut to a frontal close-up. Then Crawford, overdoing a scene in which she was supposed to sprain her ankle, actually broke it. This occurred while shooting the opening number of a back-stage musical where Clark Gable, as the show's rough-neck producer, asks a shy, slim dancer to take Crawford through the steps.

'Good evening, Mr Astaire,' she says – and Astaire, cast as 'himself', made his film debut for all of thirty seconds before Joan's mishap cut the number short. The incident was filmed and later inserted in the script, showing how tight the shooting schedule was. But Crawford's proficiency as a dancer is well demonstrated in two technically complex routines. After she and Astaire have strutted through 'The Gang's All Here' number in evening dress, they are elevated on a platform (still dancing) high above the partying throng and sail across the studio clouds to make a safe landing in *dirndl* and *lederhosen* respectively for a 'Let's Go Bavarian' number in the Austrian Alps. Drinking is the only link, but as Prohibition had just been repealed, it was a shrewdly topical touch.

Franchot Tone owed his role as a dinner-jacketed Park Avenue socialite to Crawford's lobbying; but it displeased him to have to play this social drone and, as if to show Joan how frivolous this kind of make-believe really was, he persuaded her once the shooting finished to accompany him to New York for the first night of Sidney Kingsley's *Men in White* at the Group Theater. At the curtain, he shouted at her through the ovation, 'This is where we'll be some day, you and I, in the theatre – where you belong.' To her amazement, she heard herself reply, 'Yes, of course!' A live audience always terrified Crawford: she could never adjust to facing people – even a few dozen making up the audience at a radio broadcast. 'I think I must have been scared by a red light as a child,' she once told Hedda Hopper. 'The minute that red light goes on, which means you're on the air, I freeze. With a camera, even a TV one, it's different. The camera is mother to me: if I'm nice to it, it'll be nice to me.' Yet she was at her most impressionable

Plenty of working girls knew what it was like to go hungry, but Crawford in *Sadie McKee* does something about it: she steals another customer's [illegible] in the Automat.

when she was present in a theatre and felt the enviable power of a live audience to project love across the footlights. To receive love from people, *real* tangible people, was the greatest conquest she felt she could make; and on returning to Hollywood, she instructed Billy Haines to blueprint plans for a 'Little Theater' annex to her home. Tone told her: 'You need constant challenges, Joan,' and she heard in this the voice of 'Daddy' Wood saying, 'if the job is impossible, you may never get it accomplished, but you'll grow in trying ...'

Her next film, *Sadie McKee* (11 May 1934), didn't offer much chance of growth, except to her eyebrows, which she stopped having plucked and allowed to grow into stiff bristles. She also slicked back her hair and starkly simplified her wardrobe. She was playing a housemaid abandoned by her man in the big city who marries a bibulous millionaire, but eventually turns to the puppyish son of her old and wealthy employer. If the role was Cinderella, at least her appearance was closer to life than fairy-tale. It was an unashamed 'fans' film'. Mordaunt Hall, the *New York Times* critic, noting the throng expectantly standing in line at the Capitol Theatre, reported that when the cad who had jilted Joan at the registry office 'breathed his last ... there was many a dry eye in the house'. She played this bedside scene as she remembered herself responding to the death of one of her own early boy-friends who had succumbed to pneumonia after giving up his tuxedo to keep her warm at the Coconut

Grove. Franchot Tone was showing her how to reach into herself for emotional truth; maybe Stanislavsky was being served as well as Cinderella. As for Tone's role as the rich 'young master', he felt it hardly compensated him for once more presenting the personable face of capitalism.

There is no better sign of Franchot Tone's growing influence on Crawford than her decision to try radio. He eased her into the medium whose immediacy terrified her. Tone guided and coaxed her the way a parent eases a child into the water for a swimming lesson. She had been invited to appear on Bing Crosby's show – *as herself*! Not even protected by a character role! On the evening of the broadcast, she had her doctor in attendance. Her script pages were glued on to cardboard lest her shaky hand made them rustle. Franchot Tone kept a reassuring hand on her shoulder-pad. And gripping a chromium towel-rail with her free hand to steady herself still further, she fought back her 'mike fright' and successfully swapped tight-lipped repartee with her relaxed host. She drew applause and ended the ordeal trembling, but intact. More dramatic challenges next time, Tone promised. Bing, today: tomorrow, who knew? Chekhov, maybe. The Moscow Art Theatre's productions were the talk of Tone's *avant-garde* set, a number of whom had drifted to Hollywood and now dined and discoursed on art and politics at Crawford's Brentwood home or the rented house that Tone discreetly occupied nearby.

Crawford was now receiving more personal attention from Mayer than any of his other female stars except Garbo. With Thalberg removed from control of production by his continuing poor health, as well as by Mayer's strategy of 'divide and rule' exemplified by the 'independ-

ABOVE LEFT Ladies fight over a man in *Sadie McKee* and Esther Ralston ends up getting the worst of it.

ABOVE RIGHT, BELOW and OPPOSITE Crawford's films place increasing emphasis on fashion and *Sadie McKee*, unsurprisingly, turns out to be a working girl who can wear it.

ents' with their own production units that he had brought into the studio, he viewed the upturn in Crawford's fortunes as the reward of his own shrewd showmanship and the proof of his fatherly faith in her. He personally selected *Chained* (31 July 1934) for her next film.

Chained was one of those films which F. Scott Fitzgerald screened a year or two later when he was assigned to write a Crawford screenplay tentatively entitled *Infidelity*. Watching the film, he scribbled notes to himself which, he hoped, would help him conscript her personality and abilities into forceful scenes that would *play* on the screen. 'Write hard, Mr Fitzgerald, write hard,' she instructed him. He did: and on no one was he harder than on Crawford. 'Why do her lips have to be glistening wet?' he asked himself irritably. 'Don't like her smiling to herself ... Cynical accepting smile has gotten a little tired ... She cannot fake her bluff.' But his prescription was more optimistic than this diagnosis suggested. 'Absolutely necessary that she feel her lines. Must be serious from first. So much better when she is serious. Must have direct, consuming purpose in mind at all points of the story, never anything vague or blurred.' And he concluded: 'She must be driven.' The *Infidelity* project was never completed: it foundered on censorship objections to such a provocative title, and no one was fooled by the self-serving switch to an alternative one, *Fidelity*. But from his attitude to Crawford, one suspects Fitzgerald misunderstood the nature of star acting, which has to be accommodating to the best-liked features of the star – and these are not necessarily dramatically consistent with each other. He was proved right in the long run when he asserted

Second husband, Franchot Tone, and Crawford do a radio play together.

hangers, and a designer-wardrobe featuring Adrian's sporty polo coats, a sailboat hat perched so acutely on the side of Crawford's head that it looks set to circumnavigate her skull, and a fur coat so lavishly cloaking her figure that she appears to be a willing victim of rape by a mink-pack. This was Crawford as her fans desired her: loyal, kidding, ladylike, down-to-earth, sophisticated, a good sport, drawing a disproportionate share of life's luck, yet discovering how hard it is to handle all of it, and giving up some of it with advantageous good grace.

Before 1934 was out, she had a fourth hit on the screen, another happy mating of the talents of Gable, Montgomery and herself, in a screenplay by Joseph L. Mankiewicz, who had studied the lady more professionally than had Fitzgerald. It was one of the few Crawford films based on a Broadway success. Tallulah Bankhead had created the role of a woman jilted by one suitor, consoled by another, taken off for an exploratory week-end by the first, and finally settling for matrimony with the second. Mankiewicz's script had a smart knack of connecting the best personality points of all three stars and director W.S. Van Dyke burlesqued marriage conventions as urbanely as he had done six months earlier in *The Thin Man*. One person not amused, though, was Joseph L. Breen, appointed Hollywood's moral watchdog by the Hays Office in that same year, 1934, which also saw the formation of the Legion of Decency. *Forsaking All Others* (28 December 1934) was the first film to catch it hot from the Legion. The cynical twist in the title's religiosity caught the bigot's eye and Breen asked for the more daring lines to be deleted. 'What is this new *tsatske* about censorship?' Van Dyke exploded in a cable to MGM. 'How are we going to win the Nobel Prize if we continue to be heckled like this? . . . Really perturbed about *Forsaking*. Please wire me condition of the Breen spleen. Love and kisses, The White Hope.' Despite the 'spleen', the film was a huge success.

The star who had been 'on the verge of ruin' a couple of years earlier was now so strongly entrenched in public favour that her studio had no alternative but to renegotiate her contract. For Crawford, 1934 was the year of *her* New Deal. Under a three-year agreement of 10 December 1934, MGM undertook to pay her $7,500 a week for forty-four weeks of the first year (any single extra week needed for filming would cost an additional $7,500); $8,500, the second year; and $9,500, the third year. For each film in excess of nine which she completed inside the three-year term, she would receive a $50,000 bonus. Tone's growing influence on her own readiness to branch out into radio was reflected in a personal letter from Mayer accompanying the contract. He conceded she could do four single broadcasts each year with only two conditions: sponsorship and content 'shall not be connected in any way with intoxicating liquors or photoplays'. It was then the fashion for film stars to do digest versions of up-coming or recent movies on the radio: Mayer didn't want to use up Crawford's availability for this type of promotion.

Though Franchot Tone was only on $1,500 a week, this didn't irk him so much as his constant battle for 'valid' roles. He succeeded in getting a 'loan-out' to Warners for

that Crawford 'must be driven' – but that was still ten years away. In 1934, she was not disposed to take any more risks with 'driven' characters like Sadie Thompson. And scripts that gave a hard edge to female roles were not too native to the MGM house product, which softened the studio's women stars to accord with the moral focus of Mayer and his 'tasteful' supervisors.

Chained is scarcely 'hard' writing, yet it does make capital scenes out of Crawford's customary dilemma of having to choose between two men – the charming but ageing shipping tycoon played by Otto Kruger, and Clark Gable's cheeky young globetrotter. One man she has married out of gratitude after he has divorced his wife and surrendered half his fleet for love of her; the other man wants her because, well, that's simply how life is. The film finds a breathtakingly abrupt solution: the older man makes the sacrifice that would be popular with an audience of younger film-goers, but there is just enough discreet ambiguity at the fade-out to hint that henceforth both men will share Crawford's affections, consecutively if not simultaneously. The sharp notation of the dialogue projects character, while Clarence Brown's direction precipitates cause and effect with a brisk good-humour. It may seem like heresy, but if Fitzgerald had been able to write a movie to order as well as the credited screenwriters John Lee Mahin and Edgar Selwyn, he would have been accounted a commercial success by MGM and at least an intelligent strategist by posterity.

Of course the luxurious props and sentimental sops of a Crawford film are present: ocean liners more glamorous than anything afloat, ski lodges built on the scale of aircraft

OPPOSITE Cigarette . . . drink . . . embrace – the sequence of seduction in *Chained*.

The love affair that existed off-screen gave the shipboard romance in *Chained* a more than usually authentic feeling.

OPPOSITE Director Clarence Brown (on the stage, right) directs Crawford, Stuart Erwin and Gable in a scene set in the latter's South American hacienda in *Chained*.

THE

Dramatic in fashion and gesture: Crawford holds the hemispheres in *Chained* (above) and poses on a pillar for portraitist Hurrell.

Gentlemen are Born as a newspaperman mouthpiece for the college graduates who found Depression era America had nothing to offer them. He told Mayer it was the sort of film with a fighting social conscience that MGM should be making. Mayer replied tartly that the hero in *Gentlemen are Born* had been notably successful in solving his own unemployment problem – he had married an heiress. He then sent Tone over to Paramount for *The Lives of a Bengal Lancer*. As well as his 'loan-out' value, Tone suspected that MGM tolerated his fractiousness for the sake of his 'replacement value'. If any larger male star of similar appeal needed disciplining, Tone was always an available substitute in the role. One wonders if this treatment coloured his desire to separate MGM from one of their chief assets. For having eased Crawford into her radio début, he stepped up his persuasion to embolden her to do a stage play. He was aided by an accident to E.H. Griffith, the director of Crawford's next picture *No More Ladies* (14 June 1935), which brought in George Cukor to direct her retakes. Cukor, who came to Hollywood with the Talkies as a dialogue coach, had a Broadway stage background. Crawford profited from his stern coaching in some extremely long speeches: 'He took me over the coals until I gave every word *meaning*,' she said. 'It was illuminating to watch [Franchot] work with Cukor, both of them from the theatre, speaking the same language.'[14] Cukor went on record some years later with his assessment of Crawford's dramatic potential: 'If she had started on the stage, she might equally have become a top stage actress.'[15] This experience strengthened Crawford's imaginative overdrive and she avidly accompanied Tone to New York to breathe in the reviving ozone of legitimate theatre which he always seemed to need after the stale air of Hollywood. There the two of them dined with the great theatrical couple Alfred Lunt and his wife, Lynn Fontanne; and during the evening, Crawford had a sudden vision, almost an epiphany, of what she and Franchot might achieve together, like the Lunts, as allies in the unending struggle to serve art and fulfil oneself, as theatrical partners, as husband and wife. Once again the live stage had swayed her choice of mate.

They came East again that autumn to do some radio shows. For Tone, radio had an attractiveness over and above its freedom from Hollywood hyperbole and platitude: it enabled him to claim and gain equal billing with Crawford, something their respective status at MGM precluded on the screen. But on this occasion the broadcasts were a cover for their marriage, which took place surreptitiously on 11 October 1935.

Mayer disapproved of the match. One good reason was Crawford's speedy demand that her husband be given a rise. Fortunately he had just collected the best notices of his career in *Mutiny on the Bounty*, where he played the role which Robert Montgomery turned down of an English gent press-ganged into the crew. MGM had played its 'reserve' talent; and Tone won an Oscar nomination. The studio had also made a $5,250 profit on his 'loan-outs' in 1935: a small sum, but justifying a rise to keep his wife happy. The strength of Mayer's desire to do this also emerges from the $25,000 loan he made to Tone in December, against the advice of his own legal department, which told him he needed the agreement of his board of directors. Tone had moved into Crawford's home; and no doubt the money was useful for paying a share of the lifestyle which she mainly supported. But no sooner had Tone married Crawford than he wanted them both to be up and off and out of Hollywood: a round-the-world voyage with Joan in a sailboat ('*Mutiny on the Bounty* had had its effect,' she noted dryly much later), or a back-to-nature sojourn in one of the log cabins in Canada where his youth had been spent. Anything, in short, that drew on his own resources; anywhere that diminished his physical dependence on Hollywood. It was a bad omen, and one she would have recognized except for the excitement of managing their lives as man and wife. In the first few months of each of her marriages, Crawford seems to have been unduly open to the man's influence; and now she even began toning down the publicity he thought cheapening and hateful. For her, the clamorous attention of the fans confirmed how much they loved her; for him, it simply underlined that in the service of the arts, there should be no stars at all. The new couple scouted the Connecticut woods for an East Coast home. They did radio plays together: she was the Tudor monarch to Tone's Earl of Essex in a Lux Radio Theater adaptation of Maxwell Anderson's *Elizabeth the Queen*. 'I was told I had given a good performance; it was a real conquest,' she exulted.

If MGM was suspicious of these 'conquests' and the independence they fostered, the studio was totally bewildered by the next course of self-expression that she

Crawford shows off one of the latest home gadgets, the radiogram.

embarked on enthusiastically with her husband.

Tone had a surprisingly well-developed tenor voice and he proposed to Crawford that they do opera together. As spectators, they sampled the Hollywood Bowl's repertoire; then, at home, they took to submitting after-dinner guests to an entire Wagner opera recording, Joan reading the libretto, Franchot joining in the arias. When they entertained the soprano Rosa Ponselle or the tenor Tito Schipa, Crawford sang opera selections in German, French and Italian. The scene irresistibly recalled the one in *Possessed* where she sings multilingual snatches of song to a trio of foreign dinner guests, causing a vulgar interloper to ask, 'Say, what is this – Ellis Island?' She then started serious singing lessons and made so many requests for pressings of test recordings she had made at the studio that MGM's legal department actually contacted Electrical Research Products Inc. to check whether Joan's appetite for voice-training was in violation of their copyright agreement. ERP answered that it was. In a letter throbbing with dedication, and obduracy, Crawford then appealed to Mayer's henchman Eddie Mannix: 'I assure you that I only want these pressings for my own personal use in order that I may be able to study and improve my work ... When taking lessons from my teacher, I wear them out.' Her taste was ravenously catholic, as Mannix discovered when he demanded details from the recording department. 'To date,' replied a nervous manager, 'we have sent ... for her

Mr and Mrs Franchot Tone (centre), recently married, give a party for 130 guests including (left to right) James Stewart, Leopold Stokowski and Henry Fonda.

own study purposes: four pressings of "Lamp on the Corner"; four of "You're a Sweetheart" and "I Can Dream"; four of "Du bist die ruh"; two of "Traviata"; two of "Don Giovanni"; six of "Night and Day"; one of "The Man I Used to Love"; six of "Blame It on Love"; seven of "Barcarolle"; one of "I See Your Face Before Me." And now she's requesting additional pressings: seven of "Night and Day", seven of "The Man I Used to Love" ...' No wonder MGM wondered what the hell was going on up there in Brentwood. Had its star got her heart set on a career at the Met instead of at Metro?

But Crawford's operatic dedication had its self-protective aspect, too. The studio had recently signed an artist who posed a clear threat to her. Jeanette MacDonald was in one of MGM's biggest hits, *San Francisco*, where she even had Crawford's 'steady', Clark Gable, as her leading man. She had proven she possessed dramatic as well as operatic range: her voice could span the catchiest of numbers like the Arthur Freed–Nacio Herb Brown lyric 'Would You?' to arias from *Traviata* and *Faust*. These were the rigorous tests to which Crawford was now submitting herself. If she had to compete with MacDonald, she didn't intend to be flunked by hitting a wrong note.

She paid tribute in her own way to Tone's left-wing sympathies. When Vittorio Mussolini, the Italian dictator's son, visited MGM, Crawford retired to her dressing room till he left the set. Conversely, VIPs from socialist lands were always welcome. Crawford's co-workers shook their heads in wonderment when she brought shooting to a temporary halt to greet a group of engineers from the Central Hydroelectrical Institute of the USSR sponsored by Elliott Roosevelt and piloted around MGM by Franchot Tone.

It was in this state of mind, seeking a self-conscious

importance by association, that she succumbed to the lure of playing Peggy O'Neal Eaton in *The Gorgeous Hussy* (28 July 1936). An innkeeper's daughter of the 1820s, she owed her footnote in history to a relationship with President Andrew Jackson, who reputedly sent his cabinet members packing because some of their wives openly disapproved of this vulgar but vivacious woman who had the President's ear. Jackson's Secretary of State for War, John Eaton, was conjured up to give her respectability by marriage. But she finally exiled herself to Spain, where she had obtained the Madrid embassy for her husband, and later married a nineteen-year-old Spanish dancing instructor. David Selznick tried to dissuade Crawford from playing the part. 'You can't do a costume picture: you're too modern,' he said. But producer Joseph L.Mankiewicz and director Clarence Brown differed. They saw her mind was made up. So she was buttressed by an eminent cast: Lionel Barrymore as President Jackson, and Melvyn Douglas, Robert Taylor, Franchot Tone and James Stewart as other historical personages. The film turned out a disaster. Not because of Crawford's modernity: she is at least as 'period' as anyone else, though the men have the advantage pictorially of displaying their lower limbs in form-fitting trousers, while Crawford had to harness her energies to ferrying her over-decorated skirts from one lavishly furnished room to another. The fault was that although she looked gorgeous, she was not enough of a hussy. Apart from her tavern origins, it is hard to see why the usual MGM chorus of tongue-clucking matrons disapprove of this fashionably turned-out lady disporting herself decorously in Washington DC, where everything (and everyone) comes to a halt for Barrymore's interminable State of the Union speeches. Some actors are accused of chewing the carpet; Barrymore could be convicted of chewing the flag. It is *his* film, if anyone's, to such a suspicious extent that its première, coinciding with the Democrats' National Convention in 1936, looks like an endorsement of Roosevelt's re-election ticket rather than a defence of Peggy O'Neal's reputation. Frank S.Nugent ended his acidulous *New York Times* notice: 'History compels us to accept the real Peggy Eaton's contribution to the preservation of Jacksonian democracy, but our national pride rebels at the notion of having to thank Miss Crawford for making possible such boons as Mr Cleveland, Mr Wilson and Mr Roosevelt.'

Franchot Tone was cast as John Eaton. According to Crawford, he hated the part so much that he completely clammed up about it and, after work, she felt his silent frustration at having his gifts yet again constricted by a part that was just a pendant to his wife's. 'A twenty-six line part', Crawford dubbed it in an oft-quoted fit of pique, which caused her to complain to Mayer about the waste of 'one of the most brilliant actors in the business'. Mayer's riposte is well known. He told Crawford that as one of MGM's greatest stars, she couldn't 'walk away into the sunset with some unknown actor. We *have* to have an important actor.' This is a good story, with some truth in its general attitude to star-ranking; but it is not supported by the film's internal evidence. One doesn't need to cavil over the fact that Peggy and John Eaton do not 'walk away into the sunset', but *sail away*, facing windward on the prow of a ship in a fade-out strongly recalling Greta Garbo's self-exile in *Queen Christina*. Tone's part has considerably more

Barbara Stanwyck visits and perhaps sympathizes with Crawford as she is made up for her role in *The Gorgeous Hussy*.

In between takes, Crawford feeds cooling ice-cream to Robert Taylor and the other 'boys in the bed' in the bundling sequence from *The Gorgeous Hussy*.

impact (and length) than Crawford's *reductio ad absurdum* of it to that of an escort agency hireling. He appears in no fewer than seven sequences, more than holding his own by sheer presence; and if his part is short on dialogue, this is because all the parts except for the garrulous Barrymore and the puppyish Taylor (who has the good luck both to kiss Crawford *and* widow her early on) are dramatically negligible: all reaction and no action. What made Tone so morose was the way that the role of a man brought on to history's stage to provide his wife with respectability resembled his own part in legitimizing Crawford's search for significance. It was a slightly mischievious bit of casting. She could understand his feelings; but what she could not forgive was the way he surrendered to them to the extent of arriving late on the set. 'Goddamit,' she thundered, 'you're not going to keep this entire cast waiting!'

The movies he made acted on Tone like a depressant. He had stayed away so long from Broadway that he knew this escape route would now be hard to take. He had an image, indeed he was a popular player who appeared regularly on the lists of public favourites; but it was not the kind of image or popularity he valued. He had started to take to that other depressant, alcohol. Crawford's home now boasted a cocktail bar, which was quite extensively used by her husband to ease the humiliations of the day's work. Flippant and charming on screen, he was accounted a 'disagreeable drunk' by at least one MGM producer-director who had to work with him. The 'Little Theater' in the garden of their home never saw a production staged by the Tones: there never seemed enough time between films. To get back at the Hollywood establishment, Tone became increasingly militant – though it was a bland form of militancy, more like nagging. Crawford let him persuade

her to have her contract brought under Screen Actors Guild rules. Other MGM artists whom Tone helped recruit included Judy Garland, Jeanette MacDonald and Dame May Whitty.

The life-style in Brentwood Heights, however, was not constrained by many radical tendencies. Dinner parties were usually for ten or twelve, minutely planned events, with gold-edged and handwritten place-cards and embossed menus like the one Joan shared with her half-dozen flourishing fan clubs. She had presented these with mimeograph machines to relay the latest news about her, and the menu was run off for fans who wished to 'eat like a star'. 'Fresh pineapple and strawberries topped with mint sorbet; almond soup; roast *poulet* stuffed with sage and orange slices, wild rice and garden peas; endive, watercress, lettuce and chicory salad with lemon or French dressing; *crêpes Suzette* or *crème caramel*.' For fans who could not muster the appetite (or money), there was consolation in the reminder that Joan's dietary stringency returned when the day's work began: her studio lunch was no more than a pitcher of iced water and her favourite dish – fruit salad in lime aspic. With cook, butler and downstairs maid, her home could accommodate even more lavish buffets for several hundred, if the garden area and the pool were used. But as it was the same crowd who congregated at most times, in most places, entertainment was simply an extension of working hours at a more relaxed tempo.

She seldom did anything now without its having some application to her career. Even a trip East to see the new plays served a dual purpose. Consider one unaccustomedly cordial letter written by Louis B. Mayer on 17 December 1937, to Crawford's agent Mike Levee. 'I am glad that Joan has decided to go to New York to look over the plays, and see if she can find a suitable vehicle which she is

ABOVE Franchot Tone, a dab hand at mixing drinks, and Crawford, who was introduced to them by him, show off the cocktail bar in their home . . .

enthusiastic about,' Mayer said. 'As long as she is willing to spend her money to make the trip, our company is willing to give her selection its honest consideration. As soon as you hear from her, please let me know and I will have Mr Rubin or Mr Schenck, or both, discuss the play with her there. If they reasonably agree with her choice, we will arrange to buy the play. I do congratulate her and I wish you would express to her my great admiration for the interest she is showing in attempting to find a vehicle she would be happy working in.' With a characteristically pious sigh over his 'family' of stars, Mayer added, 'If they should all show such great interest, it would be inspiring to all of us.' Perhaps, though, the last sentiment was intended ironically, since Mayer knew the purpose that had drawn such a warmly commendatory letter from him. A lot of the dollars and cents expended by Crawford on her trip East would be tax-deductible. A letter like this might be used as corroborative evidence to justify her expenses. Three years later Mayer was again asked to express support for another play-hunting trip to New York; but his legal department this time advised him to let the first letter suffice and not overdo things – 'lest it result in undoing what has been accomplished'.

Yet the right sort of vehicle for Crawford, whether it came tax-deductible or not, was increasingly hard to find as audience tastes in the mid-1930s became more fickle and film-going habits less dependable. She tried converting herself into the spoilt-silly heroines of screw-ball comedies who are jolted into a more (but not too) realistic view of life by men with a hard-working set of social values. The year 1935 saw Frank Capra's *It Happened One Night* walk off with all five of the major awards at the Oscar ceremonies, confirming what its box-office had already told the other

. . . And, of course, every day had its fashion hour too.
I Live My Life was a switch of style for Crawford. Screwball comedy with Brian Aherne frequently put her on her backside, but MGM production values ultimately reasserted themselves in the grand ball at the opera.

ABOVE With her director, Dorothy Arzner (right), and photographer George Folsey (centre), Crawford prepares a scene for *The Bride Wore Red*.

BELOW The bride also wore peasant costume (with Franchot Tone as a folkloric postman) as well as the bugle-beaded red creation (right) that gave the picture its title and much of its interest.

studios who rushed even more screw-ball comedies into production. The world now saw Joan Crawford being manhandled the way Claudette Colbert had been by Gable – except that it was not Gable who came near to spanking her in *I Live My Life* (4 October 1935), but Brian Aherne as the stuffily likeable, Pygmalion-bent archaeologist whose 'dig' she trips into on a Greek island, nearly demolishing his unearthed Praxiteles. This brings them together, with her being aroused by his disapproval of the idle rich. It was a smoothly entertaining example of the way Hollywood mediated in the class war that there might have been in a less democratic country than America, and turned it into the sex war. Franchot Tone didn't play in it, but should have – judging by Mankiewicz's dialogue at the expense of the Park Avenue set who complain that 'it's getting to be that anyone with seven or eight ponies can get to play polo'. Aherne cracks back, 'There are millions of people in this country who, if they had a pony, would eat it.' The sight of Crawford several times dumped on her backside is also an unusual pleasure – though some rules, like Adrian's fashions, could not be so lightly mocked. His wide-shouldered styles with lapels that almost touch her shoulder tips dominate Crawford to the extent of becoming part of the performance.

W. S. Van Dyke also directed her in *Love on the Run* (20 November 1936). It arrived at the end of an autumn season which saw *My Man Godfrey* (William Powell, Carole Lombard), *Cain and Mabel* (Clark Gable, Marion Davies), *Sing, Baby, Sing* (Adolphe Menjou, Alice Faye) and *Libelled Lady* (Jean Harlow, William Powell). If Crawford wasn't exactly striking out for herself, she was at least keeping abreast of the tide. She played an American heiress in Europe mixed up in a spy network and helped out of the entanglement by the very newspapermen who have hounded her on the Society pages, played by Clark Gable and (the loser, as usual) Franchot Tone. The sardonic Mankiewicz produced it, and later, with glee, showed Crawford a copy of a letter received from a Mrs Bertram Frankenstein of Massachusetts, who demanded, 'Kindly instruct your exhibitors of [this film] to refrain from the use of the line "I is Mrs Frankenstein." I realize the above-mentioned line receives a great many laughs from theater audiences and I do not wish this name to appear in a ridiculous form throughout the country.' With memories fresh in his mind of the famous libel suit brought (and won) against MGM by a surviving member of the Tsar of Russia's family, Mankiewicz passed the letter on to a studio trouble-shooter with the laconic comment, 'My friend, we have another Rasputin on our hands.'

Crawford's career at this stage exemplifies the uncertainty that MGM was feeling about her. She was still a top star, but she was approaching an awkward age, her mid-thirties, and what roles she could play had to be considered in relation to what films the public wanted to see. MGM was none too sure of either. Crawford was too mature to be a convincing working girl; too modern for a historical heroine; too easily confused in comedy with other stars who had an earlier patent on the role of screwball

Hollywood's best known woman director Dorothy Arzner and her star were disappointed by the film they made together, but took to each other. She later directed Pepsi Cola commercials for Crawford's companies.

115

comedienne. The uncertainty was compounded when Thalberg suddenly died in September 1936, and the studio faced a future in which Mayer's own preferences in stars, stories and treatment came to predominate. Wholesomeness, family sanctity, love for one's mother, respect for one's father – even when these all-American qualities were as likeably accommodated as they were in the Andy Hardy series, which Mayer initiated in 1937, they were not the best ones to enhance or advance Crawford's career. Financially, too, the studio was having a rough time. After an all-time record profit of $14,388,000 in 1935–6 (on a production budget of $22,916,999 and forty-five films) came a slump to $5,855,000 (on an investment of $26,835,000 and thirty-five films) in 1936–7. Thalberg's last two productions before his death, *Romeo and Juliet* and *The Good Earth*, together accounted for a loss of $1,500,000. Expensive risks, which included prestigious as well as off-beat productions, no longer had a place in Mayer's plans. Signs of playing safe with Crawford are apparent in the enquiry he personally addressed to Sam Eckman, MGM's London head, in November 1936. How did Eckman view Crawford's starring in a remake of *The Last of Mrs Cheyney*? This was Frederick Lonsdale's society drama of the adventuress who robs the aristocrats of their jewels and exposes their morals as paste. Eckman's reply, though favourable, should have put Mayer on his guard against the datedness of this theme: '*Last of Mrs Cheyney* one of the most successful early Norma Shearer films even in industrial areas, contrary to original opinion. Therefore favour remake.'

The Last of Mrs Cheyney (19 February 1937) was not a success. Crawford's disquiet is reflected in numerous imperious memos during shooting to the publicity department: 'I am anxious to have still No. 972/72 killed. Please advise,' is typical. In other ways too, it was a 'disturbed' production. Director Richard Boleslawski died in the middle of it; George Fitzmaurice was assigned to take over; at the last minute this was countermanded; the person who completed the film, though uncredited, was Hollywood's only woman film director at that time, Dorothy Arzner.

She and Crawford took to each other at once. Arzner was four or five years older than her star, but looked like a youth in her mid-twenties and could be mistaken for a boy. She was invariably impeccably turned out, usually in twill trousers or tweeds tailored with a chic yet masculine line. She affected a slouchy hat on the set. Yet the effect, instead of being 'butch', was the crisp statement by a talented and shrewd woman of the qualities she wore comfortably in the Hollywood studios where she freelanced. In this almost exclusively male world where people in power were concerned, exceptional female talents like Arzner and Margaret Booth, one of MGM's pre-eminent editors, were accepted, even admired, but as workers first, and then (and a long way after) as women.

It was Franchot Tone who recommended Crawford to take a look at Arzner's work. Together, they screened the last film she had directed, *Craig's Wife*, in the cinema at Crawford's home. Oddly, it was this film that Crawford herself remade (as *Harriet Craig*) some years later; even more bizarrely, it is a film that anticipates, and may have contributed to, the marked change of life that overtook Crawford as her temperament was toughened to meet the challenge of the gathering years. Harriet Craig, who wants a home of her own, symbol of security and love, gets married so as to gain her heart's desire and then, to secure her conquest, turns her husband into just another bit of the furnishings. This woman (played by Rosalind Russell in Arzner's film) patrolling the dustless rooms in all her loneliness presages the desperate withdrawal into her own shell from which a later Crawford would re-emerge toughened and regenerated.

Arzner had been assigned by MGM to direct Luise Rainer in *The Girl from Trieste*, based on an unperformed play by Ferenc Molnár. Molnár's version was about a prostitute trying to go straight, but discovering that the so-called High Society she mixed with was much more vicious than her own class. But Rainer dropped out for reasons that are still obscure. Instantly Crawford snapped up the film, whereupon, to her consternation (and, one guesses, Arzner's, too) Mayer ordered it to be rewritten as a Cinderella story for Crawford entitled *The Bride Wore Red* (8 October 1937).

Because the story's original heartlessness has not been satisfactorily masked by the blander re-write, *The Bride Wore Red* is an acutely uncomfortable film to watch. Its author's distaste for the rich constantly undercuts our sympathy for the heroine who panders to them in order to become one of them. This girl is Crawford, a cabaret singer in a tawdry Trieste cellar, sent off at the whim of a cynical count to spend two weeks in an expensive hotel in the Tyrol and win his bet that, with the right deportment and wardrobe (by Adrian, of course, and including the eponymous red creation of some 2,000 – or was it two million? – bugle beads), she can pass for a lady of breeding among the aristocrats in residence. The film makes the mistake (and Crawford's almost neurotic anxiety compounds it) of emphasizing the callous purposiveness of her imposture. With never a moment of self-mockery, but only nervous concern least her ruse be detected, she snaps at her social inferiors among the hotel domestics (her *superiors*, if the truth be known) and calculatingly grasps at the chance of marrying a rich young snob, played by Robert Young, who has unfeelingly jilted his own fiancée the minute Crawford appeared. For once, only Franchot Tone looks at home as the single man of integrity in the Alps, though incongruously cast as a flute-playing postman and even more bizarrely costumed in *lederhosen* of a length that Bavaria might dispute with Bermuda.

It is one of the few films concerned with rising above one's origins in which Crawford fails to make the grade. Possibly because, in a European setting, she is shunned for not being what she seemed; whereas, in an American milieu, according to Hollywood, status comes with successful economic assimilation and her lowly social origins would have been forgiven her.

'We were the people who made a forgetable
picture memorable.'

How exactly did MGM regard Crawford at this time? Was she, in the studio's opinion, a wasting asset or a redeemable liability? Again, the contract files provide the answer. They tell a very different story from the one that is usually printed whenever Crawford biographies refer to the notorious advertisement placed in certain periodicals in 1938 by one Harry Brandt, president of the Independent Theater Owners of America, which stigmatized Crawford as 'box-office poison' along with Marlene Dietrich, Katharine Hepburn, Fred Astaire and Greta Garbo. The MGM executive who had great influence over the contracts – and hence the status – of the studio's stars was Benny Thau, a quietly spoken producer and Mayer's confidant since Thalberg's death. He and Mayer, in their different ways, were commercial realists: neither would have ignored a star's slipping box-office rating, if they felt it was justified by diminishing talent. The fact that neither took advantage of the 'box-office poison' calumny indicates that they regarded Crawford's reverses as temporary. In fact, all the 'fallen stars' named above enjoyed a huge commercial and critical success within a year or so of Brandt's attack: Dietrich in *Destry Rides Again*, Hepburn in *The Philadelphia Story*, Astaire in *Broadway Melody of 1940*, and Garbo in *Ninotchka*. Mayer knew that the strangely touching fidelity of fans was a force in the marketplace; and it was this powerful residual loyalty that the contract Crawford signed in 1938 continues to reflect.

PREVIOUS PAGE Crawford in *Mannequin*.
ABOVE *Mannequin*: Spencer Tracy was the millionaire this time; Crawford started out, at least, as the working girl who marries him.

Certainly it reduced her compensation; but this was not evidence of a slipping reputation so much as of a declining box-office all round – the whole film industry was starting to suffer a slump as audiences declined from a high of 85 millions in the mid-1930s to the low 70 millions by 1938. Crawford was to get $330,000 a year for five years and ten weeks. (The 'ten weeks' was the period she had agreed to extend her expiring contract so as to facilitate shooting, and for this she got a sum unspecified but described as 'a good and valuable consideration'.) There was to be a limit of fifteen pictures, not more than six during the first two years and nine during the last three. 'We cannot require her to appear in more than four pictures during any contract year,' Thau's memorandum continued. 'She is to have full radio rights during the life of the contract. During such years as she elects to do a stage play, she has to have a vacation period of twelve weeks. During any year in which we require her to render her services in excess of forty weeks, she is to be paid additional compensation at the rate of $8,250 per week.' The contract provided for MGM to 'collaborate' with Crawford – probably in investment terms – if she decided to tour in a stage play: a clause that shows the strength of her reluctance to abandon her ambition to become a new Lynn Fontanne. Another clause suggested how closely she still identified with Mayer's paternalism: she was to be 'lent out' to 'majors' only – i.e., the other big Hollywood studios. 'This will prevent our lending her services to such producers as Samuel Goldwyn, David Selznick and Walter Wanger,' noted MGM's attorney Floyd Hendrickson. Nevertheless, Benny Thau accepted all these conditions, save one. She had asked that MGM 'cannot require her to render services after 5.00 p.m. except in case of emergency – the reason ... being that she wants to devote the time between 5.00 p.m. and 6.30 p.m. to her singing lessons.' Thau, who had probably had quite enough of Crawford's excursions into the opera classics, turned this down flat: otherwise, she got her way.

One event that had probably helped her get it was the excellent business being done from the start of the year by a film in which MGM's other great male star besides Gable played alongside her, their personality 'chemistry' being a good antidote to 'box-office poison'. Making *Mannequin* (21 January 1938) with Spencer Tracy had nevertheless been a disconcerting experience for Crawford. The story was familiar – over-familiar – to her. She was again a working girl who weds one man to get out of the tenement ghetto, divorces him on realizing his duplicitous nature, then finds him blackmailing her new husband, a self-made millionaire, with threats that all she was after was his money, not his love. Tracy was the millionaire. To Crawford, he was an unpredictable new breed of actor. He gave her the feeling that he was making no effort at all to project his personality by the rapid-fire notation of character-traits favoured by the acting style of the 1930s. He just seemed to walk through the scene, never changing into character, yet emerging in the rushes as holding the interest by sheer presence. This in turn required Crawford to revert from the wilful desperation of her working-girl routine when she was with the other players in the film to a far more subdued but for her less effective approach in her scenes with Tracy. She found him far from a delight to work with. A man frequently bored by movie-making, but

The stars of *Mannequin* are posed affectionately; in truth she could not get along with him on the set.

blessed by the way his indifference appeared on the screen disguised as effortlessness, he frequently resorted to malicious little tricks to relieve his tedium, like standing on Crawford's toes during a take or playing an affectionate scene between them with onion on his breath. Such pranks later met their happy match in Katharine Hepburn: but the over-disciplined Crawford sensed Tracy's disdain for the work in hand, and it reminded her of Tone's. Both men were brooders who drank heavily and often thought themselves wasted in films.

Mannequin had been in preparation since 1936 and was still an unresolved attempt to graft the stock 'working girl escapes her background' story on to the inspirational 'successful man loses all but picks himself up again' theme of the Depression. Luckily, audiences ignored its datedness and went for Tracy's amiable air of homespun integrity. Crawford thought this made nonsense of her proletarian zeal. She wasn't alone in her doubts. Frank S. Nugent said in his *New York Times* review: 'We thought at times that the script writers had the roles reversed, that Mr Tracy should have been the honest working boy, Miss Crawford the plutocrat.' The two stars never worked together again – nor wanted to. They were good for business, but not for each other.

Crawford kept on at Mayer until he arranged for MGM to buy the film rights of a play she and Tone had seen in New York. (This special purchase in itself showed how MGM valued her.) She then asked for the two other female roles in *The Shining Hour* (18 November 1938) to be played by stage actresses Margaret Sullavan and Fay Bainter. Mayer, ever protective, warned her that such experienced women could steal the picture from her. Crawford replied, 'I'd rather be a supporting player in a good picture than the star of a bad one.' Again she got her way: it was a good, intuitive decision, for the other actresses called up Crawford's reserve of self-reliance, though the play didn't transplant well to the screen. Sullavan, then married to the agent Leland Hayward, was several months pregnant during shooting. This vicarious experience of a role she herself had never played, namely 'motherhood', made its impact on the impressionable Crawford. The several occasions she and Tone tried to have a family had ended in miscarriages. It was at this time, after witnessing Margaret Sullavan's happiness at becoming a mother after three failed marriages of her own, that Crawford was seized by the desire to adopt children. Thus did the imminent arrival in the world of Brooke Hayward, the daughter who wrote so movingly about her mother's tragic life and suicide in her family memoirs, *Haywire*, inspire Joan Crawford to adopt the child who was to write so uncompassionate a set of her own family reminiscences in *Mommie Dearest* after Joan's death. Some things in life even a film script would not risk.

What deterred Crawford from immediately going ahead with her adoption plans was her divorce. Her marriage to Franchot Tone was in its last months, foundering unsalvageably on her accidental discovery, by opening the door of his dressing-room, that he was being unfaithful to

OPPOSITE Flanked by two women who had made stage reputations, Fay Bainter (left) and Margaret Sullavan (right), Crawford in *The Shining Hour* had at least the support of two male screen stars, Robert Young and Melvyn Douglas (right).

With Melvyn Douglas . . . and a suitably shining seascape.

ABOVE Crawford learning the ropes with her private movie projector.
BELOW Seven was her lucky number; she even had it on her car registration plate.
RIGHT A classic shot; no matter how long the photograph took, Crawford never lost patience.

her with a minor film actress. At Mayer's insistence, she delayed the divorce suit until after *The Shining Hour*'s release: their marriage was dissolved on 11 April 1939. But the studio did not wait that long to separate itself from Franchot Tone. Once the affections of his film-star wife had been alienated, MGM's patience with an actor whose drinking habits and troublesome nature were undercutting the value of his $2,500 a week salary swiftly snapped: on 5 November 1938, Tone was curtly informed his option was being picked up. He was offered a compensating $50,000 to co-star with Wallace Beery in *Thunder Afloat*, but chose instead to co-star for the same fee in *Fast and Furious*, a fading copy of *The Thin Man* series. Following his divorce, he was in such poor physical shape from drinking that his agent Mike Levee informed MGM that he could not accept their offer of a new film, virtually a 'B' picture, at $40,000. He returned to New York and the stage, appearing in supporting roles in twenty-nine more films before his death in 1968. There is a poignant footnote to what he would have called his years of 'servitude' at MGM. Despite a draft board classification of '4F', he applied for war work and Floyd Hendrickson was asked by the Investigative Division of the California Office of Provost Marshal to check off his opinion of Tone's 'Loyalty to the USA', 'Discreetness', 'Honesty', 'Ability', 'Home Life' and 'Personal Habits'. In every category, the MGM lawyer entered an 'Excellent'.

The divorce also inspired Adrian to tailor his only known

quip: 'Foot-loose again, Joan, and Franchot-free.'

A disproportionate amount of myth has gathered around the next film Crawford made, largely because the 1981 movie based on Christina Crawford's memoirs, *Mommie Dearest*, made it appear that *The Ice Follies of 1939* (10 March 1939) was some kind of punishment inflicted on her by a cruel studio for her slipping popularity. There is no truth in that. Yes, she herself is on record as saying, 'This was about the time my loyal public began dwindling. You can't keep 'em coming to bad films.'[16] But her new contract (set out above) shows how much faith MGM still put in her. Their trouble was finding the right film for her. While waiting for that, she had to be kept in work and the fact is that everyone in MGM's front office was enthusiastic about *Ice Follies*. All studios were then desperate to try anything novel – anything that might reverse the box-office's continuing decline. Ice shows were all the rage, so MGM signed the Shipstad and Ehrhardt company of speciality skaters to do a musical spectacular on ice. As the film put a strong accent on show-business and back-stage (or off-rink) relations, the man entrusted with this fairly costly venture was – Harry Rapf. It was this old protector of Crawford's who involved her in the project. What, she asked incredulously, could *she* do on skates? Very little, Rapf answered – and no more was required of her than that little. And indeed, though she put on skates to advertise the film, she never set those skates on ice in the film, and the movie makes a running joke in its last reel of her prudence

Ice Follies of 1939: she could leap in the air, but would not set foot on the ice.

Sidney Guilaroff (right) arranges a blond wig on Crawford while *Ice Follies* director Reinhold Schunzel looks on a little uneasily.

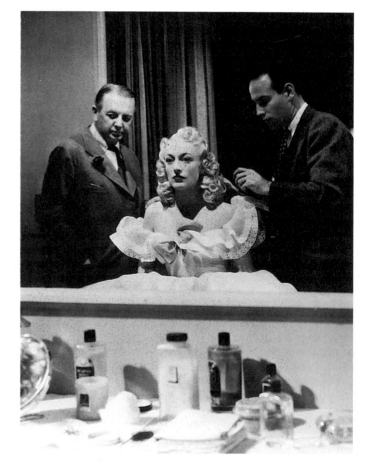

The Women: (left to right) Florence Nash, Phyllis Povah, Rosalind Russell, Joan Crawford, George Cukor, Norma Shearer, Paulette Goddard, Mary Boland and Joan Fontaine. How they all looked when they weren't being bitches to each other – George Cukor takes the cast for an off-the-set stroll.

in *not* skating. Rapf explained that MGM owned a play, aptly titled *Excess Baggage*, which would be spliced into the ice-show numbers. It was about the usual good-pal girl torn between the affections of two buddies, to be played by James Stewart and Lew Ayres. To Crawford, the part seemed a throwback to a silent-era plot, though MGM planned to add up-to-date novelty to the film by lavishing Technicolor on its last sequence where Stewart, who has turned from staging ice shows to directing Hollywood musicals, puts Crawford (the only one *not* on skates) into a Cinderella-and-nursery-rhyme ice spectacular. Direction of *Ice Follies* was entrusted to a German friend of Rapf's, Reinhold Schunzel, who had had a hit in Berlin in the early 1930s with a role-reversal comedy called *Viktor und Viktoria*. (In the course of time, *it* was to become the 1982 Julie Andrews comedy, *Victor/Victoria*: movies do swallow movies.)

'Everyone was out of their collective minds when they made *Ice Follies*,' Crawford told an interviewer, Roy Newquist, years later. But really, it was no more insane a project than many which are bludgeoned together out of bits and pieces of popular entertainment. It is true that, for Crawford especially, the film had an aspect that induced a chill which had nothing to do with its location on the ice rink. For its oddest feature is the way it exactly duplicates the circumstance of Crawford's own 'discovery' by Harry Rapf fifteen years earlier. This time she is an ice skater, not a chorine; and the Rapf figure is played by Lewis Stone,

head of a fictitious Monarch Studio, whom she has literally bumped into at the ice-show opening patronized exclusively by MGM stars, if the 'Tannoy' calls for 'Mr Gable's car . . .', 'Miss Loy's car . . .', or 'Mr Tracy's car . . .', are anything to go by. Seeking a job at the studio for Stewart, whom she has married, Crawford finds herself being quizzed on her own film chances. 'I don't want a job in motion pictures,' she tells Stone (as she told Rapf). He won't take no for an answer (nor did Rapf). 'You wouldn't.' – 'Let me see your profile . . . turn round . . . walk a little.' A moment later, in a parody of a lucky break, which is however only a slightly exaggerated replay of Crawford's own real-life good fortune, Stone is saying, 'Young lady, I think you've got what it takes to be an actress' and ordering his assistant to 'Make out a stock contract for Miss McKay, usual salary, usual options.' The salary is $75 a week, the options run for seven years (exactly the terms Crawford signed at MGM in 1925). Once her first film is a hit, her name gets changed from 'Mary McKay' to 'Sandra Lee' to give it more class (as 'Lucille LeSueur' had her name changed to 'Joan Crawford'). Soon she is a star, which leaves Stewart on the sidelines of his wife's life, fame and fortune (the way Franchot Tone was). Hollywood fantasy, of course, can put together strained marriages that the divorce courts finally sunder in real life; and *Ice Follies* ends with Stewart promoted to be motion-picture producer so as to be in his wife's studio, if not actually on a par with her stardom.

What her feelings must have been as she played these scenes, we can only speculate. She never referred to them, except for calling the film 'that dreadful thing' in her memoirs. But when one's spirits are low and one's career is faltering, it must have been profoundly dispiriting to have

With Norma Shearer in *The Women*. The hand with the nails is emblematic.

ABOVE Where the perfume counter girl can get to if she steals the right husband.
BELOW Arranged as per contract: Norma Shearer, Crawford and Rosalind Russell.

to play a part that put her, in several senses, right back where she started. It was worse than a professional set-back: it was an emotional trauma that seems, from this moment on, to have induced a sense of recklessness in her search for a part, *any* part, that would get her career moving again and reassure her about the distance she had travelled from her origins.

This recklessness led her to bid for the role of the arch-bitch Crystal in the Clare Boothe Luce play *The Women*. The studio was applying the 'safety in numbers' principle, which had shielded it from the Depression with *Grand Hotel*, and crowding the film version of this all-female tale of bitchery in hot pursuit of alimony with every top star it could muster – Norma Shearer, Rosalind Russell, Paulette Goddard, Joan Fontaine, Mary Boland and (Louis B. Mayer permitting) Joan Crawford as the perfume counter salesgirl from Blacks, Fifth Avenue, who successfully divests the Shearer character of her rich husband. Producer Hunt Stromberg still regarded Crawford as a 'dancing daughter', a 'good sport' type. Mayer regarded her almost as his 'youngest daughter'. Both men were appalled. Mayer warned, 'The role is that of an outright bitch: it could hurt your career.' When that failed to impress her, he wagged his finger and said, 'It's also a very small one, Joan.' Crawford countered, 'The woman who steals Norma Shearer's husband, Mr Mayer, can't be played by a nobody.' It was *touché* for the man who used the same argument for casting Franchot Tone in *The Gorgeous Hussy*.

Spiting Thalberg's now unprotected widow, Norma

ABOVE 'Don't lie to me. You had this private phone installed so that you could talk to a man,' purrs Rosalind Russell to Crawford in *The Women*.

BELOW 'Gee, you sure have a line,' comments Virginia Grey to Crawford.

Shearer, was a bonus for playing Crystal. Crawford even contrived to upset her rival's delivery of her lines by letting her own knitting needles go click-clack and refusing to meet Norma's eyes while 'feeding' her dialogue to her from the edge of the set for the reaction shots. Shearer's satisfaction had to be the defeat that she and the other women inflict on the gold-digging Crystal. This was the moment that caused Mayer most heartache. He knew that Shearer would walk off with film-goers' sympathies and that the cattiness of Rosalind Russell, in her first comic role, would be lapped up by female audiences. So where did that leave Crawford? Playing the 'heavy', he feared. Mayer insisted on making the character more sympathetic. Stromberg tried to oblige, with ruinous results at the film's late July sneak preview. Crawford was quickly advised to hold herself ready for re-takes and Stromberg frantically cabled Anita Loos, the screenplay's co-author, in New York: 'Wish you would please write some more links for Crawford's exit, as scenes we took are not effective or satisfying. We were wrong in agreeing that Crystal should not be defeated as she leaves the story ... She is the one character we want to see knocked for a loop for the havoc she has wrought. We distinctly want to feel that Mary's [Shearer's] strategy has exposed and stripped her and her little excursion is over, with the perfume counter calling her back.' Final editing was suspended on the film and with the laboratories urging haste in order to meet the print date, and Crawford standing by, Loos cabled a set of bitchy alternative lines of dialogue. 'Think first part of speech should be, "Well, it looks like I'm going back to Black's, Fifth Avenue ..." Second part of speech, "But you'd better come and see me because a little perfume wouldn't do you ladies any harm. So long." Or "And by the way, you ladies had better thank your lucky stars for perfume." Saying which, she takes a big sniff, salutes, says "So long, girls", and sails on out. Or "Nice to have known you ladies. I'll feel a lot more friendly towards mice. So long." Or "As far as I'm concerned, you cats, Park Avenue's just one big back alley. So long, ladies."' In the event, Crawford swept out of the film on yet another variation of the line: 'By the way, there's a name for you ladies, but it isn't used in high society – outside of a kennel.'

She did not get any additional sympathy from the audience, but the gratifyingly loud laugh she provoked may have allayed Mayer's apprehensiveness.

Her anxiety about keeping her status intact at MGM wasn't lessened by her 'hard as nails' success in *The Women*. It soon erupted again in an angry dispute over her screen credit alongside – of all people – Clark Gable. Mayer had rushed them both into *Strange Cargo* (1 March 1940), a melodrama about convicts escaping from a Devil's Island, which aspired to metaphysical significance through a Christ-figure being included in the break-out. (The only result of this was censorship trouble.) Exchanging her $40,000 designer wardrobe in *The Women* for a couple of cheap frocks bought in a chain store and emblematically dragged along the beach before being worn, Crawford played a trollopy café entertainer looking (up to a point) dishevelled and without make-up. Relations between her and Gable had been cool ever since he had unwisely galloped off along the same prestige trail that had caused her to come a cropper in *The Gorgeous Hussy*: he had invited her to co-star with him in *Parnell*. For film stars of that era to play a great historical character was regarded as a direct route to an Oscar nomination; something that the next generation of Hollywood stars would achieve by playing in 'disability biopics' about the famous casualty cases of show-business. With her own experience of history thankfully behind her, Crawford declined Gable's invitation. The likelihood is she would have liked to play the part of Parnell's mistress; but with Gable in the title role, she would have been forced into second place on the billing. The woman behind the ruin of the Irish Party was one thing; the star behind Clark Gable was a less dominant position. It was precisely over such a clash of egos that *Strange Cargo* sailed into trouble. On 10 February 1940, Floyd Hendrickson received an impassioned telephone call from Crawford. The lawyer instantly recorded it in a memorandum. From its tortured pleading one can infer Crawford's acute anxiety crisis – her fear that if she surrendered her status on even one point, in one film, it would be acknowledging her loss of power and decline in importance, and harm her future films.

'Joan Crawford called today and advised that on the title *Strange Cargo*, Clark Gable's name precedes hers,' Hendrickson noted. 'This is the first instance in which her name has been preceded in which there were only two stars.' (A film like *The Women*, starring numerous MGM artists, was specifically excluded from Crawford's contractual rights; she was paid *pro rata* by the days she was wanted for filming in it, and she accepted equal billing, second to Shearer, but in the same type-size.) 'She said it was particularly bad in this instance as she was the only female billed. She stated that in instances of this kind it is always customary for the woman's name to precede. She stated that she had told this to Joe Mankiewicz, who had told her that he thought they were working on the picture over the week-end. I explained to her that Mr Thau was the one who approved all the billings and he was unavailable. She then requested that I endeavour to contact him at Santa Anita, which I explained was impossible due to the fact that there were no telephonic connections ... Contacted Jack Rogers who stated that the title had been made up and that the picture would be ready for negative cutting no later than Monday ... Contacted Miss Crawford and advised her that the matter could rest until Monday evening, by which time I would speak to Mr Thau. She stated that five people not directly connected with the industry had called her attention to Gable's name preceding hers and one of the five had sent her a telegram.' The hapless Hendrickson, caught in this withering burst of fire, pencilled a note on his own memo: 'Explained to Mr Thau and Mr Mannix, 12 February 1940, my conversation with Miss Crawford. [They] indicated there would be no change in the title.'

Did it end there? It did not. Losing no waking moment, nor, probably, any intended for sleeping, Crawford had been on to her agent Mike Levee, who was in Florida. The first thing Eddie Mannix found, on returning from the week-end trip to Mexico, was a bundle of increasingly fraught cables from the agent, protesting against the billing. He wired back: 'Know of no promises regarding billing on *Strange Cargo*. However Mr Mayer returning to Los Angeles tomorrow and will discuss it with him.' Then, somewhat foolhardily, he added: 'Know of no better billing than "Gable and Crawford" especially taking into consideration Gable's tremendous hit and publicity after *Gone With*

the Wind.' (It had opened eight weeks earlier.) 'Am at a loss
for you to have any reason for complaining of co-star billing
Gable first, as this is not unusual with us with Gable in any
of our pictures in which he appears. Only time this has been
different was *Idiot's Delight*.' (Significantly, perhaps,
Gable's co-star was that other highly status-conscious lady
Norma Shearer.) 'Gable billed first in both *San Francisco*
and *Gone With the Wind*. No matter what we do, public will
see it that way.'

Mannix was no doubt right: but his reply begged the
question. For Crawford didn't see it that way. When
Mayer returned, she was waiting for him; and he had to
make one of his most delicate arbitrations. The outcome
was fixed satisfyingly, and permanently, on the credits of
the film when it opened a month later: 'Joan Crawford and
Clark Gable in *Strange Cargo*'.

Just to keep moving professionally now, Crawford took
risks she would once have considered unnecessarily high
gambles with her fan following. When Shearer was
unwilling to shatter her own image of unageing gracious-
ness and play a mother's role in *Susan and God*, Crawford
almost crowed with pleasure when Mayer hesitantly
offered it to her. 'If it's a good part, I'd play Wally Beery's
grandmother.' But the risk she took didn't lie in the age she
played but in the nature of the part, which required
Crawford to turn herself from a star into a character
actress. *Susan and God* (7 June 1940) was a about a silly
socialite (Gertrude Lawrence played the role on Broadway)
who catches a dose of Moral Rearmament in England and
comes home with a titled dowager guru in tow to make a
scatterbrained nuisance of herself by urging her Long
Island yachting-and-tennis set to repent and reform. But

ABOVE Mirrors were favourite props in the MGM portrait gallery: they
gave two stars for the pose of one.
OPPOSITE Crawford in 1940.

she serves herself as devoutly as God, pushing her
understandably boozing husband into a divorce. The
surprise is the accomplished and unsparing sense of self-
parody that Crawford gives under George Cukor's
direction. Got up in a country outfit of cloak, feather and a
cross-strap handbag which looks inspired by Robin Hood
and may be Adrian's self-satirizing contribution, she
doesn't trade on personality, but really creates character.
At least she does so till the story turns cravenly sentimental
and converts Susan into the Joan Crawford we all know
who can slip a disfiguring brace off her daughter's teeth,
comb out her hair and prettify the girl for a teenage beau
with the advice, 'If there's anything you want to know
about this glamour business, come to your mother'.

A Woman's Face (9 May 1941) is also a broken-backed
film. MGM were obviously only prepared to let Crawford
take half-measures with creating a new, anti-star image for
herself. Mayer was again shocked when she insisted on
playing a terribly disfigured woman who takes her
bitterness out on the world. It was a kind of hell-bent
determination on her part to undercut all those well-
protected years when MGM stars were only visible to the
world looking their impossible best. But until the film's
second half, which turns into conventional suspense,
Cukor kept Crawford reined in; he feared that scars, like
cloaks and canes, tempted players into attitudes of
flamboyance. Working with Cukor, who had come from
the theatre, was as gratifying as actually working on the

Susan and God: playing a scatterbrained society woman who gets religion and antagonizes her family (husband Fredric March and daughter Rita Quigley) and friends, Crawford received help from the costume designer in sending herself up.

stage. He stretched her, motivated her, manipulated her in a way few other directors had the nerve to do. It was *he* who stood on the sidelines, contorting his own face and body, to project the crippling sense of ugliness he wished her to absorb. Even though he might not be in her sight-line, she felt – and obeyed. Before she recounted her childhood's misery – the drunk father, the disfiguring accident – Cukor made her recite the multiplication table till she was drained of all emotion, then tell the tale likewise, counting on the audience's empathy to supply the emotion by dramatic osmosis. In short, he taught her how to use a tool-kit, rather than a cosmetics tray.

Meantime, her home life had shifted her into the new role of motherhood. Whatever its motive, her decision to adopt a child is an extraordinary one. Other childless Hollywood couples had adopted families. But it is very, very hard to find another first-magnitude star, a divorced and therefore an officially 'single' woman, pursuing a career fraught with strain, risks and set-backs, resolving to give a home and her love to an unwanted child who had neither.

However wretched that child's life later became – and if we credit Christina Crawford, she was *very* unhappy – Crawford's own maternal needs deserve compassion. No sooner had she adopted one child than she sought to draw a whole family around her. Was this an alternative reality to the MGM 'family' that she now felt no longer cherished her as much as formerly? Or a compensatory scenario, 'more significant and valid', as she might have put it, for all the career-women roles or rich and silly heiress parts she had played? Or was it simply a need for a safer kind of love – the love of children – than she had found in two

ABOVE Narcissism à la Joan Crawford as the cartoonist saw it . . .
BELOW   but in *A Woman's Face* Crawford deliberately mistreated her beauty with a hideous scar. This is a frame enlargement since MGM, which still believed in glamour, forbade any still to be made of their 'transformed' star.

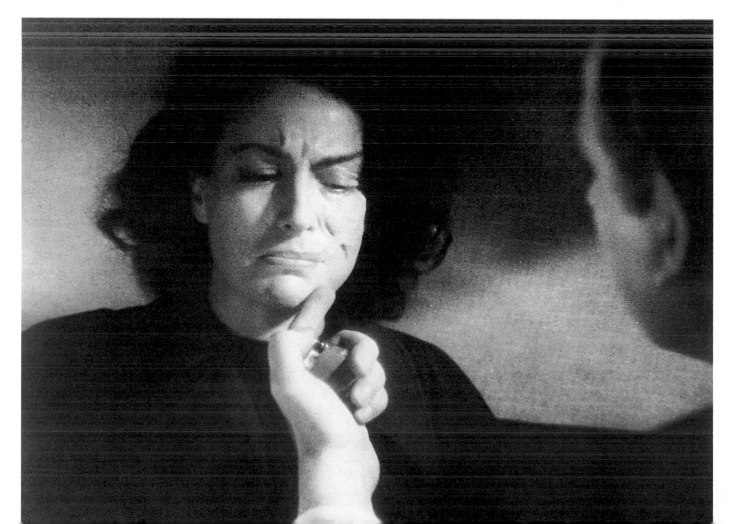

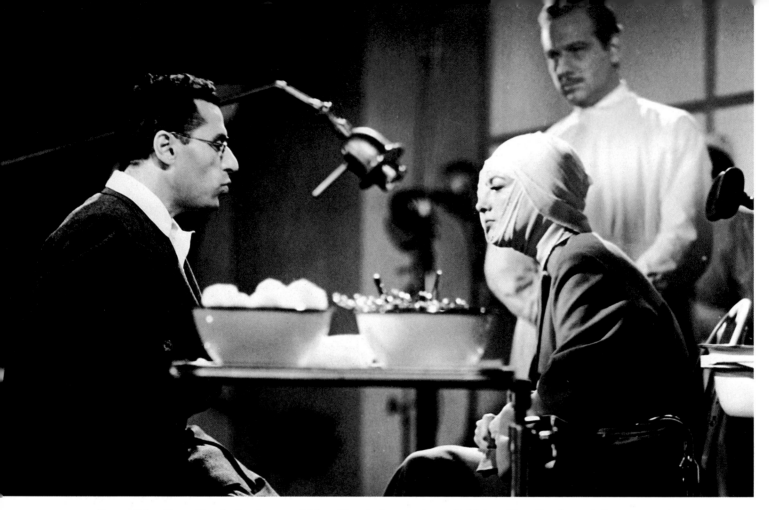

ABOVE George Cukor directs Crawford and surgeon Melvyn Douglas in *A Woman's Face*.

BELOW Publicity stills assigned stars their appropriate places in the grouping: Crawford dominates Conrad Veidt (left) and Melvyn Douglas.

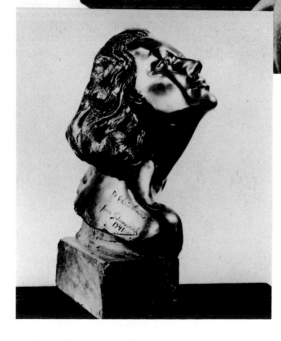

Crawford with the bust of her by Salamunich on the set of *A Woman's Face*; it was dedicated to her adopted daughter Christina.

unsuccessful marriages? Mayer need hardly have asked her if she minded playing a mother in *Susan and God*: in her own mind, she was already in the role. The baby she adopted and named Christina was born officially to unknown parents on 11 June 1939, exactly two months after the divorce from Tone. Though she had no part in the child's conception, Crawford henceforth created everything else about her in her own image: this included her name, which was at first 'Joan'. The image had to be perfect.

Perhaps because a family without a father is incomplete, hence 'imperfect', she came round to accepting the possibility of remarriage. Indeed she seems to have picked her third husband for the way he fell instantly and informally into the fatherly image. 'There was nothing of the Hollywood actor about Phillip [Terry],' she recalled, 'nothing of the exhibitionist.' The first Sunday this film actor came over to her Brentwood home and stayed for dinner, she remembered 'the candlelight, and blonde Christina in her high chair, and the deep tenor of Phillip's

ABOVE Crawford's wedding outfit for marriage to her third husband, Phillip Terry, in 1942 was conceived by MGM's designer Irene; 'two-tone beige, full gauntlet gloves in light yellow and green were the only colour notes' according to the photograph caption.

ABOVE Crawford and Phillip Terry with toys for children.

BELOW At home with little Christina and a bedtime book.

voice'. He was already cast as father, it seems, before she accepted him as husband or even lover.

Phillip Terry was born in 1907 (though he frequently subtracted five years from his age) and had a restless childhood, dragged through the Oklahoma and Texas oilfields by a father who worked as a rigger. Like Gable, he saw enough of hard, dirty work to strengthen both his muscles and his desire to avoid it in future. Just over six feet tall, with a footballer's frame and conventionally handsome good looks, he had bummed around London, picking up an English accent in acting classes that he hoped would ease him into Hollywood's Anglo-Saxon colony, which held the monopoly of screen roles requiring visible bearing and audible breeding. These were two male qualities that it always pleased Crawford to have in her vicinity: she felt they complemented her own lady-like imperatives. Exactly when she met Terry is uncertain, but it was probably in late spring 1942, as we know that she asked his opinion of her new script, *Reunion in France*. However, she may well have singled him out of the crowd while still married to Tone, for MGM started him on the stock $75 a week contract in 1937, giving him bit parts or using him as 'loan-out' material; and Crawford's income tax claims, which include lists of films she had projected in her private cinema, refer to MGM's Cossack musical *Balalaika*, in which Mayer's new discovery, a 'Hungarian Jeanette MacDonald', named Ilona Massey, starred and Phillip Terry played a dashing lieutenant. Anyhow, Crawford saw him; she got to know him; she married him – on 21 July 1942. The event attracted little notice: small wonder, since bride and groom used the names they had respectively acquired or been born

with, Lucille Tone and Frederick Kormann. The secrecy was at Mayer's bidding, for here indeed was one of MGM's great stars 'walking away into the sunset with some unknown actor'.

Crawford later put this unexpected liaison down to sheer loneliness, but her desire to complete the family circle with a father has been noted. In addition, the year or two immediately following her divorce from Tone had begun to open cracks in even the formidable Crawford façade. She had begun drinking, carrying her own discreetly concealed flask of vodka, always 100 per cent proof, to private parties. And for a person who was a stickler for self-discipline, the studio log of her absences from work now indicates a troubled spirit as well as an ailing body. In 1940, she shot only one picture, *Susan and God*, and the list of her 'illnesses' for the year ending October, 1940, scrupulously maintained on the studio files, testifies to the pressures she was under. On 27–29 November 1939, while on location at Pismo Beach for *Strange Cargo*, she was 'depressed' for three days and unable to work; on 6 February 1940, she was 'unable to make a test' for George Cukor; on 12 February, she was ill and 'unable to rehearse' for *Susan and God*; on 8–9 March, she 'looked ill and . . . we had to shoot round her', on 18 March, she had a severe cold and 'was unable to work'; on 3–4 April, she was 'depressed and ill'. She was granted leave of absence, for unspecified reasons, from 3 October 'until such time as we shall designate in writing', MGM informed her, 'provided it is not later than 11 December or earlier than 31 October'. Such pernickety itemizing of an individual's illnesses and depressive states seems the very antithesis of stardom; for this reason alone, it is worth remembering how severely regulated a star's life could be under the terms of the almighty contract. It is certainly reliable evidence of Crawford's emotional mood at a period she remained reticent about discussing later on.

A news photograph of Crawford caught a sense of disarray as well as an unemptied ashtray – an unusual oversight for such a punctilious star

ABOVE Star on the way up, Judy Garland, visits one whose career is faltering.
BELOW LEFT Crawford takes to advertising, but only Max Factor, 'the make-up of the stars'.
BELOW RIGHT The bicycle, an unlikely star vehicle, is a concession to wartime austerity that she made look fashionable.

She worried about the competition from the new generation of film-stars. On that same talent-seeking trip to Europe in the summer of 1937, Mayer had picked up not only Ilona Hajmassy (who became 'Massey') in Hungary, but also Hedy Kiesler (who became 'Lamarr') in Austria and Greer Garson (who stayed 'Garson') in England. The established ladies back in Culver City knew they had to redouble their battle for the best roles going. Crawford felt the competition at first hand when Greer Garson was co-starred with her in *When Ladies Meet* (29 August 1941) as the understanding wife who tolerates her husband's philandering with Crawford because, well, men are fools, aren't they? The long, slightly *too* long heart-to-heart chat the women share confirms the feeling that Mayer was having his 'discovery' groomed into the same ideal of self-sacrificing womanhood on which Crawford had held the patent for so long.

She took another ten-week suspension on half-pay ($3,173.70 a week); tried to adopt a baby 'brother' for Christina, only to have him reclaimed by the real mother, who had tracked her child down to the star's doorstep; and then impulsively, like someone reclaimed for the pursuit of life by someone else's tragic loss of it, she leaped into the film that was being prepared for Carole Lombard when that actress, then Clark Gable's wife, had been killed in a plane crash on 15 January 1942. She donated the whole of her fee for Columbia studios' production *They All Kissed the Bride* (30 July 1942) to various charities in memory of Lombard. But, as if manifesting her inner tensions, her performance as a career woman is unnaturally pitched towards the emasculating company harridan, rather than the comically impetuous feminist, which is how Lombard might have conceived it.

What was it like to direct Crawford at this time? Strangely enough, an answer isn't easy to find. Most of her

MGM directors have died; the ones alive at the time of writing, in particular film-maker Clarence Brown, are on record with perceptive comments, but generally of a cordially testimonial nature: they tell us little about her status in the studio in this, the last full year of her MGM stardom, or the characteristic ways she tried (or expected) to 'direct' her directors. Yet it is important to know such things, if only to make an informed guess about her up-and-down moods of elation and exhaustion in these final months. But there was a young man, a film-maker belonging to the generation not overawed by the power of stardom, whose recollection of directing Crawford in her penultimate MGM film of this period is fresh and candid.

Jules Dassin, in 1942, had just turned thirty and in his year at MGM had directed Conrad Veidt in a dual role in *Nazi Agent*, an unpretentious but highly effective wartime thriller. One day, Louis B. Mayer's arm dropped round his shoulder. Dassin had no love for Mayer: he thought him 'ruthless and tyrannical . . . and to me, Mayer's arm round your shoulder meant his hand was closer to your throat'. On the strength of a screen test Dassin had done of Mickey Rooney's new bride, a seventeen-year-old called Ava Gardner ('I told them she'd be a star,' Mayer exulted, 'the idiots have no flair – I *told* them'), the MGM chief now confided, 'I am entrusting to you one of the biggest stars.' He waited for Dassin to react, then almost whispered, '*Joan Crawford*.' Dassin was impressed, but, as he recalled, 'I still wore that cloak of snobbishness affected by people who came from the New York theatre. I showed no emotion and asked when I could read the script. Mayer was more amazed than angry, but he did shout, "The *script*! Did you hear me say 'Joan Crawford'?" . . . Word got around that my first reaction to the electrifying news "The kid gets Crawford" was to ask to read the script!'

When he did read the script of *Reunion in France* (1 January 1943), Dassin was 'aghast'. A story that posed as a courageous anti-Nazi film had Crawford as a great dress designer, 'the Coco Chanel of Paris', who would sacrifice all, face ruin and poverty to save France; Philip Dorn, then being touted as a new star, was her lover, pretending to be a collaborator but really in the French Underground; John Wayne was a crashed US pilot pretending to be Crawford's French chauffeur. Dassin was assured there would be a complete rewrite. When eventually a script conference was called, only one thing was discussed for hours on end: 'The Crawford character is broke and penniless, yet we must have her dressed richly, elegantly, in the high fashions her fans demanded of her.' When Dassin, 'after hours of costume talk', still insisted that the scenario was in need of much, much more work, Bernie Hyman led him to the window overlooking the MGM parking lot. '"Which is your car?" he asked. I pointed. It was one grade above a jalopy. He pointed to his, a magnificent Cadillac. He said, "That's my car, and I say the script is wonderful."'

The first day's shooting was disastrous. Dassin had met Crawford a few times and found her 'carefully cordial, but uncommitted, clearly waiting for my first mistake'. Dassin did not keep her waiting long. 'After a moment or so, Joan did something she had done much better in rehearsal. I called "Cut!" You'd have thought lightning had struck. A tremor went through the entire set. My assistant shouted at some non-existent electrician on high, "Stop making that noise: we had to cut the scene because of you." He pressed

ABOVE Jules Dassin, Joseph L. Mankiewicz, Franz Waxman and Crawford look at the Irene-designed playsuit she was to wear in the film about the German occupation of Paris, *Reunion in France*.

ABOVE Hollywood's idea of Germany at war: even the place setting conformed to the swastika shape.
BELOW With the two men who compete for her favours: John Wayne and Philip Dorn.

me warningly on the shoulder, but I was just too stupid to understand. Again when the scene came to be shot and Joan made the same mistake and I said, "Cut!" she wheeled around, looked at me, and walked off the set. One hour later, Mayer said to me, "You're fired ... you're off the film."'

But that night, Crawford summoned Dassin to dinner and in her well-stocked library after dinner said, 'Hey, Julie – may I call you "Julie"? – do you think I'm a bad actress?' Dassin told her he thought she was a good actress who sometimes made the mistake of 'acting the lady – or what you conceive the lady to be'. He waited for the smack on the jaw, but she said, after a minute, 'Really, is that what I do? . . . Let's start again, only don't you ever say "Cut!" to me.' '"Well," I said, "If I don't think a scene is right, what do I do?" "Just run a finger over your eyebrow." "What if you're not in a position to see it? What if your back is turned?" She said, "Brother, when I'm in front of that camera, whatever goes on anywhere on that set, *I see*." Believe it or not, all through that film, instead of saying "Cut" I'd run a finger over my eyebrow, and wherever she was, she knew it, and the scene would start again.'

On the first day of shooting, Crawford appeared with her new husband, along with a long retinue of maids, secretaries, governesses and dogs, and it seemed to some that she was determined to show Phillip Terry how little she cared for Philip Dorn, an actor she was rumoured to have been close to before filming began. This in turn affected shooting.

On the last day, Dassin was sitting high on a camera boom above a huge railroad set, preparing to track through the hundreds of extras on the platform following Crawford and Dorn. 'We began that long travelling shot,' Dassin recalled, 'with me high on the boom, and at a certain moment, with the skill of a basketball player, with a movement of her hip, Crawford gets Dorn right out of the frame – just flips him out of the shot! I became furious.' Forgetting he was on a weighted boom, Dassin jumped off the camera ... 'The men went flying all round me as the boom flew up. I put myself in front of Joan ... Now, I was raised in Harlem and the street fighter spirit came out in me and I heard myself saying to her, "I'm going to punch you in the jaw." Then she did something astonishing. She was wearing one of those famous Crawford hats. She ripped off her hat, threw it to the ground, threw her bag to the ground, sticks out her jaw, and says, "Go ahead." I get paralysed. I don't know what the hell to do. It's about 10.30 a.m. ... hundreds of extras ... I can think of only one thing to do. I call "Lunch!" and walk off the set.'

Back in his office, with Philip Dorn in the corner weeping, Dassin remained defiant – but Mankiewicz prevailed on him to finish the film, by conveying all directions to Crawford through the cameraman. 'At the end of the day, she came to me and said, "Hold out your hand." She put into my hand a lovely gift, a pair of cuff-links, and she said, "I enjoyed working with you." And I said, "You bitch ... that is *really* a nasty thing to do." After that they became friends, though they never again worked on a film together.

In retrospect, it emerged that Crawford shared Dassin's

OPPOSITE In her last MGM film, *Above Suspicion*, the face of the later Crawford begins to show itself.

Farewell to fashion and MGM: Crawford in one of the last publicity photographs taken at her old studio in 1943.

opinion of *Reunion in France*; if anything, she was even more extreme in her dismissal: 'If there is an afterlife, and I am to be punished for my sins, [it] is one of the pictures they'll make me see over and over agin.'[17]

Compared with this débâcle, what was to be the last film of her long, eighteen-year-reign was warmly received. *Above Suspicion* (17 September 1943) co-starred Fred MacMurray in a well-paced, Hitchcock-type thriller about a young married couple conscripted into Intelligence by the British Foreign Office who elude the enemy in a parody pursuit through Europe. Asked if she understands what is expected of her, Crawford (with memories of half-a-dozen movies glinting through her patriotism) replies, 'I know, climb through a train window, fire off a gun in a deserted theatre, whistle "Annie Laurie" backward and Boris Karloff will fall out of a closet with an apple in his mouth.' (The ever prudent MGM required Karloff to sign a release authorizing the use of his name.) Almost unbelievably, though, the movie ran deeply into censorship trouble on two fronts. One was an objection, strenuously maintained by the Hays Office, to the unpunished killing of a Nazi agent by a British Intelligence officer. War or no war, there was a morality that transcended the Allies' ends – the Hollywood Production Code. The other objections were to

Crawford's role. The Code office demanded of MGM: 'Please change the line "What are you doing tonight?" on account of its unacceptably sex-suggestive inference – this scene should of course be played without any unacceptable suggestion of sexual frustration on the part of Miss Crawford . . . The following dialogue also seems unacceptably sex-suggestive and hence could not be approved in the finished picture: "Think of what we're going to do." – "I am."'

Crawford wasn't directly involved in this pre-production argy-bargy, but in her prevailing mood of frustration and belligerence, the bickering depressed her the way that similarly obtuse and obdurate complaints by the Legion of Decency about the morality of *Two-Faced Woman* dispirited its star, Greta Garbo. Both women, whose very presence in an MGM picture should have been the guarantee of its moral integrity, felt themselves blemished by the objections. Crawford found it wasn't fun any longer to fight for the last inch of permissiveness as she had done when she was a symbol of 'Flaming Youth'. It brought her age home to her: it was another sign of stagnation. If Mayer valued her – and he *did* – it seemed more for old time's sake than any new public image which the studio had been able to develop for her by choice of pictures and roles. On 2 April 1943, with MGM's consent, she arranged to take six months off and consider any offer made to her for a picture elsewhere. She retired to her home and shut herself away. Hitherto, she or her agent had picked up her weekly salary cheque. Now she did not even bother to come in; it was sent by post.

Sometime after April, she informed Mayer that she wanted to quit MGM. Her old restlessness had got the better of her: she simply couldn't sit still, do nothing and wait. The decision to leave was hers and hers alone. Nicholas Schenck spoke of holding her to contract; it was Mayer who persuaded his boss not to try and squeeze the last dollar and cent from a woman who had made them millions. So on 29 June 1943, by mutual consent, the contract between Loew's Inc., producer, and Joan Crawford, actress, was terminated for a consideration of $100,000 in lieu of a new picture.

Crawford drove through the front gate of the studio as usual on that day and, true to her nature, alone and with her sleeves rolled up, cleared out her dressing-room, emptied her personal possessions into valises, washed the small kitchen, vacuumed the carpets and plumped the cushions. Then she loaded her belongings into the car and drove herself through the rear gate without a backward glance. There was a subdued atmosphere all afternoon in the executive building. Said someone who was there that day: 'It was as if we'd lost a part of our history.'

For someone indentured to one master for eighteen years now suddenly finding herself 'at liberty', what Joan Crawford did on leaving MGM showed extraordinary purposiveness. She knew exactly what she wanted to do. Furthermore, to do it, she was prepared to wait ... to sit things out, to muster her strength for another one of those phased 'renewals' which characterize her life and career. Two days after coming off MGM's payroll, she was put on Jack Warner's at $500,000 for a three-picture deal. But it was to take all of two years before she found the picture she was after. Meanwhile, all the left-over energy that sends other women back to work after home-making and child-bearing was building up its creative head of energy. Her home became a bunker of fortitude.

For the first time in her life, she had no studio to report to regularly. It was Phillip Terry whom she now saw off to his day's work at the studio – he had signed an RKO contract – and later his patriotic night shift at a munitions factory. Yet how Joan worked, too! Hollywood's domestics had emigrated from Beverly Hills to better-paid war work or else had been drafted into the Services. But the household chores that absorbed her energy and compressed the empty hours were welcomed by Crawford. She shut down half her house's twenty-seven rooms, dug up the turf where she used to host buffet suppers for hundreds of celebrities, planted a vegetable plot for victory and took to using a motor-bike for getting to the grocery store with Christina

PREVIOUS PAGE Crawford in the late 1940s.
BELOW Stars in their austerity courses: Crawford rides in the sidecar with Phillip Terry to do the shopping and hoes a row for victory in her back yard.

and her new baby 'brother', an adopted boy named 'Phillip', strapped in the sidecar. She even found time to set up a day nursery for fifty youngsters whose mothers were on shift work. It required a week's hard scrubbing and painting to put the rented premises in shape; but it was like being back at St Agnes's Academy in her own childhood, serving at tables, washing up crocks, making cots for the tots ... Only this time, she wasn't an outcast, treated like a slavey: she was needed, accepted, in charge – in a word, *loved*. 'Fatherless', she had found a step-parent in the MGM studio; now she invented the whole experience of motherhood in a way that she was to feed into many of the films she made over the next fifteen years. In this period was incubated the maternal instinct that she could play off so effectively against the increasingly masculine grain of her character and appearance. When Dana Andrews in *Daisy Kenyon* (26 December 1947) offers to give up his wife and family out of love for her, Crawford recoils in horror: 'Marriage can't be all over, if children are a part of it still.' From now on, with increasing frequency, she gives the feeling that inside every career woman she plays is an imprisoned mother – and she knows just the moment to let us hear her beating to get out.

Her house-cleaning even spread to her career. She got herself a new agent, Lew Wasserman, buoyed up by his insistence that she *wasn't* 'through'. But the rightness of any part she was offered had to be felt by her before she would endorse a return to work. Taking pay for not working made her uncomfortable; and after a few mediocre proposals by Warners, she had herself taken off salary. Crawford had become a very good judge of a script. It wasn't all feeling, either, all 'instinct'. Nor did ego play as preponderant a part as might be assumed. Professionally,

she was able to analyse a script's opportunities from a broader-based vantage-point than the size of her own role. The point is illustrated pithily in a letter written to Hedda Hopper in 1953. This time, though, her decision to turn down the role proposed was complicated by her friendship with Jill Winkler, the woman who had sent her a pilot script for a projected TV series. (Mrs Winkler was the widow of an MGM publicist who had been killed along with Carole Lombard in 1942.)

Crawford wrote:

It's now 11.30 p.m., on the Saturday night after I finished the picture [*Johnny Guitar*], and I can't call you naturally at this hour. But I did want to talk to you about it. I think Jill's idea with Lally Bower's script is very interesting. And the suggested prospectus of future scripts is fine, too. The only thing I feel – and I must be honest with you, Hedda – I feel that Jill will not be able to get any star to play this part. It's actually plain narration. The star part is inactive. It brings in a lot of interesting characters – like soap-operas – and, believe me, no-one loves soap-operas more than I . . . God, I've been doing them all my life! Cinderella stories and soap-operas – they make an awful lot of money. I think it's a brilliant idea for an unknown or someone who's done a couple of pictures – but certainly not for a star (and this is merely my opinion). I think that is why Irene Dunne's show is off the air. I think it is also why I hear so much criticism about *Letters to Loretta*. (Mind you, I haven't seen the latter, I'm only quoting.) God, just tell me what I should

Mother of many (though none of them her own) looks after children at the wartime day nursery she helped to establish.

tell Jill and how I should go about it. I'll take it from there, dear. God bless – and thank you again for your belief in not only a devoted friend, but, as Billy Haines calls me, an iron reindeer in a Victorian garden. My name, however, is still [signed] Joan.

Maybe in those mid-1940s, Crawford sensed how time was running in her favour, despite her age. *Mrs Miniver*, which starred her MGM replacement, Greer Garson, proved that 'war films' were box-office: female film-goers got a cathartic satisfaction out of such stories which made them feel that they, too, in their way, were fighters in a man's world. With many male stars by then in uniform, women stars were coming to the fore as the embodiment of their sex's endurance and influence, though not always as supportive and domesticated as Mrs Miniver's.

At the very time the Allied armies had Germany encircled, Hollywood itself was capitulating to the Teutonic strain of *émigré* directors, Wilder, Preminger, Siodmak, Sirk and Lang among them, who set the tone for the *film noir* of the 1940s, the era's dark, violent and fatalistic movie genre in which women played forceful, frequently ambivalent roles as agents of seduction and destruction. At Warners, Crawford found herself in an aggressively masculine stronghold, where women's responses had to be strong-willed and unsentimental to survive the latent or overt male chauvinism. Their sex was granted a statutory courtesy, but none of the courtier-like worship of immaculate femininity which was the MGM way of simultaneously idolizing and categorizing its female stars. In Michael Curtiz, Crawford inherited a Warner director with a callous disregard for any star's status, whatever their sex. Curtiz was good at 'encounter' scenes

OPPOSITE The come-back performance that won her the Oscar: Crawford in *Mildred Pierce* with Zachary Scott.
ABOVE A very different scene from MGM's glamorously lit sets, Crawford and Jack Carson in the *film noir Mildred Pierce*.

on screen; and off-screen, too, he had a habit of recharging himself for work by deliberate acts of provocation, manoeuvring for the upper hand on the film set in the belief that those who fought back would take an extra shot of adrenalin into the scene they were playing. His first act on seeing Crawford clad in a plain house dress for her first major Warner role in *Mildred Pierce* (28 September 1945) was to rip the back of it from shoulder to waist line with the scream, 'You and your damn Adrian shoulder-pads!' It didn't matter that the dress had no shoulder pads at all: he was serving notice that Crawford's days as a glamorous MGM clothes-horse didn't impress him. Instead of provoking a blazing row, or inducing a nervous breakdown, this act of humiliation was just the therapeutic thrust Crawford needed to propel her into a new role – and a new phase of her life.

Whatever life at Warners might be like, gone for ever were her protected days at MGM. There, Louis B. Mayer had once summoned Jules Dassin to his office. He had viewed the rushes and now showed the director a single frame enlargement from them. A tree's leaves cast pretty shadows intentionally upon Crawford's face. But Mayer bawled, 'Take them the f—— off! People all over the world pay a lot of money to see Joan Crawford. I don't want you to put any goddam shadows on her.' Warners, which some called 'the home of shadows' by virtue of the low-slung lamps that enveloped the fateful figures of the *films noirs*, liked to see its stars darkly. *Mildred Pierce*, which Crawford began as she turned forty, presented her literally and figuratively in a new light.

'The role of Mildred was a delight to me,' said Crawford in a magazine interview, 'because it rescued me from what was known at MGM as the Joan Crawford formula. I had become so hidden in clothes and sets that nobody could tell whether I had talent or not.'

Though MGM had groomed her, there was actually more of Crawford's own background and drive in the Warner tradition that honoured proletarian struggle than

in the MGM tradition of validating middle-class aspirations. And in James M. Cain's story, there was a lot of Crawford. Published in 1941, it was about a tough, resourceful, working-class woman who interprets life as a power struggle and uses energy, brains, nerve and ruthlessness to build a career on the ruins of her marriage. On Crawford's own admission, 'It was the easiest role I ever played.' The most prophetic, too. The theme of a success-drive which inspires a mother to over-protect her daughter and get no thanks for it – it was a fateful one for Crawford, too. The American Dream of providing one's children with greater opportunities for success than one had oneself fell to pieces in Crawford's case the way it did in Mildred's: in both film and real life, the child was driven to an extreme act of rebellion. In the film, the daughter pays for her mother's sins by shooting her lover; in life, Christina Crawford made her mother's sins pay off by assassinating in print Mommie Dearest.

Film-stars of an obsessive disposition tend to remake the world in the image of their own expectations; and much that is beyond dispute about Joan Crawford emphasizes this aspect. The change of life she underwent from the mid-1940s was strongly conditioned by the nature of the roles she played in this period. Nowhere is this so evident as in her ambivalent attitude to love, marriage and children. Children *en masse*, other people's children, were given devotion, creature comforts and constant attention by her at the war-time nursery crèches; her own children, on the other hand, had to be hardened to resist the insecurities that their mother had had to battle against all her life. It was a commendable desire to give a child a line to follow in a world that was seen as a harsh, unjust and competitive place, much like a movie studio. But Crawford undoubtedly overdid it, the way Mildred Pierce overdid it. Her own need was greater than her children's, just as Mildred's ambitions were more 'driven' than *her* child could appreciate or forgive. 'You know something?' Christina Crawford once said to a reporter whom a confident Crawford had urged to get the child's view of her adoption, 'I think that people who adopt a child feel a need for security just as much as the child feels that need.'[18] 'Just as much as,' one may ask, or 'more than'?

Mildred Pierce delivers a stinging slap of rebuke to her daughter for looking down her nose at her mother's humiliating struggle to get to where she has and take her family with her. 'Get out before I kill you,' she rasps. Children in Crawford's films are like the pelican's brood: while their mother is cherishing them, they eat her heart out. '*Mildred Pierce* – Don't Ever Tell What She Did', ran the advertising teaser designed to sell the film. Thirty years and more after the film, Christina was to tell everyone 'what she did'.

'I loved every scene with Ann Blyth as my daughter,' said Crawford later, 'except where I had to slap her and she had to slap me back. I have a phobia about slapping, dating back to my childhood, when my father [she must mean her step-father here] once slapped me for telling a lie at the dinner table. After I slapped Ann, I burst into tears and found myself apologizing frantically. Later, it wasn't quite so

OPPOSITE The fashion habit is, however, hard to break: Crawford in a publicity still for *Mildred Pierce*.

Giving her adopted daughter Christina swimming lessons in the pool at her Brentwood home.

hard to have Ann slap me, but my head was shaking as the scene faded out, and then it was Ann who was remorsefully apologizing.'

There is no point in rehashing the painful life story presented by Christina, who certainly did not apologize for anything she had to say about her adoptive mother in her 1978 book, *Mommie Dearest*. But there is one aspect of it that becomes plain in the context of Crawford's life at this time, yet was overlooked in the scandal created by Christina's 'revelations'. It is this: Joan Crawford made no secret of the rigorous, often humiliating physical discipline she inflicted on her children, who came to include two more adopted daughters, Cathy and Cindy, called 'the twins', though they were not actually related. (She added them to the family after her divorce from Phillip Terry: at which point she changed her adopted son's name from 'Phillip' to 'Christopher'.) Plenty of Crawford's contemporaries knew, and not a few disapproved of, the stern task-master who ruled the family circle. She was so sure her attitude to the rearing of children was the right one that she did not hide it from strangers, but even commended the benefits of punishment so confidently that her visitors blenched. The 'public' children of war-workers elicited a traditionally maternal response from her because it was what the public, *her* public expected. She didn't see any contradiction between this and the way she treated her own family, and for a long time she was shielded from criticism by the orthodox approach of Press interviewers. Reporters in the 1940s colluded with the studios on whom they depended for access to the stars: they burnished images, they didn't

(yet) deface them. Editors were also in fealty to what the readers believed, or wanted to believe, about the stars. Newspaper people in front of whom Joan's children conducted themselves like docile circus animals, trained in obedience and devotion to the ring-master, invariably kept their own opinion of the 'performance' to themselves. Later on, of course, the children's open rebelliousness broke into print, with news stories about Christina's unhappy schooldays, or Christopher running away and being put in a reformatory. But luck was still on Joan's side. Such examples of ingratitude from 'children who had everything' were consolation to thousands of other American parents in the 1950s whose family life was suffering post-war traumas and whose offspring had at last found a role-model for their restlessness in the romantic teenage *angst* of the late James Dean. 'So Joan Crawford, too, had her family problems . . .' they felt.

Even so, once the scandal magazines, trading on the love-hate relationship with the stars and undeterred by any indebtedness to Hollywood and its favours, began publishing stories openly hostile to Crawford, criticism of her wasn't confined to the media. It can be measured by the increase in letters, often anonymous, received by gossip columnists like Hedda Hopper. Her files bulge with denunciations of Crawford for callousness, hypocrisy and much else of the same painful nature which Christina Crawford's book was to give the imprimatur of 'inside knowledge' years later when 'Mommie' wasn't there to rebut the charges. This kind of 'hate mail' reached its peak in 1958 around the time Joan's mother died; and many letters now ironically charged Crawford herself with being an ungrateful child!

'As you know by now, Mrs Anna LeSueur, mother of Joan Crawford, died at 6.30 a.m. this morning [August 15], brought on by a stroke and bad heart,' ran one typical letter to Hedda Hopper. 'However, I think a more truthful story would be to say that she died of a broken heart. It is three years since Joan has even "bothered" to see her Mother . . . The only person who cared what happened to her, besides her friends, was her son Hal LeSeur [*sic*], Joan's brother, who lived with his mother at 105 S. Mansfield Avenue in Los Angeles and struggled to help her out . . . after his "dear sister" prevented him from getting jobs on TV and the movies . . . [Joan's] eldest daughter lives in a cold-water flat in the Bronx, strictly on her own, and I'm sure a much happier person . . . This is the great Joan Crawford!'

Another letter received at the same time also illustrates the feelings of deception and affront, now being stoked by the new-style *Confidential*-type scandal magazines. 'Just thought you would like to know that Joan Crawford's Mother passed away at 6.30 a.m., Friday. Joan is *en route* to Bermuda. She knew her Mother was ill, but said she had an important business meeting . . . She never came to see her Mother while she was ill in hospital, and she was told about it the day her Mother entered hospital. Said she would come soon. What kind of woman is Joan Crawford anyway? She hasn't seen her Mother in over three years and puts her son in a school for distrubed [*sic*] children; she certainly isn't a mother or she would have taken her son into her own custody. She is to blame for the way he is as she has shoved

him around constantly and he has never known what it is like to have a home and parents to stand by him and help him out with his problems . . . She had ordered the casket closed; she didn't have the nerve to face her Mother alive . . . What are Mrs LeSueur's friends going to think of Joan Crawford now?'

What Hedda Hopper thought of her, she did not record – either for her readers, or privately. But this last letter is followed in its file by a crisply typed note of thanks dated 29 August 1958. 'Hedda Darling, Thank you so much for your beautiful expressions of sympathy. It was so sweet of you to send the lovely large spray of gladioli, stock and roses to Mother's funeral. We are so deeply grateful to you. The flowers were exquisite. I know Mother would have adored them. She looked so beautiful. I placed her in the private gardens at Forest Lawn, in the sun, surrounded by the lovely flowers and the shrubbery which she loved so much. Love [signed] Joan."

The phrase 'born again', though by no means newly minted, has acquired a somewhat counterfeit ring in recent years: it is hard to forget the past reputations of some of those who lay the loudest claim to it. But there is no doubt that Joan Crawford was born again, in several senses, in *Mildred Pierce*; some would say *as* Mildred Pierce. However, this is not the way it looked when the first notices appeared. Contrary to popular belief, the qualities that later made the movie a classic were not at all blindingly obvious to some of the reviewers in 1945. A few even disliked it. Their reasons were confused; but, partly, it was disbelief that any mother could let herself be so dominated by her daughter's snobbishness and selfishness that she would hazard her own love, and possibly even her life, when the daughter shoots her lover and mother tries to take the blame. In the *Herald Tribune*, Howard Barnes dismissed it as 'windy melodrama . . . a laggard and somewhat ludicrous movie . . . Miss Crawford is handsome as a matron. She is self-sacrificial beyond belief. Unfortunately, she never breathes emotional intensity into a role which demanded just that.' *Time* magazine labelled it 'just another tear-sodden story of Mother Love'. What made the film a huge box-office hit was Crawford's star presence in it. This overrode all critical carping about 'reality'. Her audience had stayed loyal to her. Curiosity about her comeback in a dramatic role was intensified by the association which many fans made between her and Mildred. 'Actor and role mutually determine each other,' Edgar Morin said in writing of the mythic means by which a star is born. Mildred, it seemed, had been fermenting for years inside Joan Crawford. Now she came 'of age' – at precisely the time of life when the woman who incarnated her had most need of her. Against formidable competition from Ingrid Bergman, Greer Garson, Gene Tierney and Jennifer Jones, the film won Crawford her first Academy Award as 'Best Actress' at the 1946 Oscar ceremonies.

A few weeks later, on 25 April 1946, she filed a petition for divorce from Phillip Terry. She testified, as was now her custom, that her grounds were not any infidelity on his part; it was his interference with her work. 'For the first year and a half of our marriage, I was never allowed to entertain or go out of the house at night' – pleasures which she characteristically defined as essential to employment, rather than enjoyment. 'Consequently, I lost many valuable contracts in the motion-picture field.' This was

OPPOSITE An adopted son joins the family; first called Phillip, his name was changed to Christopher after the divorce from Phillip Terry.

ABOVE *Humoresque* marks the start of Crawford's menopausal melodramas: she spots her *protégé*, John Garfield.

BELOW With Van Heflin in *Possessed*, a story that leads into madness.

also a handy means of explaining away her protracted absence from the screen. But the testimony that elicited many an ironic smile in Hollywood concerned the faith that she implied she possessed in her husband's business judgement: 'He would tell me I was wrong about a script many times when I felt I was right. I turned down script after script because of his criticism.' To those at the studios who knew Crawford, this was more than a little hard to credit. It was enough for the court. The divorce settlement has not been made public; but for the first time it involved Crawford paying over a sum that, she claimed, almost destroyed her financially. Because of her large fees, her lifestyle had been lavish; her savings were low; and she had had herself removed from the Warner pay-roll until she felt she could *earn* the money. Her tax papers even suggest she was very short of ready cash, for they include a claim prepared by her agent for a refund for the year 1940 when she was at MGM. She said she had spent $25–30,000 on clothes and had provided her own wardrobe, either as required by contract or because she wished to advance her career by a presentable appearance. It was unfortunate that she had made only one picture in 1940, *Susan and God*, and the records failed to disclose if she had provided her own wardrobe for it. A Revenue inspector visited MGM and with the help of the studio head of wardrobe (and a magnifying glass) examined a master set of all the stills of the film and checked off 'all dresses, coats, negligés and nightgowns' Crawford had worn. All turned out to be costumes provided by Loew's Inc. The claim was disallowed.

The roles that Crawford plays in the next ten years show great skill at keeping in step with the emotional insecurities experienced by those largely female audiences who made many of them into box-office successes. She showed the ultimate loyalty of star to fans: she grew old along with them. But as she did so, the screen registered the cracks in the self-reliance of the Crawford characters opening wider and wider. Now it is the career woman who develops a mid-life crisis. The pictures are structured dramatically round Crawford going to pieces, even though the ending decrees that she must pull herself together if she elects to go on living. If not, she must at least take leave of life with conviction. Jerry Wald, who produced *Mildred Pierce*, had come to movie-making out of journalism and he brought with him a box-office penchant for pushing a theme (like a news-story) as far as it would go against the conventions of the times. He shaped her next two films, *Humoresque* and *Possessed*, then encouraged her to go to Twentieth Century-Fox, where Otto Preminger, another convention-breaking film-maker, produced and directed *Daisy Kenyon*.

Love in all three of these films is essentially something to be mistrusted. If Crawford feels its stirrings, then the past conditioning of a loveless marriage in *Humoresque* (24 December 1946) brings on her fears that it will 'mix me up again'. And indeed it does when John Garfield, as the musical prodigy she makes into her *protégé*, exhibits such unshakeable fidelity to his muse in the violin strings (as well as to a younger girlfriend) that Crawford resolves to sink herself non-competitively in the Pacific Ocean to the crescendo of the 'Liebestod' from *Tristan and Isolde*. If an unmarried man in these films professes to be in love with her, she fears he is using her; if he is a married man, then he

Crawford models a pearl necklace as part of Warner Brothers' tie-ups.

is 'running away from responsibility'. She is invariably granted the luxury of suffering; it is frequently the men, paradoxically, who finish up victims. She may be harassed and confused, indeed she may go right round the bend as she does in *Possessed* (29 May 1947) and land in a psychopathic ward, but her crack-up is simply there to put her into a more interesting state of feminine determination – and she shoots her lover, played by Van Heflin, because he can't muster the same devotion for her that she can for him. (He has, in addition, been romancing her step-daughter: a touch of *Mildred Pierce*'s tainted family.) In *Daisy Kenyon*, Dana Andrews and Henry Fonda, as the two men in competition for her love, are practically emotional dependents whose inability to make up their own minds throws responsibility for the choice directly on to her.

The old, capable, level-headed Joan rarely surfaces in these turbulent melodramas of the menopause, though when she does, she proves herself still highly satisfying. After her car accident in *Daisy Kenyon*, which is merely introduced as a somewhat extreme means of clearing her head – what a good shake does for other women – she disinterestedly warms her stockinged feet at the fireside while her lovers quarrel over who will make her his wife. The cool spectator look on Crawford's face – the look of a woman who never gets into a mood she can't fight her way out of – signifies there is nothing like a crisis to show what is going on inside people. For a moment, Joan is herself again.

But if witnesses are to be believed, the real Joan was by no means herself. Tensions were starting to affect her daily

behaviour in previously unheard of ways. She suffered temperamental flare-ups during shooting; she refused to be photographed during her menstrual period lest her condition was reflected in her looks; and guests at her home noticed that she was increasingly 'directing' her children in the roles of 'extras' to her stardom – it was not motherhood, but motherdom. Some Hollywood hosts also noted that she tended to come to their parties later and later – she who had once been such a stickler for punctuality – and sometimes left early, making her children the excuse, but departing in the company of a male guest who had not been her escort to the party. Her need to be loved had become a form of sexual hygiene. Hedda Hopper, sympathizing with this need, took care to supply an extra male guest at suppers to which she invited Crawford: she would feel well rewarded for her unspoken complicity by the note sent round the next day. 'Hedda Dear, It was the most beautiful party ever. – I thank you for asking me. – I'm sorry I was late – and had to leave early. – I have all four children home – alone – no nurse – no cook – Just your devoted Joan.'

Crawford eventually found a steady friend and lover in a film industry lawyer, a social lion as well as a legal tiger, whose temper was as strong as her own, and sometimes as violently expressed. Their battles continued for several years interspersed with exhausted truces and cordial peace treaties. To what a jealous extent this man took his amorous custody of Crawford can again be glimpsed in the Hedda Hopper 'Intelligence' files which a multitude of fans kept supplied with up-to-date fact and gossip. These informants were nothing if not scrupulous in reporting incidents to Hopper that now read like nostalgic vignettes of the Beverly Hills *mores* of those times. In a letter dated 19 May 1948, one Betty Hunt wrote:

> This evening I was out sightseeing with my relatives, who are visiting from Cincinatti. We drove past various movie stars' homes, including Jack Benny, Ronald Colman, Ginger Rogers, etc., then we drove past Joan Crawford's home and stopped the car so our visitors could see more plainly. We pulled away and drove over to Rockingham to see Shirley Temple's home, when a car pulled along side us and forced us off the road. ——, who I recognized from seeing his picture in movie magazines, got out of the car and asked us what we meant stopping in front of Joan Crawford's home. We said we were sightseeing. He tried to open the car doors and fortunately they were locked. He wanted my brother and cousin to get out of the car to 'take a poke' at them as he said. We drove round his car and went back to Sunset, he followed us and tried to force us off the road again. However as we stopped for Sunset traffic, he said if he ever saw us on Bristol Avenue again, we would be sorry. I have always been a terrific fan of Joan Crawford's and admired her, but I'll never see another of her pictures.

There were happier notes to Hedda Hopper – from Crawford herself. But they testify to the happiness that comes from locking pressures out. It was as if she was backing away from an intolerable strain which required

In *Sudden Fear* Jack Palance matches his murderer's glare against hers.

tighter and tighter self-control in order to preserve herself. She used to set off in her car, all alone, except for her French poodle Cliquot, driving herself hundreds of miles at a stretch farther and farther into Northern California's wilderness areas, experiencing the reviving contact with strangers who would quite often turn out to be fans of hers. It was like a queen sallying out into her realm without the visible appurtenances of her rank to see her subjects and test their loyalty. It was going back to the well-spring of love which she had tasted on that first day when 'I found that incredible thing, a public'. Hedda Hopper logged the telephone calls that Joan used to make to the columnist in the form of nightly progress reports:

> Crawford has been having great time staying at motels all the time. Gets up in the morning, goes to nearest lunch counter, then on her way. Doesn't know who gets more attention, she or Cliquot, but is quite sure dog has slight edge. Raving about courtesy of truck drivers who get in the middle of the road if they think car in back is dangerous to pass, but immediately pull over and wave you through if the road is clear ahead. When she gets back wants to do an article about truck drivers. Staying at Lake Louise for a few more days, then coming down the coast, will take her a week to drive down. Greatest experience of her life, has been wanting to do it for years. Calls home and talks to kids every night. Strong reaction

OPPOSITE Confrontation scenes are what Crawford's later movies thrive on: (above) with mink and gun, she takes the measure of Sydney Greenstreet in *Flamingo Road*, and (below) in hostess gown, she orders Wendell Corey about the house in *Harriet Craig*.

of people in little towns where she stops. They aren't sure whether it is or isn't. In one coffee shop she heard two guys making a bet as to whether it was her or not – she bent over to the guy who bet against it, and told him to save his money.

These hasty notes of Hopper's are gratifying to read: they catch Crawford for once in a genuinely happy and relaxed mood, at ease with herself and her legend, and even kidding both a little. But her sense of freedom was quickly banished once she was back in the world of studio politics and career moves. A disconcerting change was taking place in Crawford as a result of all these pressures, some of them self-created, some of them inevitable to anyone who is passing through the middle age of the emotions. A remark recorded by a recent biographer, Bob Thomas, indicated the source of the trouble. It came from David Miller, director of *Sudden Fear* (7 August 1952), who told her with wary reluctance, and then only at her insistence, 'In your last few pictures, Joan, you've played not only the female lead, but the male lead as well.'[19] Painful to hear, but true; and not only true on the film set. At home with her children, she was playing the father and over-compensating for the lack of a man's hand in rearing them – though, if Christina's account is to believed, the reluctant Phillip Terry was frequently ordered to deal out physical punishments. In her films, her talents were hardening into the mould of an emasculating woman. This didn't deprive her of sex-appeal; but it converted what she had of that into such things as 'power' and 'control'. Put together, these are potent parts of her screen appeal; but they are also responses to a Warner Brothers world of male values by a star who has discovered the advantage of exemplifying them. *Flamingo Road* (6 May 1949), *The Damned Don't Cry* (7 April 1950) and *Harriet Craig* (2 November 1950: shot at Columbia, who owned the remake rights to the 1937 version) all feel like darkening admonitions of a neurotic descent into Crawford's 'panic period', in which the roles are fashioned to exploit her emotional dependence, usually on a much younger man who treats her roughly, treacherously and sometimes murderously.

Sudden Fear, which she left Warners to make for an independent producer, thereby sacrificing $800,000 in contractual fees from the studio, casts her as a famous playwright (though actually she conducts herself more like someone *on* the stage than someone who writes for it) who turns down Jack Palance for the leading role because he does not look like the romantic type she seeks. He pursues her with a charm he apparently didn't have when she fired him, woos her, marries her, then plots to take her life. A scared Crawford is an awesome sight: her stretched face holds terror the way a sponge holds water. Fear, in short, is what she increasingly employs to hone the edge of femininity back on to a performance that was, as Miller observed, becoming too masculine. *Sudden Fear* was a huge hit – of which she owned a percentage – and tapped the latent fears of women fans who, like her, were finding life turning into loneliness. Her films capitalize on this as increasing age separates her from the supply of roles once available to her. It induces a neurotic zig-zag feeling in her emotional life. The male stud to whom she attaches herself boosts her self-confidence – she can still attract younger men, she is implicitly saying – while the agony of mind and body to which his treacherous nature subjects her keeps her female audience suffering along with her. *Female on the Beach* (19 August 1955) is another picture that puts her in peril from a gigolo type. The man in all such cases must be morally weaker than Crawford. But her seduction by him must be emotionally strong and fulfilling to her, until she realizes how her nature has trapped her. *Autumn Leaves* (1 August 1956) is the masterpiece of this genre, with its carefully graduated revelation that the crew-cut lad she has married after years of caring for her father is a liar, a thief, an ex-convict, a near-bigamist, a latent killer and, in addition, is rapidly reverting to infantilism. But Crawford will not accept that anything or anyone is beyond her love. She has him committed to a mental hospital and from then on is depicted by Robert Aldrich, a director whose taste for sadism so perfectly matches his star's capacity for masochism, frenetically revolving in her mind the last question one would have expected to find there – Will the cure kill his love for her?

She had still a few years to go – but it was bound to happen – before another young stud with whom she is infatuated in *I Saw What You Did, I Know Who You Are* (21 July 1965) proved that the cure for love was indeed lethal by administering it to her with a carving knife.

Crawford also underwent a disconcerting physical change during these years. The contours of her face, understandably altering with the onset of middle-age, began to reassert themselves in a strikingly aggressive fashion. Her features became more pronounced, more masculine, suggesting some radical disturbance taking place in her metabolism, upset perhaps by the tensions of life and the melodrama of her movie roles. With her hollowed-out cheeks, her accentuated eyebrows, her eyeballs almost starting out of their sockets, her mouth (by no means outsize in itself) which she now enlarged to rapacious extremes by obliterating its natural outline with heavily applied lipstick, she came to resemble the only known picture of her father, Thomas LeSueur, who had fled the family circle before she had been born.

In 1953, eleven years after she had left MGM, Crawford gave in to the temptation to 'come home'. After her success in *Mildred Pierce*, she had had a highly emotional tribute paid her by a tearful Louis B. Mayer. He chastised his producers for letting her go when she was supposed to be 'all washed up'. He made them sit penitentially through a screening of that Academy Award-winning Warner Bros movie. Now seven years later, when she had turned 'independent', and was able to receive motion-picture offers from any source, Benny Thau of MGM sent her a script entitled *Why Should I Cry?* which soon became *Torch Song* (12 October 1953). Accompanying it was a deal for two pictures at $125,000 each. Much, much less than she had been getting; but now she was nearly fifty and felt in need of the softening touch of a 'woman's picture'.

If the studio didn't give her prime rates of pay, it was eager to accord her all the privileges of stardom: first-place billing, name above the title, and her own key make-up man, Eddie Allen, provided she met the bill for what his skill did to features that were now stretched round her bones as if they had been eroded from within, intensifying her sense of domination to an uncomfortable degree. (His bill for 'cosmetic application' came to $1,871.64, and she paid it after nudging by MGM's accounts department.) Dore Freeman, a Western Union telegram boy in the 1930s whom she had had MGM recruit after a timely interjection from him had bailed her out of trouble at an inquisitive press conference, was now a top publicist at the studio and he arranged a red carpet all the way from the main gates to the three dressing-rooms, the ones normally occupied by Lana Turner, Kathryn Grayson and Ava Gardner, which had been redecorated for her exclusive use. The MGM gateman greeted her with her favourite gardenia; stars sent gift-wrapped 'welcome back' presents and the sound stage looked like a florist's shop. Among the gifts was a decorated basket of Pepsi-Cola bottles with a silk-ribbon legend twined round the handle which said, 'A Soft Drink Turneth Away Wrath'. It came from Alfred N. Steele, president of Pepsi-Cola, whom she had met briefly three years earlier. He was to become her fourth and last husband almost exactly two years later.

But it was not to Pepsi-Cola she turned that first day on the set. After presenting each crew member with a red carnation, she and director Charles Walters, who had entered films as a choreographer and was Crawford's personal choice for this story of a ruthless Broadway dancer trying to stay at the top, adjourned to the star's dressing-room(s). Out came her vodka flask.

To stiffen her confidence still futher, it had been agreed to shoot her Broadway rehearsal sequences first. Walters, as well as directing, also played her stage partner. In this role, he loyally let himself be rebuked for clumsiness ('Stay behind and practise till you're perfect') while actually covering up any lack of precision on Crawford's part by timely masking and 'lifts'. Crawford's voice wasn't any longer judged good enough to let her do her own singing. On the film's release, this became an embarrassingly reiterated Press query and Howard Strickling was obliged to issue advice to MGM branch managers: 'Joan Crawford did not do her own singing in *Torch Song*, but for obvious reasons de-emphasize this in publicity.' (Her singing was dubbed by India Adams.) *Torch Song* was a weepie with music. Crawford the bitch goddess, insecure, lonely, in

PREVIOUS PAGE Crawford in the last weeks of her life portrayed by John Engstead.
ABOVE Aged nearly fifty and ready for an MGM home-coming in 1953, Crawford's face now shows the characteristic features of her father.

need of love but fearful of lowering her emotional defences, discovers a long-time admirer in her blind accompanist played by Michael Wilding. Back in the days when he had sight and a music-critic's column, he wrote a review of her that reads like a love letter. Now his blind devotion opens her own eyes to the possibilities of a kinder world.

Through all this Crawford stalks like the last representative of a protected species: every line is uttered square-jawed with a snarl that says, 'People will only do what you want if you hit them first.' She drives her associates into breakdowns and greets her producer with the cruel communiqué, 'I've made a few changes.' She must have known the story well. It was her own experience: the constant vigilance needed to stop others making off with your limelight, the family dependents who sap one's energy ('Make out a cheque,' is her weary response), the professional day made up of cynical rebukes ('Your idea of art is the fruit in the slot machines'). She herself behaved much like this during filming, judging by the testimony of Michael Wilding. The first scene they shot together was the last shot in the film: when the pianist kisses her. Wilding quipped that it was the first time he had kissed a woman before they were introduced. She made no response. They never were introduced off-screen, yet their relationship in the story is so well pitched that it staunches the script's tear ducts every time the lachrymose flow threatens to dampen the players.

Crawford didn't leave for home when the day's shooting ended. (She asked for no close-ups after 4.30 p.m.) Instead,

ABOVE Flowers and a basket of soft drinks greet her on arrival at the old studio, MGM.
BELOW Crawford puts her feet up on the set of *Torch Song*, but still suggests who's boss.

she slept at the studio. It had become a refuge from the problems that home now held. Her adopted family were still there, but at a distance: she could telephone them nightly, assure them of her love; they were out of sight, though not out of hearing. It was the dialogue of motherhood, and much more comforting to rehearse than practise. Totally alone, she walked the empty sets of *Torch Song* by night, thinking: 'One of the most wondrous places in the world is the night studio, quiet, shadowed, the vast equipment standing idle, the city of a million fantasies and as many combined talents, ready to spring into being at daybreak.'[20] What did home hold to compare with this?

Speaking to Hedda Hopper some years later, she forgetfully referred to *Torch Song* as 'my first Technicolor picture', a mistake often repeated by biographers, who also forget, or have perhaps not seen, the last Technicolor reel of *Ice Follies*, shot fourteen years earlier. But the hues used in *Torch Song* were unusually subdued – beige, olive, saffron and smoky blue – and threw her red hair into prominence as if it were the beacon of the film-title. Physically, she was still remarkable: waist twenty-five inches, weight 127 lbs. To Hopper, she added reflectively: 'You know, the great thing about our business is that we're allowed to see ourselves as others see us. Some of the new kids see themselves and say, "Oh gee, I look pretty good." They don't know that what they are seeing is the loving photography – all the singing, posture, dancing lessons they have taken. Where else could you get all these? *And* the publicity? They believe it. They're going to be awful lonely hearts – they're going to be awful lonely with all those goddam clippings.' Love and loneliness: the two poles of the film world she occupied.

JOAN CRAWFORD

With Michael Wilding as her blind accompanist in *Torch Song*; he recorded later that they did not exchange a friendly word during filming.
OPPOSITE Director Charles Walters, who also played the role of her dance partner, takes Crawford through the steps at the start of shooting.

ABOVE and BELOW Two of the more exotic stage numbers in *Torch Song*, her first all-Technicolor film.

A sign of Joan Crawford's coming to terms with her age was her increasing willingness to speak her mind, sometimes vehemently, sometimes appreciatively, about the new generation of promising talents. Her well-known comment about Faye Dunaway is, of course, ironic in view of the fact that Dunaway played Crawford in the 1981 movie *Mommie Dearest*. 'Of all the actresses,' she told Roy Newquist, 'only Faye Dunaway has the talent and the class and the courage it takes to make a real star.'[21] This was uttered in the late 1960s or early 1970s, but ten years earlier her opinions, as Hedda Hopper set them down, were as perspicacious and much pricklier. Audrey Hepburn: 'I think everybody in the industry should open their arms to this child and say "Come in and help us." Someone said to me the other day, "Isn't it a pity she doesn't have her teeth straightened?" I said, "What does it matter? I didn't even notice her teeth."' Shelley Winters: 'I think she gave a sensitive performance in *A Place in the Sun* and she's not a sensitive girl socially. But if one director can get it, it's there – it may be latent. She should do another performance like that with another director.' Leslie Caron: 'In a class with Audrey Hepburn. People say she's not pretty. Who cares? She has talent. Pier Angeli is another – if she doesn't rely on her beauty.' Jean Simmons: 'Our greatest young talent outside of Hepburn.' Of course such budding stars conformed to the traditional screen values by which Crawford set high stock: she endorsed them warmly because they represented the continuance of a sort of film industry that was 'home' to her. Much tarter were her remarks about a star who looked like a home-breaker. Marilyn Monroe's burlesque of innocence was considered by Crawford an affront to womanhood (or, at least, that section who called themselves 'ladies'). She publicly criticized Monroe for behaving like a lewd *ingénue* when the latter appeared 'half-naked' at a film industry reception. Monroe's apology now carries an undertone of irony which it did not have in 1953: 'I've always admired [Miss Crawford] for being such a wonderful mother ... Who better than I knows what that means to homeless little ones?'

In spite of MGM's high hopes for *Torch Song* ('We are all very thrilled following preview,' cabled Howard Strickling, 'you are absolutely wonderful'), the film was only a modest success. MGM paid her $125,000 in eighty-three instalments (to lighten her tax burden), but either couldn't find or was unwilling to submit any ideas for her second film and the contract lapsed after October 1954. The lady, meanwhile, had found her own role: she purchased the film rights to *Johnny Guitar* (27 May 1954) while the novel was still in its galleys. It was a role-reversal Western in which two feuding women, a feisty saloon-owner and a greedy cattle baroness, replaced the familiar male antagonists. While retaining what Bosley Crowther referred to as 'her technically recognized sex', this allowed Crawford to appear *en travesti*, gun-belted, top-booted

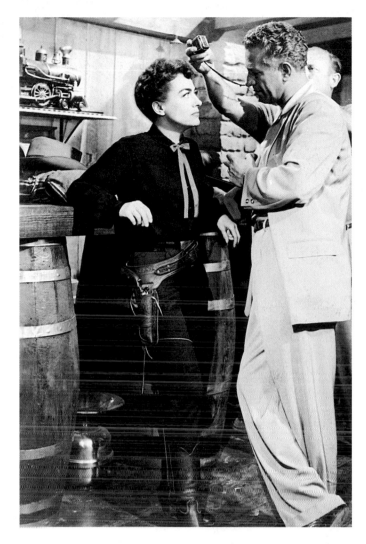

RIGHT Nicholas Ray tenders direction to a fully-armed star in *Johnny Guitar*.
BELOW Even at bay with Sterling Hayden, Crawford shows the enemy a fierce face.

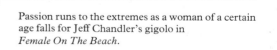

Passion runs to the extremes as a woman of a certain age falls for Jeff Chandler's gigolo in *Female On The Beach*.

and cord-breeched, almost as often as Garbo had assumed male attire in *Queen Christina*. The genre was ideal for the 'encounter scenes' that were now a pre-fabricated part of a Crawford script; but this time, the presence of Mercedes McCambridge as her prairie rival generated friction on location that escalated into a trial of strength in which, it seemed, the lady who came out of the collision looking the biggest smithereen would regard herself as the winner. Crawford called her co-star a 'witch' and later claimed McCambridge had been casting spells on her – an improbable supposition, but a prophetic piece of forward-casting, since it was McCambridge who provided the grotesquely frightening *basso profundo* voice of the demon in *The Exorcist* some twenty years later. Crawford attempted, successfully, to exorcize this malign presence by reducing McCambridge's role and expanding her own. But lady-like disdain was restored upon returning to civilization. 'Dig away,' she wrote to Hedda Hopper, 'and get out from under this so-called feud. What year do you want to emerge? I've said before, Darling – it takes two to make a feud. Well, I hope she's happy if she thinks she's two. As I said once, I'm raising four children. I haven't time to raise another on the film set.'

Alfred Steele began courting Joan Crawford soon after his divorce from his first wife early in 1955. This time there was no Louis B. Mayer around to disapprove of the match. Not that he would have been likely to do so. For in making Al Steele her fourth husband, Crawford might be said to have married her 'Mr Mayer'. When she later wrote that Steele was someone who 'could measure the community of people whose livelihood and happiness stemmed from him and his stubborn belief that people *can* work together as a team', she might have been writing, in an idealized fashion, maybe, about Louis B. Mayer. And when she wrote that 'what I didn't realize about Alfred was that he not only loved business, he lived, ate, slept and breathed it ... His social life and business life were one and the same',[22] she might have been writing about herself. Mayer, Steele and Crawford: all three had started on the bottom rung and climbed to the top, each was an American success story. Steele was four or five years older than his wife, but, like him, she trailed the glamour and power of big business wherever she went. Like Mayer, he was a corporate decision-maker who backed his opinion with his executive muscle – and, if occasion arose, with his forearm muscle as well. This brought him into argumentative conflict with Crawford in the way that she and Mayer had sometimes clashed: and as she had done with Mayer, she deferred to him – at least in the early stages – a characteristic of her three earlier marriages, too. For example, although she had not travelled by plane ever since a rough trip back to Los Angeles from location on Catalina Island had made her vow never to set foot in anything higher off the ground than the drawing-room of a Pullman carriage, she agreed there and then, on 9 May 1955, to fly with Alfred in the Pepsi-Cola plane to Las Vegas and get married the next day.

He was the first of her husbands who was not a film actor: therefore their interests were complementary not competitive. She felt safe in letting herself be referred to as 'Mrs Alfred Steele' – this husband wouldn't capitalize on her stardom to get himself bigger roles or better credits. Both of them were dedicated to work: for them, a honeymoon meant a week at a Pepsi-Cola convention. For him, there

Matriarchal passion smites the family (Lucy Marlow) in *Queen Bee* (above); at home discipline was strict too.

was the aura of being married to one of the world's most famous women; for his business, the commercial advantage of having her endorse the product, which she did ubiquitously and imperiously, insisting on Pepsi-Cola dispensers being installed on the sound stages wherever she was working. And what did *she* get out of the relationship? Dora Alfred, author of *You're Better Than You Think*, put it succinctly in a letter to their mutual friend Hedda Hopper: 'For the first time in her life, Joan ... found instant security with a man. For the first time in her life, perhaps, she could be a feminine woman, leaning on the strength of her man. Doug Fairbanks Jr was too young when they married to give Joan that instant support, and her other husbands were also actors and consequently subject to the ego conflicts within themselves.' Crawford even made Steele's business interests into the structure of the love rituals she had spent her life erecting around herself. Her fans were now expected to transfer their loyalty to Pepsi-Cola on the 'love me, love my product' pattern. Opening endless bottling plants replaced the personal appearance tours that had once marked the *première* of a Crawford film. She treated workers and management with the minute attentiveness lavished on the technical crews who had protected her so well and for so long in the film studios.

A personal note. I visited her in London in August, 1969, when she was sixty-five and just finishing her eighty-first and last movie, *Trog*. Calling at 5.30 p.m. precisely, as arranged, at her rented apartment in Grosvenor House, I was admitted by Crawford herself wearing a white terry-

Three for the family album: (above) Crawford and her fourth husband, Alfred Steele; (below and opposite) the new arrivals in the household, the adopted 'twins' Cathy and Cindy.

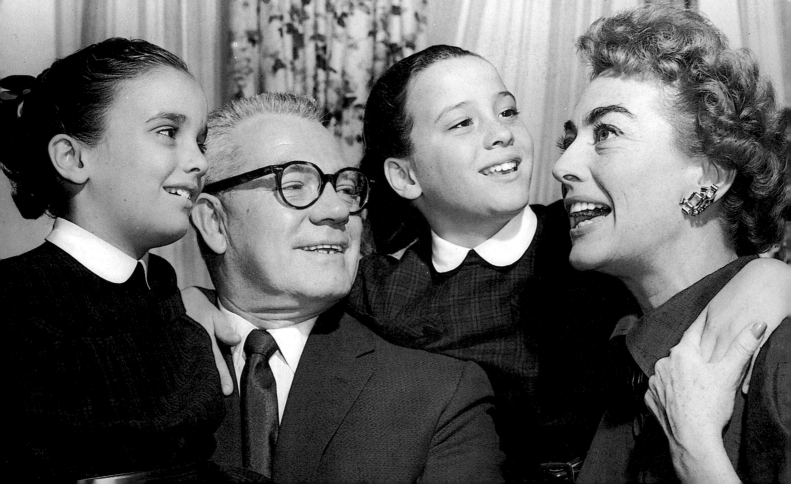

168 towelling gown, her newly-washed hair still swathed in a towel-turban: she had given her maid the evening off, she explained. The picture was that of a *grande dame* in *déshabille*, but not too *grande* a one to have forgotten how to treat her servants or be embarrassed to do her own chores. For erected in the middle of the elegant living-room was a common kitchen ironing-board: on it was the silk gown she planned to wear later that night when she received half-a-dozen Lebanese managers and their wives from Pepsi-Cola's Beirut bottling plant. As we talked, she kept ironing and re-ironing the dress: it became obvious that it was something for her hands to do. She refreshed herself from a tumbler of clear liquid. I guessed it contained the vodka I was drinking. She had prepared her fall-back position lest the dialogue languish, for the relatively small budget of the film on which she was engaged apparently allowed her no personal publicist, and we were alone. On the ironing-board was a stapled sheaf of papers. At one stage she passed them over. It was a list of her engagements to open bottling plants in America and it went right up to 21 December. Slightly at a loss, I said, 'Lucky you left Christmas for the children.' (In retrospect, *not* a well-chosen remark.) She paused, the iron hovering dramatically a millimetre above the silk fabric. Then: 'Oh, Mr Walker, the children are all grown up ... I use Christmas for cleaning out the New York apartment.' An hour later, the Pepsi-Cola guests arrived, large beefy men with liquid brown eyes and wives to match, plainly in thrall to the Presence at the ironing-board. Two hours later, when I left, the iron was still going up and down, up and down, the tumbler of clear fluid had

been replenished out of sight in the kitchenette, and no hour had apparently been set for dinner.

For Crawford, Pepsi-Cola served a very practical purpose beyond the new identity it gave her. Now that she was an 'independent' film-maker, with no major studio to manage her publicity and personal appearances, or attend to the dozens of privileged perquisites she claimed as the dues of stardom, the Pepsi-Cola organization acted as a sort of studio – but a studio with only one star. She pushed its products and it kept her in the style and prominence to which she had always been accustomed. The movie companies which produced her films in the years during and immediately following her marriage to Alfred Steele found they had a tycoon on their hands as well as a star. A nine-page booklet of detailed instructions went out to all Columbia Pictures branch managers in the seven cities in the United States and Canada which Crawford visited in January 1964, on a fourteen-day publicity tour for the movie *Strait-Jacket* (22 January 1964). Crawford's power infiltrates every instruction in Roger Caras's schedule:

Miss Crawford will be travelling by the Pepsi-Cola executive aircraft. Two people will accompany her: Mr Bob Kelly, PR representative for Pepsi-Cola in New York; Miss Anna Brinke ('Mamacita') Miss Crawford's maid. She does not speak English. The following hotel accommodations are to be prepared. The top suite (including three bedrooms) in the hotels indicated. This should be the best suite available. A single room for Mr Kelly is to be reserved on the same floor. The *three*-bedroomed suite is for Miss Crawford and Miss Brinke. The single is not to be part of the suite, but is to be nearby. A special Press conference room or suite is to be promoted from the hotel. Press conferences described below are *not* to be held in the Crawford suite. Press suite to be the size of a normal hotel luncheon room. The two pilots of the Pepsi-Cola plane will have a single room each in the hotel. The following special arrangements are required at each hotel ... There may be no deviations. A uniformed security officer is to be assigned to the door of the hotel suite twenty-four hours a day. You are *not* to use a city policeman and you are *not* to use the hotel detective. This security officer should be hired from Pinkerton ... There is to be a man there twenty-four hours a day, I repeat.

The following items are to be in the suite prior to Joan Crawford's arrival: cracked ice in buckets; lunch and dinner menus; pen and pencils and pads of paper; professional-size hair-drier; steam iron and board; one carton of Alpine cigarettes; a bowl of peppermint Life Savers; red and yellow roses; case of *Pepsi* Cola, ginger ale, soda. There is to be a maid on hand in the suite when Miss Crawford arrives at the hotel. She is to stand by until Miss Crawford dismisses her. The following liquor is to be in the suite when Miss Crawford arrives: two-fifths of 100° Proof Smirnoff vodka (NOTE: THIS IS NOT 80° PROOF AND IT IS ONLY SMIRNOFF); one-fifth Old Forester bourbon; one-fifth Chivas-Regal scotch; one-fifth Beefeaters gin; two bottles Moët & Chandon

LEFT Crawford waiting her turn, for once, at a rehearsal for the Royal Film Performance in London, 1956.
OPPOSITE Mr and Mrs Steele spend a quiet evening in their new home.

Champagne (Type: Dom Perignon). Miss Crawford will be met in an air-conditioned, chauffeur-driven, newly-cleaned Cadillac. Instruct your chauffeurs that they are not to smoke and that they may not at any time drive in excess of forty miles an hour with Miss Crawford in the car. Miss Crawford will be carrying a minimum of fifteen pieces of luggage . . .

The instruction bulletin ended on a note of combined grandeur and economy:

Miss Crawford is a star in every sense of the word; and everyone knows she is a star. As a partner in this film, Miss Crawford will not appreciate your throwing away money on empty gestures. *You do not have to make empty gestures to prove to Miss Crawford or anyone else that she is a star of the first magnitude.* If the detailed instructions above have given you the impression that money is no object, then carefully note the following, because exactly the opposite is true: The detailed instructions above are to tell you how far you may go. They are very explicit for the precise purpose that we do not want money over and above that required . . . to be spent. WATCH THE COSTS OF THIS TOUR. NEITHER MISS CRAWFORD NOR THIS OFFICE [at Columbia Pictures] WILL APPRECIATE YOUR THROWING MONEY AWAY. YOU ARE ACCOUNTABLE FOR EVERY CENT YOU SPEND – WATCH IT – AND SUBSTANTIATE IT!

Let anyone beware who stood between Crawford and the love she thought her due: even as her career began to deteriorate, she hung on to power. She kept faith with her public by being there – one sometimes wished she had not also been required to *do* something. In the final series of films she was in the habit of engaging a different publicist for each one, partly so as to retain control, partly because she believed a publicist would work harder if she stressed how big a chance this was for him – 'Do yourself some good, representing me.' One unlucky publicist ordered off some fans who had gathered downstairs in the New York hotel where she was staying while completing a film's post-synching. He mentioned this soon afterwards while pouring the after-work vodka – 'You don't want to be bothered by those people after a hard day.' The blow she aimed at him knocked the drink from his hand. He was shamefacedly sent down to invite the fans hanging on in the lobby up to her suite. After apologies and autographs, Crawford said to her aide, 'Please see my friends out.' When he returned, she met him at the door of the suite. 'And now, see yourself out, for good.'

In the same way, the many kindnesses she showed to people were inextricably linked to her own status. Her favours were imperious ones: they brooked no refusal. Two people who felt the full force of her 'bounty' were her former director at MGM, Jules Dassin, and Melina Mercouri, the Greek actress who starred in several of his European movies and later became his wife. In the early 1960s, they ran into Crawford in New York. Melina Mercouri had become world-famous with Dassin's *Never on Sunday*. Crawford instantly tried to set up a dinner-party for that Saturday. Mercouri declined politely – Saturday was her birthday. Instantly, the dinner was inflated to a full-scale birthday party. They gave in. But a few hours before the party, Dassin pulled a back muscle,

was in great pain, could not move. A frantic Mercouri summoned medical attention, then collected enough wits and words of English to call Crawford and report that the guests of honour would not be at the party. Dassin, lying on his couch of pain, heard her reaction at the other end of the line, it was so explosive. 'Joan screamed "You can't do that to me!" Remember *Dinner at Eight*? It was nothing to this. Remember Billie Burke in *Dinner at Eight*? Joan played that role, only like a Dead-End Kid. She shrieked, "I have invited people from all over America. I have Senators and Congressmen coming. You can't do that! I'll send you Kennedy's own doctor." And she did send a doctor, but still I couldn't move. Crawford told Melina to come without me, but she just would not leave me . . . So there was no birthday party for Melina. The next day, early in the morning, I am being carried out of the suite to undergo medical therapy. We open the door. And there, placed right outside, in front of the door, alone in the corridor, with no note or anything else to explain its surrealist presence, is an *enormous* birthday cake. On the icing on top it read, "TO DEAR MELINA".'

Yet once again the rupture was healed . . . friendship was repaired . . . and Dassin recalled that 'till the very end, a Christmas message would come from Joan, always the first to arrive. Never a card, but always a letter, embossed with candles and holly and other seasonable emblems, and a little sentimental message, "Thinking of you . . . Merry Christmas . . ." and so on. First one of the year, always.'

After the Steeles were married, they briefly inhabited Al's 'bachelor' pad on Sutton Place South, then Steele acquired two apartments at 2 East 70th Street, just off Fifth Avenue, and converted them into an eight-room duplex decorated – by Billy Haines, naturally – in film-star style. The children were lodged in a nearby hotel whenever they visited New York from California. Steele was dismayed to find that the bill for purchase and refurbishment, which came to well over $300,000, was being charged to him personally, not to the Pepsi-Cola company. As much as anything, this drain on his resources accounted for his wife's acceptance of a role in *The Story of Esther Costello* (5 November 1957), another protective mother part, as a wealthy American who rescues a deaf-and-dumb girl from Irish squalor only to see her exploited for gain by Crawford's husband, played by Rossano Brazzi. It was her first British-made movie and a happy exercise. She had first feared the British press because, as she told Hedda Hopper, 'They always ask "How old are you?" or "How much money do you make?"' Instead, she was fêted by fans and critics and honoured with a Café Royal luncheon by the same feared newspaper people. She was also asked to appear in a 3-D movie. 'I like people coming out of the screen,' she replied, 'but I prefer them coming out of that screen on their own personality.'

In April 1959, this period of stability was abruptly terminated with Al Steele's unexpectedly sudden death from cardiac arrest. Despite his $125,000 a year salary, he had been living too high for his means, and debts and taxes consumed all of his $600,000 estate. 'JOAN CRAWFORD FLAT BROKE' the headlines cried, picking up an indiscreet remark of hers to Louella Parsons. Not quite 'flat', but broke enough to sell up her California home, move into a smaller apartment and take a supporting role as the office Gorgon of Rona Jaffe's drama about the temptations and

With two of her closest friends, Crawford arrives in New York from Los Angeles.

fates of Manhattan career girls, *The Best of Everything* (8 October 1959). It was a lifeline thrown her by her *Mildred Pierce* producer Jerry Wald. Even so, she tied her own status-knot in it by insisting on billing that set her apart from the leading players. Adversity had its uses . . .

Formidable compensation was at hand. Not just the $60,000 a year fee she was henceforth to get from Pepsi-Cola, whose board she joined as a non-executive director with special responsibility for publicity, but in the shape of a novel which arrived from producer-director Robert Aldrich. He sought her opinion on it. Inside twenty-four hours she had not only cast herself in *What Ever Happened To Baby Jane?* (6 November 1962), but she had mentally cast Bette Davis to play opposite her.

Crawford had had her mouth-whetting taste of Gothic melodrama as early as *Queen Bee* (22 November 1955), but in that film she had played the role of an active bitch, for which she now cast Davis, reserving for herself the part of *Baby Jane's* passive victim. *Queen Bee* was one of her most successful recent movies: its writer-director Ranald MacDougall had been among the hands which worked on *Mildred Pierce* (how many things led back to *that* film!) and had pushed Crawford's compulsive domesticity to cannibalistic extremes as a matriarch who disposes of her family once they have served their purpose the way other women empty ash-trays after a party. The film imputes her lack of feeling to a lack of love and offers her the self-indulgence of atonement once she feels wanted again, followed by the positive luxury of retribution in a car crash the minute she starts to lead her new life while clad in her old style of mink wrap, evening gown and diamond bracelet. Feeling she had a surfeit of bitchiness, she settled for sympathy and suffering in *Baby Jane* as one of the two reclusive sisters, former Hollywood stars, now locked into a mutually loathing relationship in their shuttered mansion. Bette was the witch-like sadist, Joan the wheelchair-bound masochist. It was a movie that fed on the public's love-hate relationship with yesterday's movie stars who have become today's mental cases.

This time there was no quarrelling over the first-billing credits. 'Bette gets [it], of course,' Crawford told Hedda Hopper during a dinner party which the columnist held for her and Davis. 'She plays the title role: no problem about it.' She had only once before appeared in a film with Davis, *Hollywood Canteen* (15 December 1944), a war-time turn-out by all Warner Bros stars, in which Crawford played herself and danced graciously with a GI on leave, and Davis played the canteen's president. They had had no scene together; now in *Baby Jane*, there was hardly a scene where they were not together. They worked at much reduced fees. A film in which the combined ages of both leading ladies topped the century mark was a risky undertaking. (Davis was actually four or five years younger than Crawford.) Davis accepted $60,000 up-front money plus 5 per cent of the producer's net profit; Crawford, with Pepsi-Cola as her fall-back banker, settled for $30,000 plus 15 per cent of the producer's net. It proved to be one of her best investments: within two weeks of its national release, the film had recovered its $825,000 cost and went on to gross $9 million, of which Crawford's share was nearly a million dollars.

Aldrich callously exploited every misogynist angle to the story; but what gave *Baby Jane* its appalling but indeed almost pardonable sense of fitness was the sight of stars who were rumoured to be real-life rivals condemned to live in vengeful propinquity to each other. It supplied the Punch and Judy show with a dimension of reality and illusion that would have interested Pirandello. Both reality and illusion combine with the personalities of the two players to produce an indelible impression of a couple of indestructible women who know of no other way to live except as film stars, even though their days of glory belong to the dead past.

Crawford had more than one cause for tight-lipped satisfaction . . . According to the story, her character's fame in the movies had surpassed her sister's and in order to show Joan at the height of her stardom, the producers applied to MGM for an excerpt from Crawford's 1934 film *Sadie MacKee*. In one of the last MGM memos directly bearing on their own great star's movie career, an MGM executive, one R.L.Mayer (not Louis B.'s ne'er-do-well youngest brother, Rudi, but, given Hollywood's endemic nepotism, quite possibly a relative of L.B.'s), expressed grave doubt about the wisdom of granting the request. Ever protective of MGM talents, he noted in a cautious internal memo: '[*Baby Jane*] is an extremely distasteful and downbeat subject. Since clips from an MGM picture will be used, there is at least the intimation that these girls [the Crawford and Davis harridans] worked at MGM in the Thirties. I do not mean to indicate that this presents any legal problem, but it may at least be something that you want to consider.' Perhaps the studio was less concerned that one of its stars should have come to the un-pretty pass of turning into a living freak than that *Sadie McKee's*

commercial value for re-release or television rental might be impaired. Aldrich and his producers had to guaranteee that no disparaging remarks would be made in *Baby Jane* about 'our motion picture' since 'they could affect our product and may conceivably be resented by Clarence Brown who directed [it]'. The fee charged was a nominal $7.50 a foot for 138 feet. As for Bette's 'Baby Jane' character, who was supposed to have been a Hollywood flop in the 1930s, Aldrich displayed an even more acidulous taste for Davis's old films and chose excerpts from two she had made in 1933. One was *Ex-Lady*; the other was *Parachute Jumper*, in which her co-star was none other than Douglas Fairbanks Jr, at that time still Joan Crawford's husband!

Bette Davis told Hedda Hopper at that pre-production dinner on 16 July 1962 that 'she had never really known Joan, had never met her'. Yet they knew each other's nature as if they were sisters. The styles they showed at the dinner-table typified the place each knew she had secured over a successful lifetime, longer than they might have hoped for in any other occupation: those whom stardom does not destroy, it preserves for an impressive span of time. Joan arrived wearing 'a dark dinner suit, her hair swirled up on top of her head and held there with a diamond pin – diamond ear-rings – elaborate diamond watch. In contrast [Bette] wore a simple black crêpe dress, no ornaments.' Joan had vodka on the rocks – 'She brought her own flask. Joan: "I say if you're going to have a drink, have what you want."' Jules Dassin, if he'd been present, might have chided her, however, for 'acting the lady'. Talk turned to her insistence on being treated like one. She named a TV producer whom she had recently called and for whom she had volunteered to do six plays 'without charge'. He came round to see her. 'He admired my apartment,' Crawford continued, 'and suggested we could make wonderful music together. When I said, "Why don't you take your wife to dinner? Pick up the phone and call her," he said he never took his wife to dinner. But he did call some girl – when she evidently wanted to know where he'd pick her up, he told her to take a cab and meet him.' Joan shrugged, as if saying to Bette, 'How different in our time.' Bette said nothing. Dinner over, 'Joan left first. Her chauffeur had been waiting for her. Bette called her secretary and asked her to come for her.'

At one point in the evening, their hostess noted, 'Crawford started putting lipstick on, Davis followed suit.' Hopper recorded, '... *The Women!*'

Davis received an Academy Award nomination for *Baby Jane*: Crawford, in the less showy role, did not. But she turned her disappointment to a bitchy advantage worthy of record by arranging to accept the 'Best Actress' Oscar if the star who won it wasn't at the ceremony. When the absent

OPPOSITE ABOVE and BELOW A feast for sadists, a banquet for masochists: Crawford and Bette Davis show their worst sides to each other as the film star sisters in *What Ever Happened To Baby Jane?* Joan gets something nasty for her breakfast and Bette finds it's her turn to slap.

BELOW After her husband's death, Joan valued the company of film stars like Glenn Ford.

174

ABOVE *The Caretakers*: no longer nervous about competing youth, old star poses with neophyte Susan Oliver.
RIGHT Crawford in a leotard and nearly sixty shows she still has her trim figure in *The Caretakers*.

Anne Bancroft won for *The Miracle Worker*, Crawford sailed past Davis, who was waiting in the wings, with barely an 'Excuse me', shared the proxy applause and the next day's pictures in the papers, whose inattentive readers might well have concluded that Joan Crawford had won her second Oscar.

Such events perhaps explain why relations between the two stars deteriorated during their attempted re-teaming two years later for *Hush ... Hush, Sweet Charlotte*. Crawford went into hospital suffering severe stress, and, while there, heard on the radio that Aldrich had replaced her with Olivia De Havilland. Aldrich's discourtesy was 'unforgivable'. 'But I'm glad for Olivia,' she added, 'she needs a good picture.'

If she recalled it in the years ahead, that two-edged remark must have wounded her. For *Baby Jane* happened to be Crawford's last 'good' picture. She was to make five more feature films in her lifetime, each a deeper retreat into a neurotic aspect of late middle-age, their very titles tracing her descent into the exploitation market of the horror film. With a hair-style that looked as if snakes had been insinuated into her curling locks along with the setting lotion, she played the aptly named Lucretia, head nurse of a psychiatric clinic in *The Caretakers* (21 August 1963) where the executives are as disturbed as those in the wards. Insanity was also employed to give a cutting-edge to her performance as a mental patient on parole in *Strait-Jacket*, a sort of axe-murderess emerita. In *I Saw What You Did, I Know Who You Are*, she received the blade instead of swinging it, having a bread-knife stuck through her while trying to protect two children from the killer. In *Berserk* (10 January, 1968: also known as *Circus of Blood*), she appeared in tail-coat, fish-net tights and leotard as a circus

owner accused of murder, her trim figure in the ring asserting its power with a bull-whip but making a discomfiting contrast with the sixty-three-year-old face that her raked-back hair style cruelly exposed. *Trog*, her last movie, featured her as a scientist who mothers a prehistoric baby monster.

Into most of these cheap movies – she was paid at most $50,000 a picture, sometimes less – she somehow managed to import a kind of perverted protectiveness as a mother, or mother-figure, sacrificing herself for the sake of her young of whatever genus they happen to be. She draws on something more innate than the vulgar or banal scenarios ever had it in mind to suggest. The theme of the ungrateful child – in two of them, mother is accused of the murders that her daughter did – not only echoes *Mildred Pierce*, but anticipates the real-life twist that was to turn her own adopted child's book into what many interpreted as an act of posthumous revenge.

It is hardly necessary to ask why she made such movies: they were a way of stopping time as well as filling it. Like the guest roles she played in TV films (one directed by Steven Spielberg) each was a challenge that made her do her best in the hope that another *Baby Jane* might resurrect her. She had made it a principle of her iron will never to look back; but now, in indirect ways, her concluding years were filled with hankerings for Hollywood. She had moved from the extravagant Steele residence into a roomy but less impressive apartment at the Imperial House on East 69th Street: she had it decorated in greens, whites and lemon yellows to simulate the dominant colouration of Southern California and the 'old' Hollywood. She was said to watch all her old films on TV to test her memory of co-stars and scenes. On more formal occasions, she appeared at the evenings arranged by the New York publicist John Springer in which clips from her old films were interspersed with questions from the audience. One is grateful that she experienced the merciful compensation of such a long life, which is to be 'discovered' by an age-group a couple of generations removed from her own – so that when she looked at the sea of faces of her fans 'out front', she did not have to see herself reflected in the ageing and wrinkled countenances of her contemporaries but in the fresh and often very youthful faces of the young. She had become a cult.

When the idea was somewhat diffidently put to her that she might narrate a sixty-minute programme celebrating Garbo, which BBC Television was preparing in 1969, she responded inside an hour. Garbo was the only star for whom she would gladly perform this service. She accepted a fee rather less than $10,000, and asked if it would be all right with the author to alter parts of his narration. He wryly recalled the remark she had once made that a writer's words were dead ones until 'they were brought to life by me'. Her sole contribution, as it turned out, was a wistful interpolated anecdote expressing Garbo's own regret at having no scene to share with Crawford in *Grand Hotel*. I was happy to defer to her nostalgia; but the programme had hardly been transmitted when the harder-headed Crawford reasserted herself. 'Please,' she said in a letter to me 'let me know what the ratings were.'

Age did not tempt her to relax her rigorous professionalism. As her life drew to a close, it became more regimented than ever: even in seclusion, she imposed a discipline on

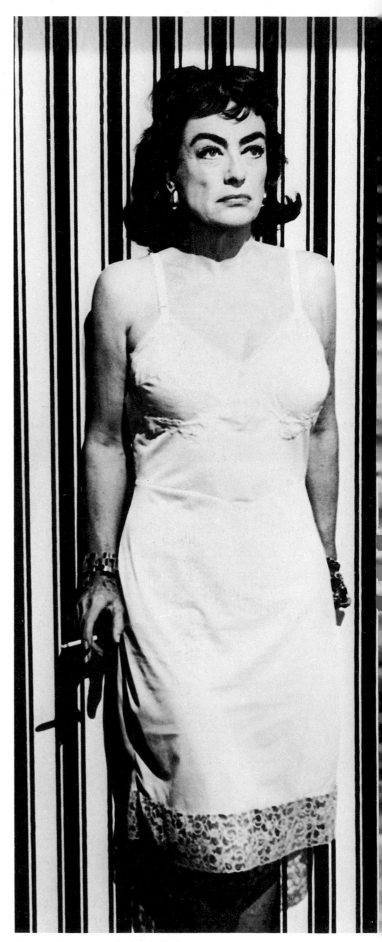

Suspected murderess in *Strait-Jacket*.

herself and her day that preserved something essential in her that would have broken down had she consciously acknowledged the need to retire. The generator stopped only when she did.

Money was tighter now. Pepsi-Cola, seeking a new, younger image for its product, had retired her from active duty; and though her $60,000 fee was continued as a lifetime pension, the company had stopped her $40,000 a year expenses, her $12,000 secretarial budget, her $1,500 accommodations allowance, even her $40 a week hairdressing money. She was also exceedingly generous with the funds she still had coming in; her revival of her Christian Science faith was accompanied by regular donations to that church.

She moved into a still smaller apartment in Imperial House. It held few visible mementoes of Hollywood: mainly the bust of herself done by Yucca Salamunich on the set of *A Woman's Face* in 1941. (One wonders if it still carried the inscription 'To Christina' etched on its bronze base.) Shortly before her death she was told that Christina was planning to write a book about her. It apparently made no impression on her.

She had been accustomed to despatching some 70,000 letters a year, most on the familiar small sheets of light-blue writing-paper with the simple heading JOAN CRAWFORD. These now tapered off, along with the 5–6,000 messages of good-will sent at Christmas. She who had celebrated every red-letter event in the calendar with a pin-up photo in her starlet days, now took no notice of anniversaries. Her greetings gradually stopped arriving. Her personal maid, Mamacita, did not return to her after one vacation in Europe. Her butler, who had been a doorman at Saks of Fifth Avenue before she 'found' him, stayed loyally by her until he felt inhibited by his own infirmities. Her neighbours down the corridor saw most of her, and that only now and then. She did not take incoming telephone calls, but would return some of them after her answering service had vetted them. Her spiritual faith in human will-power dissuaded her from entering a nursing home or committing herself to the care of other people in hospital. But will-power could not cure the cancer that began to pull down her health irretrievably in the last year or so, though it was of a simple cardiac arrest that she died, while the nurse who had been brought in for the terminal fortnight of her life was making her morning tea. Shortly after 9.30 am, on 10 May 1977, Joan Crawford stopped breathing.

Four days earlier, she had arranged for her pet dog to be adopted by friends. A few months earlier, she had remade her Will, naming individual beneficiaries and medical charities. Sums of $35,000 and $10,000 respectively went to her secretaries in Los Angeles and New York; $5,000 each to Monty Westmore, the make-up artist, and long-time friend Michael O'Shea; and $77,500 to each of her adopted daughters, the 'twins' Cindy and Cathy, whose understanding of their mother seems to have been aided by the independent lives they succeeded in establishing for themselves. The Will ended with the unforgiving words: 'It is my intention to make no provision herein for my son Christopher or my daughter Christina for reasons which are well known to them.'

The value of so long a life and career to the one who leads it is the feeling it conveys that there was no time when Joan Crawford was not a star. As an actress, her range was not

Her last two films were made in England: *Berserk* (also entitled *Circus of Blood*) cast her as a circus owner suspected of murder; and *Trog* (below) as a scientist who mothers the last representative of a prehistoric species as if it were her own child.

Six faces of the later Crawford – and two supplied by Faye Dunaway, who played her in the film *Mommie Dearest*.

Dunaway is third from left in the top row and second from left in the bottom row.

wide, but it was accurate, never less than professional, sometimes remarkable, occasionally unique. Her personality held no mystery that she could exploit the way that Garbo's fusion of reclusive beauty and reluctant stardom was exploited. For the intangibles of charisma, Crawford substituted the visible features of character: energy, control, forcefulness and dedication, in virtually all her roles. And she succeeded in creating something as solid and inherently American and of her own time as Garbo's subtler essence was international and timeless. The eulogy of Crawford that George Cukor pronounced at the Academy of Motion Picture Arts and Sciences spoke of her as being 'in the perfect image of the movie star, and, as such, largely the creation of her own indomitable will'. In that lies the essential explanation of her, which renders it unnecessary to ask who the real Joan Crawford was, or if, indeed, there ever was a real one. She subsumed herself so completely into her roles that an archaeologist would have embarked on a useless quest if he sought the remains of her true being. Perhaps, at the end, even she had ceased to understand where it once lay. It lay in so many roles . . . in the gauche chorus-line newcomer desperate to make good pictures . . . in the headstrong 'dancing daughter' of the flapper era . . . in the resolute working girl using sex-appeal to rise to riches . . . in the romantic beauty gowned by Adrian for the ocean liner and the Manhattan penthouse . . . in the sophisticated playgirl driving rival lovers to distraction . . . in the dauntless mother overly protective of an ungrateful family . . . in the bitches of violent melodrama and the freakish victims of *grand guignol*.

In forty-five years of making movies, she got through many roles, many lives. She took the material others provided, but made it her own; yet she herself was no one's invention – no one's but her own. How could it have been otherwise? she once asked an interviewer, genuinely puzzled that such a question should ever have been put to her. 'You manufacture toys,' she declared, 'you don't manufacture stars.'

An unaccustomed sense of tranquillity softens one of the most
famous faces in the cinema: the picture was taken by John Engstead
within a few weeks of Joan Crawford's death.

FILMOGRAPHY

The following list includes selective credits of all major features, in order of their release, in which Joan Crawford appeared. I have included some production details which I think throw an interesting light on the workings of a studio like MGM.

SILENTS

1925

1 Pretty Ladies
MGM

Story by Adela Rogers St Johns
Adapted by Alice D. G. Miller
Director: Monta Bell
Cameraman: Ira H. Morgan
Cast: Zasu Pitts, Tom Moore, Ann Pennington, Lilyan Tashman, Bernard Randall, Helen D'Algy, Conrad Nagel, Norma Shearer, George K. Arthur, Lucille LeSueur (Joan Crawford), Paul Ellis, Roy D'Arcy

2 The Circle
MGM

Play by W. Somerset Maugham
Adapted by Kenneth B. Clarke
Director: Frank Borzage
Cameraman: Chester A. Lyons
Cast: Eleanor Boardman, Malcolm McGregor, Alec B. Francis, Eugenie Besserer, George Fawcett, Eulalie Jensen, Creighton Hale, Otto Hoffman, Buddy Smith, Joan Crawford, Frank Braidwood, Derek Glynne

3 Old Clothes
MGM

Story by Willard Mack
Producer: Jack Coogan, Sr
Director: Eddie Cline
Cameraman: Frank B. Good
Cast: Max Davidson, Lillian Elliott, Joan Crawford, Alan Forest, James Mason, Stanton Heck, Jackie Coogan

4 Sally, Irene and Mary
MGM

Musical play by Eddie Dowling and Cyrus Woods
Adapted by Edmund Goulding
Director: Edmund Goulding
Cameraman: John Arnold
Cast: Constance Bennett, Joan Crawford, Sally O'Neil, William Haines, Douglas Gilmore

1926

5 The Boob
MGM

Adapted by Kenneth Clarke from the story by George Scarborough and Annette Westbay
Director: William A. Wellman
Cameraman: William Daniels
Cast: Gertrude Olmstead, George K. Arthur, Joan Crawford, Charles Murray

6 Tramp, Tramp, Tramp
FIRST NATIONAL

Story by Frank Capra, Tim Whelan, Hal Conklin, J. Frank Holliday, Gerald Duffy and Murray Roth

Produced by Harry Langdon Corp.
Director: Harry Edwards
Cameramen: Elgin Lessley and George Spear
Cast: Harry Langdon, Joan Crawford, Edwards Davis

7 Paris
MGM

Story and direction by Edmund Goulding
Cameraman: John Arnold
Cast: Charles Ray, Joan Crawford, Douglas Gilmore

1927

8 The Taxi Driver
MGM

Story by Robert Terry Shannon
Adapted by A. P. Younger
Director: Harry Millarde
Cameraman: Ira H. Morgan
Cast: Joan Crawford, Owen Moore, Douglas Gilmore, Marc MacDermott

9 Winners of the Wilderness
MGM

Story by John Thomas Neville
Director: W. S. Van Dyke
Cameraman: Clyde De Vinna
Cast: Tim McCoy, Joan Crawford, Edward Connelly, Frank Currier, Roy D'Arcy, Chief Big Tree

10 The Understanding Heart
MGM

Story by Peter B. Kyne
Adapted by Edward T. Lowe, Jr
Director: Jack Conway
Cameraman: John Arnold
Cast: Joan Crawford, Rockcliffe Fellows, Francis X. Bushman, Jr, Carmel Myers

11 The Unknown
MGM

Story by Tod Browning.
Scenario: Waldemar Young
Director: Tod Browning
Cameraman: Merrit Gerstad
Cast: Lon Chaney, Norman Kerry, Joan Crawford

12 Twelve Miles Out
MGM

Play by William Anthony McGuire
Adapted by Sada Cowan
Director: Jack Conway
Cameraman: Ira H. Morgan
Cast: John Gilbert, Ernest Torrence, Joan Crawford, Betty Compson

13 Spring Fever
MGM

Play by Vincent Lawrence
Scenario: Albert Lewin and Frank Davies
Director: Edward Sedgwick
Cameraman: Ira H. Morgan
Cast: William Haines, Joan Crawford, George K. Arthur, George Fawcett

1928

14 West Point
MGM

Story by Raymond L. Schrock

Director: Edward Sedgwick
Cameraman: Ira H. Morgan
Titles: Joe Farnham
Editor: Frank Sullivan
Cast: William Haines, Joan Crawford, Neil Neely, William Bakewell

15 Rose Marie
MGM

Operetta by Otto Harbach and Oscar Hammerstein II
Scenario and direction: Lucien Hubbard
Cameraman: John Arnold
Cast: Joan Crawford, James Murray, House Peters, Creighton Hale, Gibson Gowland, Polly Moran

16 Across to Singapore
MGM

Story by Ben Ames Williams
Director: William Nigh
Cameraman: John Seitz
Cast: Ramon Novarro, Joan Crawford, Ernest Torrence

17 The Law of the Range
MGM

Story by Norman Houston
Scenario: E. Richard Schayer
Director: William Nigh
Cameraman: Clyde DeVinna
Cast: Tim McCoy, Joan Crawford, Rex Lease, Bodil Rosing, Tenen Holtz

18 Four Walls
MGM

Story by Dana Burnet and George Abbott
Director: William Nigh
Cameraman: James Howe
Cast: John Gilbert, Joan Crawford, Vera Gordon, Carmel Myers

19 Our Dancing Daughters
MGM (Cosmopolitan Production)

Story and scenario by Josephine Lovett
Director: Harry Beaumont
Cameraman: George Barnes
Cast: Joan Crawford, Johnny Mack Brown, Dorothy Sebastian, Anita Page, Nils Asther, Dorothy Cummings

20 Dream of Love
MGM

Play *Adrienne Lecouvreur* by Eugène Scribe and Ernest Legouvé
Director: Fred Niblo
Cameraman: Oliver Marsh and William Daniels
Cast: Joan Crawford, Nils Asther, Aileen Pringle, Carmel Myers

1929

21 The Duke Steps Out
MGM

Story by Lucien Cary
Adapted by Raymond Schrock and Dale Van Every
Director: James Cruze
Cameraman: Ira H. Morgan
Cast: William Haines, Joan Crawford, Karl Dane, Tenen Holtz, Eddie Nugent

22 Our Modern Maidens
MGM

Story and screenplay by Josephine Lovett

Producer: Hunt Stromberg
Director: Jack Conway
Cameraman: Oliver Marsh
Cast: Joan Crawford, Rod LaRocque, Douglas Fairbanks, Jr, Anita Page

TALKIES

23 Hollywood Revue of 1929
MGM

Dialogue by Al Boasberg and Robert Hopkins
Producer: Harry Rapf
Director: Charles F. Reisner
Cameramen: John Arnold, Irving G. Reis and Maximilian Fabian
Cast: Conrad Nagel, Bessie Love, Joan Crawford, William Haines, Buster Keaton, Anita Page, Karl Dane, George K. Arthur, Gwen Lee, Ernest Belcher's Dancing Tots, Marie Dressler, Marion Davies, Cliff Edwards, Charles King, Polly Moran, Gus Edwards, Lionel Barrymore, Jack Benny, Brox Sisters, Albertina Rasch Ballet, Natacha Natova and Company, The Rounders, Norma Shearer, John Gilbert, Laurel and Hardy

24 Untamed
MGM

Story by Charles E. Scoggins
Adapted by Sylvia Thalberg and Frank Butler
Dialogue by Willard Mack
Director: Jack Conway
Cameraman: Oliver Marsh
Titles: Lucile Newmark
Cast: Joan Crawford, Robert Montgomery, Ernest Torrence, Holmes Herbert, John Miljan, Gwen Lee

1930

25 Montana Moon
MGM

Story and screenplay by Sylvia Thalberg and Frank Butler
Dialogue by Joe Farnham
Director: Malcolm St Clair
Cameraman: William Daniels
Cast: Joan Crawford, Johnny Mack Brown, Dorothy Sebastian, Ricardo Cortez

26 Our Blushing Brides
MGM

Story by Bess Meredyth
Screenplay by Bess Meredyth and John Howard Lawson
Additional dialogue by Edwin Justus Mayer
Director: Harry Beaumont
Cameraman: Merritt B. Gerstad
Cast: Joan Crawford, Anita Page, Dorothy Sebastian, Robert Montgomery, Raymond Hackett, John Miljan, Hedda Hopper, Albert Conti

27 Paid
MGM

Play *Within the Law* by Bayard Veiller
Adapted by Lucien Hubbard and Charles MacArthur
Dialogue by Charles MacArthur
Director: Sam Wood
Cameraman: Charles Rosher

Cast: Joan Crawford, Robert Armstrong, Marie Prévost, John Miljan

1931

28 Dance, Fools, Dance
MGM

Story by Aurania Rouverol
Dialogue by Aurania Rouverol
Director: Harry Beaumont
Cameraman: Charles Rosher
Cast: Joan Crawford, Lester Vail, Cliff Edwards, William Bakewell, William Holden, Clark Gable

29 Laughing Sinners
MGM

Play *Torch Song* by Kenyon Nicholson
Dialogue by Martin Flavin
Director: Harry Beaumont
Cameraman: Charles Rosher
Cast: Joan Crawford, Neil Hamilton, Clark Gable, Marjorie Rambeau

30 This Modern Age
MGM

Story *Girls Together* by Mildred Cram
Dialogue by Sylvia Thalberg and Frank Butler
Director: Nicholas Grinde
Cameraman: Charles Rosher
Cast: Joan Crawford, Pauline Frederick, Neil Hamilton

31 Possessed
MGM

Play *The Mirage* by Edgar Selwyn
Adapted by Lenore Coffee
Director: Clarence Brown
Cameraman: Oliver T. Marsh
Cast: Joan Crawford, Clark Gable, Wallace Ford, Skeets Gallagher

1932

32 Letty Lynton
MGM

Novel by Marie Belloc Lowndes
Adapted by John Meehan and Wanda Tuchock
Director: Clarence Brown
Cameraman: Oliver T. Marsh
Cast: Joan Crawford, Robert Montgomery, Nils Asther, Lewis Stone
The archives at MGM – and, one suspects, every other big Hollywood studio – show how commonplace were the claims for plagiarism. Freelance writers, rank amateurs, occasionally 'published authors' could be counted on to pester, threaten and sometimes actually sue the studio for allegedly using their idea/character/plot/dialogue, etc., in a film, usually one which was being heavily publicized and/or grossing large box-office receipts. Few of these actually came to anything. Some were obviously the work of cranks, others had a nuisance value which led the studio to make token 'payments in settlement' without admitting the claim; but all, from the illegible scrawl of the 'Sunday writer' to the letter-headed claims of law firms on behalf of prominent clients, were duly filed and are in the vaults to this day. The law suit resulting from MGM's 1932

production of *Letty Lynton* was somewhat more serious. As stated in the text, the screenplay was based on Mrs Belloc Lowndes's novel of that name, which had been inspired by the case of Madeleine Smith, the alleged Edinburgh poisoner. But a suit charging MGM with plagiarism was subsequently brought on behalf of the author of the play *Dishonored Lady*, which told the same story, and which the studio had not acquired because the Hays Office refused to allow this 'lubricious' title to be used for a film. Unfortunately, it proved possible to establish that an aspect of the play had been *inadvertently* incorporated into the film script and it looked, for a time, as if MGM would have to surrender the $600,000–$700,000 which the film had earned for the producers. This gave Mayer and Thalberg many anxious moments, for it was indeed an enormous sum to forfeit in those days. On appeal, though, it was decided that while inadvertent plagiarism was still plagiarism, the proportion of a text plagiarised in this fashion or the contribution it made to the work in dispute should be related to the sum of damages finally awarded. Thus MGM were spared having to pay over *all* the *Letty Lynton* profits; but the case may account for the relative rarity of this particular film's public exhibition up to the present time.

33 Grand Hotel
MGM

Novel and play by Vicki Baum
Director: Edmund Goulding
Cameraman: William Daniels
Cast: Greta Garbo, Joan Crawford, Wallace Beery, John Barrymore, Lionel Barrymore, Lewis Stone, Jean Hersholt

34 Rain
UNITED ARTISTS

Play *Rain* adapted by John Colton and Clemence Randolph from the story *Miss Thompson* by W. Somerset Maugham
Screenplay by Maxwell Anderson
Director: Lewis Milestone
Cameraman: Oliver T. Marsh
Cast: Joan Crawford, Walter Huston, William Gargan, Beulah Bondi

1933

35 Today We Live
MGM

Story by William Faulkner
Screenplay by Edith Fitzgerald and Dwight Taylor
Director: Howard Hawks
Cameraman: Oliver T. Marsh
Cast: Joan Crawford, Gary Cooper, Robert Young, Franchot Tone

36 Dancing Lady
MGM

Novel by James Warner Bellah
Screenplay: Allen Rivkin and P. J. Wolfson
Producer: David O. Selznick
Director: Robert Z. Leonard
Cameraman: Oliver T. Marsh

Cast: Joan Crawford, Clark Gable, Franchot Tone, May Robson, Winnie Lightner, Fred Astaire, Robert Benchley

1934

37 Sadie McKee
MGM

Story by Vina Delmar
Screenplay by John Meehan
Producer: Lawrence Weingarten
Director: Clarence Brown
Cameraman: Oliver T. Marsh
Cast: Joan Crawford, Gene Raymond, Franchot Tone, Edward Arnold, Esther Ralston

38 Chained
MGM

Story by Edgar Selwyn
Screenplay by John Lee Mahin
Producer: Hunt Stromberg
Director: Clarence Brown
Cameraman: George Folsey
Cast: Joan Crawford, Clark Gable, Otto Kruger

39 Forsaking All Others
MGM

Story by Edward Barry Roberts and Frank Morgan Cavett
Screenplay by Joseph L. Mankewicz
Producer: Bernard H. Hyman
Director: W. S. Van Dyke
Cameramen: Gregg Toland and George Folsey
Cast: Joan Crawford, Clark Gable, Robert Montgomery

1935

40 No More Ladies
MGM

Play by A. E. Thomas
Screenplay by Donald Ogden Stewart and Horace Jackson
Producer: Irving Thalberg
Directors: Edward H. Griffith and George Cukor
Cameraman: Oliver T. Marsh
Cast: Joan Crawford, Robert Montgomery, Charlie Ruggles, Franchot Tone

41 I Live My Life
MGM

Short story *Claustrophobia* by A. Carter Goodloe
Developed by Gottfried Reinhardt and Ethel Borden
Screenplay by Joseph L. Mankiewicz
Producer: Bernard H. Hyman
Director: W. S. Van Dyke
Cameraman: George Folsey
Cast: Joan Crawford, Brian Aherne, Frank Morgan, Aline MacMahon, Eric Blore, Fred Keating, Jessie Ralph, Arthur Treacher, Hedda Hopper
Preparation of the trailer for *I Live My Life* was complicated when someone realized that Brian Aherne's co-starring status below the title might give rise to an unhappy innuendo. The problem was resolved when an official in the studio trailer department assured Howard

Dietz: 'Purposely eliminated the word "with" because trailer would then read, "Joan Crawford . . . *I Live My Life* . . . with Brian Aherne." Afraid of laugh from audience on this.'

1936

42 The Gorgeous Hussy
MGM

Novel by Samuel Hopkins Adams
Screenplay by Ainsworth Morgan and Stephen Morehouse Avery
Producer: Joseph L. Mankiewicz
Director: Clarence Brown
Cameraman: George Golsey
Cast: Joan Crawford, Robert Taylor, Lionel Barrymore, Franchot Tone, Melvyn Douglas, James Stewart, Alison Skipworth, Louis Calhern, Beulah Bondi

43 Love on the Run
MGM

Story by Alan Green and Julian Brodie
Screenplay by John Lee Mahin, Manuel Seff and Gladys Hurlbut
Producer: Joseph L. Mankiewicz
Director: W. S. Van Dyke
Cameraman: Oliver T. Marsh
Cast: Joan Crawford, Clark Gable, Franchot Tone, Reginald Owen

1937

44 The Last of Mrs Cheyney
MGM

Play *The Last of Mrs Cheyney* by Frederick Lonsdale
Screenplay by Leon Gordon, Samson Raphaelson and Monckton Hoffe
Producer: Lawrence Weingarten
Director: Richard Boleslawski
Cameraman: George Folsey
Cast: Joan Crawford, William Powell, Robert Montgomery

45 The Bride Wore Red
MGM

Unpublished play *The Girl from Trieste* by Ferenc Molnár
Screenplay by Tess Slesinger and Bradbury Foote
Producer: Joseph L. Mankiewicz
Director: Dorothy Arzner
Cameraman: George Folsey
Cast: Joan Crawford, Franchot Tone, Robert Young, Billie Burke, Reginald Owen

1938

46 Mannequin
MGM

Unpublished story by Katharine Brush
Screenplay by Lawrence Hazard
Producer: Joseph L. Mankiewicz
Director: Frank Borzage
Cameraman: George Folsey
Cast: Joan Crawford, Spencer Tracy, Alan Curtis, Leo Gorcey
Among the major Hollywood studios, MGM was probably the one that attached most importance to calling a film by the 'right' title. This sometimes involved top executives in seemingly endless memos

and cables, and in elaborate 'deals' with other studios which had registered the desired title against future use. It shows the minutiae of studio management that from his New York office, on 9 October 1936, J. Robert Rubin should cable Louis B. Mayer at the studios some three thousand miles away: 'Notice in studio bulletin you are using title *Mannequin* and expect to release picture in April. Remember I wired you some time ago we could not use title, as Paramount held Fanny Hurst novel of the same title . . . As long as we must change title, why not do it now?' On 2 November 1936, Frank Whitbeck of the studio story department cabled Howard Dietz, head of Loew's publicity and advertising, 'Mankiewicz enthusiastic over title *Class* for *Mannequin*. Please wire your reaction.' It was negative; *Marry for Money* was suggested as an alternative. This did not find favour at MGM, which suggested *Saint or Sinner*, although Joseph L. Mankiewicz, who was producing the film, felt it was 'not smart enough'. In what now seems like a trial of strength between East and West Coasts, Dietz, on 22 March 1937, cabled Howard Strickling, the studio's publicity chief; 'Mr Rubin's office advises *Three Rooms in Heaven* available for use. Therefore, will this be final for Crawford picture?' MGM did some quick but thorough research on whether *Three Rooms in Heaven* or any like title had been used on any other dramatic property and discovered it was free from prior use. However, studio forces held out for *Mannequin* and on 23 September 1937 Paramount graciously (and for some future favour it could call in) granted MGM permission to use *Mannequin*. Someone in the other camp may have been just as tenacious for, apparently, theatre managers were polled and on 18 October 1937, an MGM memo notes: 'Representatives of 500 theatres thought *Mannequin* should not be used.'

On 10 November 1937, Whitbeck sent Howard Dietz a weary-sounding cable: 'Both Mr Katz and Mr Mannix utterly opposed to title *Shop Girl* . . . They agree that while *Mannequin* may not be best title, it is best so far suggested.' It was over a year since it had *first* been suggested; it stood.

47 The Shining Hour
MGM

Play by Keith Winter
Screenplay by Jane Murfin and Ogden Nash
Producer: Joseph L. Mankiewicz
Director: Frank Borzage
Cameraman: George Folsey
Cast: Joan Crawford, Margaret Sullavan, Robert Young, Melvyn Douglas, Fay Bainter

1939

48 The Ice Follies of 1939
MGM

Story by Leonard Praskins

Screenplay by Leonard Praskins,
Florence Ryerson and Edgar Allan Woolf
Producer: Harry Rapf
Director: Reinhold Schunzel
Cameramen: Joseph Ruttenberg and
Oliver T. Marsh
Cast: Joan Crawford, James Stewart,
Lew Ayres, Lewis Stone

49 The Women
MGM

Play by Clare Boothe Luce
Screenplay by Anita Loos and Jane
Murfin
Producer: Hunt Stromberg
Director: George Cukor
Cameramen: Oliver T. Marsh and Joseph
Ruttenberg
Cast: Norma Shearer, Joan Crawford,
Rosalind Russell, Mary Boland, Paulette
Goddard, Phyllis Povah, Joan Fontaine,
Virginia Weidler, Lucile Watson,
Florence Nash, Muriel Hutchinson,
Esther Dale, Ann Morris, Ruth Hussey,
Dennie Moore, Mary Cecil, Mary Beth
Hughes, Virginia Grey, Marjorie Main,
Cora Witherspoon, Hedda Hopper
The British Board of Film Censors raised
objections to one of the sequences in *The
Women*. The MGM memos show how
seriously an apparently trifling matter
was taken at the studio. On 7 November
1939, Hunt Stromberg, the producer,
cabled Arthur Loew at MGM's Broadway
office: 'We have made eliminations in
fight scene in *The Women* to comply with
objection to exhibiting women's legs. But
to make clear the succeeding scene, where
Paulette Goddard is applying iodine to
her leg, it is necessary to retain that one
big close-up of Rosalind Russell biting
her. This is a mere flash of just about
three feet, two of which are holding on
Russell as she comically contemplates
biting [Goddard]. Then the next foot of
film shows her biting and there is so little
opportunity to see leg in such one-foot
flash that certainly we should be able to
leave this in. Please send copy of this wire
to Eckman, or whoever handles British
censors, and see if this can be done, as
otherwise [reason for] Goddard applying
iodine will be lost and, besides, we would
lose terrific laugh, as audiences howl with
delight when Russell bites her and
assuredly there is nothing offensive in a
one-foot flash of that kind.'

1940

50 Strange Cargo
MGM

Book *Not Too Narrow, Not Too Deep* by
Richard Sale
Screenplay by Lawrence Hazard
Producer: Joseph L. Mankiewicz
Director: Frank Borzage
Cameraman: Robert Planck
Cast: Joan Crawford, Clark Gable, Ian

Hunter, Peter Lorre, Paul Lukas

51 Susan and God
MGM

Play by Rachel Crothers
Screenplay by Anita Loos
Producer: Hunt Stromberg
Director: George Cukor
Cameraman: Robert Planck
Cast: Joan Crawford, Fredric March,
Ruth Hussey, John Carroll, Rita
Hayworth, Nigel Bruce
In the days before location shooting
became routine, studios like MGM had to
take considerable pains to get all proper
and desirable clearances in order to
reproduce buildings, well-known
landmarks, etc., on the studio set for the
required scene. The would-be recipients
of the resulting publicity were not always
as obliging as the studio hoped. Thus in
the pre-production period of *Susan and
God*, MGM's New York office was asked,
on 15 January 1940, to send the studio as
soon as possible photos of 'doorman,
waiters, busboys, barman at Racquet
Club, New York City'. The studio also
wanted to copy the painting *Les
Lavandières* by Auguste Renoir. The
governing board of the Racquet Club
refused permission for the club to be
featured or even named in the picture: it
was presumably wanted for a scene in
which Fredric March's drinking habits,
increased by his wife's absence, were to
have been amusingly demonstrated.
Then permission to copy the Renoir
painting was refused. So MGM requested
permission to copy a Grant Wood owned
by the film's director, George Cukor,
who had bought it five years before when
a gallery had sent it to the Coast for
Katharine Hepburn's inspection.
'Picture is of sheep grazing on hill with
round, squatty trees in background,' a
studio executive wired D. O. Decker,
who replied that the 'copyright positions
of paintings is very vague'. Decker had
one of those ideas that are so sensible they
seldom are hit on as solutions to a
problem: 'It occurs to us that . . . our
artist could draw something from
imagination which would be perfectly
safe and probably, as used in picture,
would be as good as any [copy] he would
have made of any famous painting.
Difficulty is artists are rather
temperamental. Shall we try and locate
[Grant] Wood and obtain his written
permission?' This was pondered; then it
was decided not to use any painting at all.
But Decker was not let off. 'In *Susan and
God*', he was now informed, 'we need the
services of a nightingale . . .'
Nightingales, though possibly even more
temperamental than artists, have little
direct say in such matters. A Victor
Recording (No. 20968B) resolved
Decker's quest easily and, we may
assume, reasonably cheaply.

1941

52 A Woman's Face
MGM

Play *Il Etait Une Fois* by Francis de
Croisset
Screenplay by Donald Ogden Stewart
Producer: Victor Saville
Director: George Cukor
Cameraman: Robert Planck
Cast: Joan Crawford, Melvyn Douglas,
Conrad Veidt

53 When Ladies Meet
MGM

Play by Rachel Crothers
Screenplay by S. K. Lauren and Anita
Loos
Producers: Robert Z. Leonard and
Orville O. Dull
Director: Robert Z. Leonard
Cameraman: Robert Planck
Cast: Joan Crawford, Robert Taylor,
Greer Garson, Herbert Marshall, Spring
Byington

1942

54 They All Kissed The Bride
COLUMBIA

Story by Gina Kaus and Andrew P. Solt
Screenplay by P. J. Wolfson
Producer: Edward Kaufman
Director: Alexander Hall
Cameraman: Joseph Walker
Cast: Joan Crawford, Melvyn Douglas,
Roland Young, Billie Burke

55 Reunion in France
MGM

Screen-story by Ladislas Bus-Fekete
Screenplay by Jan Lustig, Marvin
Borowsky and Marc Connelly
Producer: Joseph L. Mankiewicz
Director: Jules Dassin
Cameraman: Robert Planck
Cast: Joan Crawford, John Wayne,
Philip Dorn

1943

56 Above Suspicion
MGM

Novel by Helen MacInnes
Screenplay by Keith Winter, Melville
Baker and Patricia Coleman
Producer: Victor Saville
Director: Richard Thorpe
Cameraman: Robert Planck
Cast: Joan Crawford, Fred MacMurray,
Conrad Veidt, Basil Rathbone, Reginald
Owen
As well as raising questions of taste
(noted in the text), the Production Code
Administration raised one extraordinary
objection to the script of *Above Suspicion*
which casts a minor, but interesting,
sidelight on Hollywood's attitude at this
time to the war in Europe. Geoffrey M.

Shurlock, head of the PCA, wrote to Louis B. Mayer on 23 April 1942: 'We have read the script for your proposed picture *Above Suspicion* and regret to say that it contains one element which is in violation of the Production Code and which would not be approved in the finished picture.' He identified this as the murder of a Nazi agent by a character in the film who 'at the end of the story goes unpunished'. MGM executives Eddie Mannix and Al Lichtman, as well as the film's British producer Victor Saville, pointed to the nature of the conflict then raging in Europe. On 4 May 1942, the PCA replied: 'The fact that the victim is a Nazi still does not give [Mr Shurlock] power to alter the Code. There are a number of pictures coming up in which Nazis are killed by civilians without punishment.' Shurlock urged MGM to appeal for a ruling to the PCA's board of directors – 'without which ... I will reject all such pictures'. An internal MGM memo of the same date noted: 'While technically the situation involved indicates that the murderer is freed and [it] would therefore be in violation of the Production Code, we feel that today this would not constitute breach of morality, but would in fact be acceptable by all elements of American society.' William A. Orr, of MGM's New York office, sent a memo, dated 18 May 1942, to J. Robert Rubin: 'I had read the story before talking to Governor Milliken [secretary of the PCA] and that made me suggest the idea that while the Code prohibits unpunished murder or unpunished serious crime, it seems to me that even a Code reviewer could fairly say that under all the circumstances described in the script, these killings were guerrilla or undeclared war rather than murder or individual crime ... no one could kick about such a definition these days of numerous undeclared wars ... I asked [Governor Milliken] whether he could consider the shooting of a Nazi in the Jugoslavian mountains as murder or as war because, technically, the Mikhailovitch are individuals, though roughly organised killers without a national status or government. He said he felt that killing in that section of the world would be considered as war, but that it differed somewhat from the killings in our country.' The dispute rumbled on over the months until finally, on 13 October 1942, Carl E. Milliken himself wrote to J. Robert Rubin: 'It is to be noted that the objection to the shooting of the Nazi German officer is not primarily because of the act itself, but because "this murder is not only unpunished, but is condoned and made to seem right and acceptable".

'It is to be noted also that the murder is committed as an act of revenge, because "Thornley" believes that the woman in whom he is interested has been ill-treated in a concentration camp of which "Col. Jerrold" is the officer-in-charge. This situation involves a double violation of the Code, not only because of the unpunished murder but because revenge as a motive appears to be justified. It is to be noted that no element of war psychology properly enters into consideration of this script. The locale of the story is Germany in the period before England and Germany were at war. "Thornley", the sympathetic character who murders "Col. Jerrold", is not an officer of the English army – he is merely an ordinary Englishman travelling in Germany. In the discharge of its duty, the PCA could obviously take no position other than that indicated in the letter of 23 April.'

1944

57 Hollywood Canteen
WARNER BROS

Screenplay by Delmer Daves
Producer: Alex Gottlieb
Director: Delmer Daves
Cameraman: Bert Glennon
Cast: Joan Leslie, Robert Hutton, Dane Clark, Janis Page. Guest stars: Andrews Sisters, Jack Benny, Joe. E. Brown, Eddie Cantor, Kitty Carlisle, Jack Carson, Joan Crawford, Bette Davis, John Garfield, Sydney Greenstreet, Paul Henreid, Peter Lorre, Ida Lupino, Irene Manning, Joan McCracken, Dennis Morgan, Eleanor Parker, Roy Rogers and Trigger, Barbara Stanwyck, Jane Wyman

1945

58 Mildred Pierce
WARNER BROS

Novel by James M. Cain
Screenplay by Ranald MacDougall
Producer: Jerry Wald
Director: Michael Curtiz
Cameraman: Ernest Haller
Cast: Joan Crawford, Jack Carson, Zachary Scott, Eve Arden, Ann Blyth

1946

59 Humoresque
WARNER BROS

Story by Fanny Hurst
Screenplay by Clifford Odets and Zachary Gold
Producer: Jerry Wald
Director: Jean Negulesco
Cameraman: Ernest Haller
Cast: Joan Crawford, John Garfield, Oscar Levant, J. Carroll Naish

1947

60 Possessed
WARNER BROS

Story *One Man's Secret* by Rita Weiman
Screenplay by Silvia Richards and Ranald MacDougall
Producer: Jerry Wald
Director: Curtis Hernhardt
Cameraman: Joseph Valentine
Cast: Joan Crawford, Van Heflin, Raymond Massey, Geraldine Brooks

61 Daisy Kenyon
20th CENTURY-FOX

Novel by Elizabeth Janeway
Screenplay by David Hertz
Producer-director: Otto Preminger
Cameraman: Leon Shamroy
Cast: Joan Crawford, Dana Andrews, Henry Fonda

1949

62 Flamingo Road
WARNER BROS

Play by Robert and Sally Wilder
Screenplay by Robert Wilder
Producer: Jerry Wald
Director: Michael Curtiz
Cameraman: Ted McCord
Cast: Joan Crawford, Zachary Scott, Sydney Greenstreet

63 It's A Great Feeling
WARNER BROS

Story by I. A. L. Diamond
Screenplay by Jack Rose and Mel Shavelson
Producer: Alex Gottlieb
Director: David Butler
Cameraman: Wilfrid M. Cline
Cast: Dennis Morgan, Doris Day, Jack Carson. Guest appearances by: Gary Cooper, Joan Crawford, Errol Flynn, Danny Kaye, Patricia Neal, Eleanor Parker, Ronald Reagan, Edward G. Robinson, Jane Wyman

1950

64 The Damned Don't Cry
WARNER BROS

Story by Gertrude Walker
Screenplay by Harold Medford and Jerome Weidman
Producer: Jerry Wald
Director: Vincent Sherman
Cameraman: Ted McCord
Cast: Joan Crawford, David Brian, Steve Cochran

65 Harriet Craig
COLUMBIA

Play *Craig's Wife* by George Kelly
Screenplay by Anne Froelick and James Gunn
Producer: William Dozier
Director: Vincent Sherman
Cameraman: Joseph Walker
Cast: Joan Crawford, Wendell Corey

1951

66 Goodbye My Fancy
WARNER BROS

Play by Fay Kanin
Screenplay by Ivan Goff and Ben Roberts
Producer: Henry Blanke
Director: Vincent Sherman
Cameraman: Ted McCord
Cast: Joan Crawford, Robert Young, Frank Lovejoy, Eve Arden

1952

67 This Woman Is Dangerous
WARNER BROS

Story by Bernard Firard
Screenplay by Geoffrey Homes and George Worthing Yates
Producer: Robert Sisk
Director: Felix Feist
Cameraman: Ted McCord
Cast: Joan Crawford, Dennis Morgan

68 Sudden Fear
RKO

Novel by Edna Sherry
Screenplay by Leonore Coffee and Robert Smith
Producer: Joseph Kaufman
Director: David Miller
Cameraman: Charles Lang, Jr
Cast: Joan Crawford, Jack Palance, Gloria Grahame

1953

69 Torch Song
MGM

Story *Why Should I Cry?* by I. R. Wylie
Screenplay by John Michael Hayes and Jan Lustig
Producers: Henry Berman and Sidney Franklin, Jr
Director: Charles Walters
Cameraman: Robert Planck
Cast: Joan Crawford, Michael Wilding, Gig Young

1954

70 Johnny Guitar
REPUBLIC

Novel by Roy Chanslor
Screenplay by Philip Yordan
Producer: Herbert J. Yates
Director: Nicholas Ray
Cameraman: Harry Stradling
Cast: Joan Crawford, Sterling Hayden, Mercedes McCambridge

1955

71 Female On The Beach
UNIVERSAL

Play *The Besieged Heart* by Robert Hill
Screenplay by Robert Hill and Richard Alan Simmons
Producer: Albert Zugsmith
Director: Joseph Pevney
Cameraman: Charles Lang
Cast: Joan Crawford, Jeff Chandler

72 Queen Bee
COLUMBIA

Novel by Edna Lee
Screenplay and director: Ranald MacDougall
Producer: Jerry Wald
Cameraman: Charles Lang
Cast: Joan Crawford, Barry Sullivan

1956

73 Autumn Leaves
WILLIAM GOETZ/COLUMBIA

Story and screenplay by Jack Jevne, Lewis Meltzer and Robert Blees
Producer: William Goetz
Director: Robert Aldrich
Cameraman: Charles Lang
Cast: Joan Crawford, Cliff Robertson

1957

74 The Story Of Esther Costello
VALIANT FILMS/COLUMBIA

A Romulus Production from the novel by Nicholas Monsarrat
Screenplay by Charles Kaufman
Producer and director: David Miller
Cameraman: Robert Krasker
Cast: Joan Crawford, Rossano Brazzi, Heather Sears

1959

75 The Best Of Everything
20th CENTURY FOX

Novel by Rona Jaffe
Screenplay by Edith Sommer and Mann Rubin
Producer: Jerry Wald
Director: Jean Negulesco
Cameraman: William C. Mellor
Cast: Hope Lange, Stephen Boyd, Suzy Parker, Martha Hyer, Diane Baker, Brian Aherne, Robert Evans and guest stars Louis Jourdan, Joan Crawford

1962

76 What Ever Happened To Baby Jane?
SEVEN ARTS/WARNER BROS

Novel by Henry Farrell
Screenplay by Lukas Heller
Director-producer: Robert Aldrich
Cameraman: Ernest Haller
Cast: Bette Davis, Joan Crawford, Victor Buono

1963

77 The Caretakers
UNITED ARTISTS

Story by Hall Bartlett and Jerry Paris, based on the book by Daniel Telfer
Screenplay by Henry F. Greenberg
Producer and director: Hall Bartlett
Cameraman: Lucien Ballard
Cast: Robert Stack, Polly Bergen, Joan Crawford, Janis Paige, Herbert Marshall

1964

78 Strait-Jacket
COLUMBIA

Screenplay by Robert Bloch
Producer and director: William Castle
Cameraman: Arthur Arling
Cast: Joan Crawford, Diane Baker, Leif Erikson

1965

79 I Saw What You Did
UNIVERSAL

Novel by Ursula Curtiss
Screenplay by William McGivern
Producer and director: William Castle
Cameraman: Joseph Biroc
Cast: Joan Crawford, John Ireland, Leif Erikson

1968

80 Berserk
COLUMBIA

Story and screenplay by Aben Kandel and Herman Cohen
Producer: Herman Cohen
Director: Jim O'Connolly
Cameraman: Desmond Dickinson
Cast: Joan Crawford, Ty Hardin, Diana Dors, Michael Gough, Judy Geeson, Robert Hardy, Geoffrey Keen

1970

81 Trog
WARNER BROS

Story by Peter Bryan and John Gilling
Screenplay by Aben Kandel
Producer: Herman Cohen
Director: Freddie Francis
Cast: Joan Crawford, Michael Gough

BIBLIOGRAPHY

Like Garbo, Monroe, Dietrich and Davis, Crawford has attracted many biographers. The following list – by no means exhaustive – includes some of the more interesting titles.

CRAWFORD, JOAN: *A Portrait of Joan* (Doubleday, New York, 1962). An autobiography written with Jane Kesner Ardmore and taking the story up to her last husband's death. Catches the authentic success-drive of the subject.

NEWQUIST, ROY: *Conversations with Joan Crawford* (Citadel, Secaucus, 1980). Extensive running-interview, conducted between 1962–77, which catches Crawford in unusually relaxed and forthright mood.

CASTLE, CHARLES: *Joan Crawford, The Raging Star* (New English Library, London, 1977). Valuable insights by her intimates and contemporaries and particularly good on Crawford's last years.

THOMAS, BOB: *Joan Crawford* (Simon & Schuster, New York, and Weidenfeld & Nicolson, London, 1978). The most up-to-date general life of Crawford.

QUIRK, LAWRENCE J.: *The Films of Joan Crawford* (Citadel, New York, 1968). Filmography with credits and selected review quotes.

CARR, LARRY: *Four Fabulous Faces* (Galahad, New York, 1970). Lushly illustrated picture album of Crawford and contemporaries (Swanson, Garbo, Dietrich) with shrewdly worded commentary.

LAMBERT, GAVIN: *The Slide Area* (Hamish Hamilton, London, 1959). A collection of short stories with Hollywood backgrounds, one of which, 'The Closed Set', is a thinly veiled account of Crawford as superstar and superbitch.

CAREY, GARY: *All the Stars in Heaven* (Dutton, New York, 1981; Robson, London, 1982). The most recent, and extensive, account of Louis B. Mayer's MGM, which gives a good picture of the studio's changing policies and Crawford's place in them.

MARX, SAMUEL: *Mayer and Thalberg* (W. H. Allen, London, 1978). Study of the two moguls, with material on Crawford.

THOMAS, BOB: *Thalberg* (Doubleday, New York, 1969). Biography, with relevant Crawford material.

LAMBERT, GAVIN: *On Cukor* (W. H. Allen, London, 1973). Extensive interview covering the director's long career and including his comments on Crawford and the films of hers which he directed.

HARVEY, STEPHEN: *Joan Crawford* (Pyramid, New York, 1974). A compact but comprehensive study of the star and her films.

NOTES TO THE TEXT

1 *A Portrait of Joan*, an autobiography with Jane Kesner Ardmore (Doubleday, New York, 1962), p. 22.
2 *A Portrait of Joan*, p. 43.
3 Caption to an MGM publicity still, circa 1935.
4 *A Portrait of Joan*, p. 30.
5 *A Portrait of Joan*, p. 62.
6 *A Portrait of Joan*, p. 63.
7 *Our Movie Made Children*, Henry James Forman (Macmillan, New York, 1935), p. 64.
8 *A Portrait of Joan*, pp. 63–4.
9 *Photoplay*, August 1929.
10 *A Portrait of Joan*, p. 69.
11 *The Celluloid Muse*, Charles Higham and Joel Greenburg (Angus & Robertson, London, 1969), p. 156.
12 *A Portrait of Joan*, p. 95.
13 *Joan Crawford, The Raging Star*, Charles Castle (New English Library, London, 1977), p. 55.
14 *A Portrait of Joan*, p. 108.
15 Cukor on Crawford in *Joan Crawford, The Raging Star*, p. 87.
16 *Conversations with Joan Crawford*, Roy Newquist (Citadel Press, Secaucus, 1980), p. 84.
17 *Conversations with Joan Crawford*, p. 89.
18 *A Portrait of Joan*, p. 151.
19 *Joan Crawford*, Bob Thomas (Weidenfeld, London, 1978), p. 178.
20 *A Portrait of Joan*, p. 162.
21 *Conversations with Joan Crawford*, p. 155.
22 *A Portrait of Joan*, p. 179.

ILLUSTRATION SOURCES

INDEX